Table of Contents

Download supplemental learning materials from Essential Education.

 Visit the Essential Education website to find additional learning materials, including new workbook sections.
http://www.essentialed.com/downloads.php

Essential Writing & Language Skills

Interactive Practice Workbook

Authors

Maya Moore

Teresa Perrin

Jenni Romano

Nancy Schnog

Senior Consultants

Bonnie Goonen

Susan Pittman-Shetler

Published by Essential Education

Essential Writing & Language Skills

ISBN 978-1-940532-02-8

Seventh printing, November 2019

For more information, contact:
Essential Education Corporation
895 NW Grant Avenue
Corvallis, OR 97330
Phone: 800-931-8069

Cover Design: Karen Guard

Essential Education provides innovative, effective HSE test preparation and
adult learning programs centered on the learner's needs.
For more information, please visit http://www.essentialed.com/educators/.

Introduction

The *Essential Writing & Language Skills* workbook will give you a foundation in planning, drafting, and finalizing writing. Your purpose in writing will vary, from passing a standardized test to applying for a job to writing a report or paper. Good writing skills will help you succeed in all types of writing tasks. Through this workbook, you'll learn to develop what you want to say and to express it clearly. After all, that's the purpose of writing—to develop and communicate ideas.

One important area of writing is analyzing and evaluating what you read. In the workplace, you will need to not only understand reports but read them with a critical eye. Discerning the best contracting bid or product description is an essential skill. In higher education, you will need to write original papers that reference and evaluate books, research papers, and other works. This workbook will give you practice writing about what you read.

As you practice writing, you will develop a good writing process:

- **Plan:** Read, research, brainstorm, and identify your central idea.

- **Draft:** Outline and write a beginning, middle, and ending.

- **Evaluate:** Throughout the writing process, evaluate your work. As you evaluate, continue to plan, revise, and edit your draft.

- **Submit:** When your writing is done, proofread, format, and publish your work.

A writing process will give you a structure to develop your ideas around a strong central idea, to make decisions about organization and language, and to edit and finalize your work. You'll also learn about what makes good writing, from understanding your audience's point of view to developing tone and style.

This writing book contains practice problems that involve several levels of knowledge and thinking.

★ If an exercise has one star, it is testing your ability to recall and use specific skills, such as grammar and language use.

★★ If an exercise has two stars, it asks you to interpret, summarize, or do other tasks that require some analysis. A two-star problem is checking to see if you have acquired a skill or concept.

★★★ If an exercise has three stars, it asks you to think strategically to answer a question or respond to a prompt. These exercises will require short or extended responses.

> *Technology Tip*
>
> As your writing improves, practice using a keyboard. Set a goal to type 20 to 50 words per minute.

You can use this workbook on its own, by working through each section, to improve your writing skills. The practice in this workbook will reinforce the skills you already have and develop new ones. You'll learn by applying those skills to many different situations. Practice helps you improve quickly because you're actively using the skills you're learning.

This workbook is also a good supplement to classroom learning or online courses, including Essential Education courses such as GED Academy™ and Essential Skills Online. You don't need to go through the workbook in one particular order. Instead, use whatever section teaches the skills you're currently learning. If you're in a class, your teacher can help you choose the best sections to study.

Take your time working through the exercises in this book. They're meant to enhance your thinking skills and to give you practice with many writing tasks so that you can develop strong writing for any situation. If your writing speed is slow, work to increase your speed as you work through the book. Many Check Your Skills short answers and extended responses include target times to help you prepare for timed exams.

The Writing Process

Developing a strong writing process is the key to improving your writing. The writing process helps you develop content and focus on what you want to say. Good organization, specific details, and a strong central idea all come from using the writing process to plan, draft, and evaluate your writing. The steps of planning, drafting, and evaluating are not strict chronological steps. You will return to planning and drafting as you evaluate your writing.

There are many types of writing, from work reports to advertising to song lyrics to letters. You will approach a short task, such as an email, differently from a lengthy research paper. In both cases, you will plan, draft, and evaluate before you finalize what you've written and hit "send" or "print."

 Plan

Planning is the first step of the writing process, but you will return to planning as you draft and evaluate your work. Planning includes researching, reading, developing a central idea, brainstorming, and organizing your ideas.

 Draft

Drafting doesn't happen all at once. Developing an outline and organizing your ideas makes writing your draft easier.

 Evaluate

Evaluating, revising, and editing can be a long task or a short one, depending on your writing task. Evaluate as you plan and draft, and based on your evaluation, revise and edit your work.

Submit

When you are satisfied with what you've written, it's time to finalize it. Review your work one last time to catch minor errors. For example, you might need to format a paper, put the bibliography in the proper format, print your final draft, and turn it in to your instructor.

The writing process is critical for formal writing tasks: college entrance essays, college papers, exams, work reports, documentation, and memos. No matter what writing task you approach, the writing process will help you find something meaningful to say and express it well.

This section includes an overview of the writing process and a section on each step in the process: **Plan, Draft, Evaluate**, and **Submit.**

Plan, Draft, Evaluate

Connections

Have you ever...

- Had trouble starting a writing assignment?
- Written an important email to a supervisor or client?
- Composed a letter to your senator or representative?

Writing isn't just churning out words. To write successfully, you use a **process.** Whether you are emailing a client to describe company policies, writing a New Year's message to all your family, or composing a research paper for a college class, writing involves making many decisions. You choose your length, topic, words, and tone. All of those decisions affect your message and your reader.

Consciously following a writing process helps you make deliberate choices to write effectively. Use a four-step writing process to improve your writing.

 Plan: Examine your task. Who is the audience? What is the purpose? Research your topic, read and examine source materials, brainstorm ideas, and think through what you want to say.

 Draft: Prewrite and compose your work. You might start with a central idea, some supporting ideas, and evidence or examples. Then, fill in details, connections, transitions, and conclusions.

 Evaluate: As you work, evaluate your writing. Is it successful? Does it communicate? Continue to plan, revise, and edit your draft.

 Submit: When your work is ready, make final changes and publish. That might mean posting your work on your blog, submitting a paper to your professor, or mailing a letter to a company.

Use the first three steps together. As you **plan**, prewrite and evaluate. As you **draft**, plan and evaluate. As you **evaluate**, plan, rewrite, and edit.

Plan, Draft, and Evaluate Your Writing

The writing process helps you approach writing thoughtfully so you can improve your skills. You will make conscious decisions as you plan, draft, and evaluate.

Imagine you need to make a recommendation to your boss about which printer to purchase for the office. You work in a busy office that prints up to 1,000 pages per day. Examine the table and write a recommendation, including your reasoning.

	Price	Speed (Pages per Minute)	Monthly Workload	Ink Cost (Cents per Page)
Printer A	$459	24 ppm	70,000 pages	4.2
Printer B	$624	28 ppm	50,000 pages	2.3

Plan

First, examine your task. What is your purpose? Who is your audience? Is this a formal or informal task? What do you need to read and understand? What do you want to say? Strategies that help you think through writing tasks and plan your writing include:

- Defining purpose and audience

- Brainstorming

- Researching

Writing doesn't occur in a vacuum. Developing good ideas and strong content depends on reading and investigating as well as thinking and prewriting.

Technology Tip

If you are working on a computer, keep a copy of your prewriting as you write so you don't lose your ideas.

? **1.** Determine which printer to recommend. Give two reasons why.

You might recommend Printer B. Although it is more expensive, it will cost 1.9 cents less per page in ink. At 1,000 pages a day, the savings is $20 per day. Printer B is also slightly faster.

Draft

When you start writing, you won't usually just sit down and begin composing sentences. First, develop a structure or outline, and fill in some important details and ideas. Then, complete your draft. Even a short project will have a beginning, a middle, and an ending.

? **2.** Draft a response with a beginning, middle, and ending to recommend a printer.

You might write:

> I recommend Printer B because it will be more cost effective. Printer A costs approximately $175 less than Printer B, but Printer B has an ink cost of 1.9 cents per page less than Printer A. At 1,000 pages per day, the savings in ink will be approximately $20 per day. It will take less than two weeks to recoup the extra cost of Printer B. Workload and print speed are minor factors. Both printers can handle our monthly workload (about 30,000 pages) equally well, but Printer B has a slightly faster print speed. Printer B is clearly the best choice based on the available data.

Notice that this paragraph has a beginning (stating the recommendation), a middle (giving specific evidence), and an ending (summing up the recommendation).

Evaluate

All writing can be improved. During and after writing, evaluate your work and make changes:

- **Read critically:** Approach your text with fresh eyes to improve it.
- **Revise:** Make changes to organization, tone, and content.
- **Edit:** Reorganize, improve language, and clear up confusing passages.

? **3.** Review your paragraph. Make revisions to improve it.

You might clarify ideas, improve the organization, or add details.

Submit

Submit

When you are satisfied that your writing is ready, proofread to make any final corrections and format your work in its final form. Then publish your work—send your email or letter, submit your paper, or post your blog entry.

? **4.** Proofread your paragraph and make any final corrections.

Make a note of common errors in your writing to help you catch mistakes when you proofread. In an office, the final step would be to send or give your recommendation to your boss.

Practice It!

Use your understanding of the writing process to complete the following exercises.

 1. Sharon needs to write a paper about the history of ranching in her state. How can she plan before she begins to write?

 2. Andrew has been assigned to write an essay about the U.S. Congress for a civics class. How can he decide on a more specific topic?

 3. Ralph is writing a report for work to analyze productivity in his department.

    a. What does Ralph need to think about before he begins writing?

    b. How can Ralph approach writing the report to keep it organized?

    c. How can Ralph evaluate his writing?

 4. Mauricio intends to write about nuclear-powered submarines for a science paper. He has made a list of information he knows about submarines and has found three books about how they function.

    a. Where is Mauricio in the writing process?

    b. What advice would you give to Mauricio to proceed?

The Writing Process

Plan

Brainstorm twice for unfamiliar topics. First, brainstorm questions about the topic. Research and then brainstorm again, including ideas and more questions.

Use the following passage for exercise 5.

Solar flares have a direct effect on the Earth's atmosphere. The intense radiation from a solar flare travels to Earth in eight minutes. As a result, the Earth's upper atmosphere becomes more ionized and expands. Long-distance radio signals can be disrupted by the resulting change in the Earth's ionosphere. A satellite's orbit around the Earth can be disturbed by the enhanced drag on the satellite from the expanded atmosphere, and satellites' electronic components can be damaged.

Source: Adapted from "Why Study Solar Flares?" at The Solar Flare Theory Educational Web Pages by NASA's Goddard Space Flight Center. http://hesperia.gsfc.nasa.gov/sftheory/studyflare.htm

 5. Explain possible advantages of being able to predict solar flares.

   a. 💡 **Plan:** What is the purpose and audience? What will you write?

   b. ✏️ **Draft:** Draft a paragraph to fulfill this writing task.

   c. ⚙️ **Evaluate and** (Submit) **:** Evaluate your paragraph to revise and edit it.

6. How does revising your work as you evaluate it differ from proofreading work that you are finalizing?

Use the following letter to the editor for exercise 7.

I strongly disagree with last Sunday's editorial against the city's plan to close the Bradley Branch Library. Libraries do have valuable services, but they are being replaced by services available over the Internet. Is the Bradley Library bustling with readers every day? I doubt it, otherwise the city would not choose to close it. It is natural that when people can download unlimited ebooks from the Internet and browse unlimited websites, the city should reduce its number of libraries. Patrons can travel a little further to another branch.

 7. Critique the argument in this letter to the editor. Is the reasoning sound? What are possible counterarguments?

    a. **Plan:** What is the purpose and audience? What will you write?

    b. **Draft:** Draft a paragraph to fulfill this writing task.

    c. **Evaluate and** [Submit]: Evaluate your paragraph and revise it.

8. Imagine that you are planning to write a blog post to share a recipe. How would you use the writing process?

Check **Your Skills**

Use the writing process to write short responses to the following exercises.

1. Lee is writing a blog post describing how to build a shed. He begins to draft his post. Two paragraphs later, after describing the steps, he runs out of things to say. His post seems too short, and he's not sure what to do. Describe how Lee can use the writing process to improve his writing and revise his blog post.

Write your answer below or type your response on a computer. Take approximately 25 minutes to respond.

The Writing Process

Evaluate

Don't be afraid to revise. Revision is not a failure. It is an opportunity to make good writing even better. The best writers became great writers by learning to revise— again and again.

Use the questions on page 329 to evaluate your response.

The following passage is from the book *Are Women People?* by Alice Duer Miller. The book is a collection of short passages and poetry in support of giving women the right to vote.

Use the following passage for exercise 2.

The Logic of the Law

In 1875 the Supreme Court of Wisconsin in denying the petition of women to practise before it said: "It would be shocking to man's reverence for womanhood and faith in woman … that woman should be permitted to mix professionally in all the nastiness which finds its way into courts of justice."

It then names thirteen subjects as unfit for the attention of women—three of them are crimes committed against women.

Source: From *Are Women People?* by Alice Duer Miller, 1915.

 2. Explain and critique this passage as an argument that women should be allowed to argue cases before courts. Write your answer below or type your response on a computer. Take approximately 25 minutes to respond.

Remember the Concept

Plan, Draft, Evaluate before you submit.

The Writing Process

Submit

Use the questions on page 329 to evaluate your response.

FOCUS
Plan

Planning your writing involves thinking about what to write, gathering and organizing information, and developing your ideas. The process of planning helps you think more clearly about your writing. Planning can include:

- Researching information

- Brainstorming ideas

- Developing a topic

- Finding details

- Organizing your writing

With a little planning, you can accomplish any writing task more easily, quickly, and successfully.

There are many ways to approach planning. Reading and researching is an important part of your planning. Good content is key to successful writing. Even if you know your topic well, reading and researching can provide you with evidence and details, as well as new ideas.

To develop your ideas, you might make charts, diagrams, or drawings. You can make notes, create outlines, brainstorm, or put together a bulletin board that you can modify and rearrange. Consider many options, and then choose the best planning methods for your writing. From a complex visual notebook to a few notes typed into your computer, planning can greatly improve your writing.

An important area of planning is organization. Everything you write has structure. Your ideas should be organized logically, within a beginning, middle, and ending. You should plan your organizational structure before you begin writing.

This section includes lessons that will help you get started with planning.

- **Determining Purpose and Audience**
  Understanding the purpose and audience of your writing task is important. Who will read your writing? What will they expect? What you write will depend on your purpose and audience.

- **Reading and Thinking for Writing**
  To prepare for writing, you will need to read and research. You will also need to think about what you will write. By reading and thinking, you will develop good content for your writing.

- **Choosing an Organizational Structure**
  Learn a strategy for determining an organizational structure for your writing. Good organization is the foundation of good writing. Strong organization means having a central idea with supporting ideas and details in a logical order leading to a conclusion.

Determining Purpose and Audience

Have you ever . . .

- Customized your résumé for a specific job?
- Recognized your teacher's point of view in assigning a class writing assignment?
- Written a poem for your mom?

Every time you write, you are writing for a reader. The first two questions for a writer are, "Why am I writing?" and "Who will read my writing?" The choices you make in your writing depend on your purpose and your audience.

Purpose and audience are closely related. There are four general purposes in writing:

- **Persuade**—Do you need to convince your audience to agree with you?
- **Inform**—Do you need to convey information?
- **Narrate**—Do you need to tell a story or describe events?
- **Explain**—Do you need to clarify a difficult concept?

However, a general description of your purpose isn't enough. You need to know your specific purpose and how your audience relates to that purpose. To describe the relationship between your purpose and your audience, ask the **KEYS** to understanding your audience:

- What does your audience already **Know**?
- What does your audience **Expect**?
- What do **You Share** with your audience?

KEYS to Purpose and Audience

Making conscious decisions about your purpose and audience focuses your thinking so that every word you choose is deliberate and effective.

Imagine you are writing a résumé to apply for a job.

Determine Your Purpose

What is your primary purpose for writing? Your primary purpose may include elements of other purposes. For example:

- **Persuade:** When you persuade, you also inform your audience of facts to help convince them or include a narrative to illustrate a point.

- **Inform:** When you inform, you also explain why the information is important or include a story to keep the reader interested.

- **Narrate:** In the telling of a story, you inform or explain key concepts.

- **Explain:** To explain a difficult concept, you convey information. Explaining takes this one step further, answering "why" questions.

1. What is your primary purpose when you write a résumé to apply for a job?

The primary purpose of a résumé is to persuade. It includes information and some explanation, but the goal is to persuade the hiring manager to call you to arrange an interview.

KEYS to Understanding Your Audience

Sometimes you will have limited information about your audience. Answering the KEYS questions will help you focus on the relationship between your purpose and audience.

What Does Your Audience Already Know?

Identify your audience's existing knowledge related to your purpose. You don't want to overexplain or underexplain.

2. What would a hiring manager know about you, the job opening, and the company?

A hiring manager knows a lot about the company and the job opening. He or she likely doesn't know you at all. In order for your résumé to persuade the manager to interview you, your résumé should focus on giving information about you and relating that information to what the manager knows: the company's needs and the job opening.

What Does Your Audience Expect?

You may not have as much information about your audience's expectations as you might like. However, anything you can determine about your audience's expectations will be helpful to you as you write. If you were the reader, what would you expect? What would you want?

? **3.** What does a hiring manager expect from a résumé?

A hiring manager will expect to learn about your skills, experience, and how well you can do the job.

What Do You Share with Your Audience?

What do you have in common with your audience? Answering this question will help you connect with the audience. In your writing, you can address both your similarities with and differences from your audience.

? **4.** What do you have in common with the hiring manager?

You may both share an interest in the same career field and perhaps similar work experience. You are both interested in the same company. You want to work for the company, and the hiring manager does work for the company.

Describe Your Purpose and Audience

Once you have thought about the KEYS questions, put together what you know. Describe your purpose and your audience.

? **5.** Describe your purpose and audience when you write a résumé.

You might write:

> When you write a résumé, your purpose is to get a job interview. To accomplish this, you need to communicate your skills, experiences, and attributes to a hiring manager, your main audience. The hiring manager does not know you. His or her goal is to fill a specific position with a good employee, so it is important to connect your skills and experience to the hiring manager's needs.

 1. Imagine you receive a letter that reads, "Vote no on Proposition 65! It will allow businesses to dump unlimited amounts of chemical waste into our city's landfill instead of requiring them to dispose of waste at hazardous material sites." What is the primary purpose of this letter?

    a. To inform

    b. To narrate

    c. To persuade

    d. To explain

2. Which of the following pieces of information would the writer of the letter want to know about the voters in your city?

    a. What they already know about Proposition 65

    b. How much they already pay for waste disposal

    c. If they expect the city to dispose of hazardous waste safely

    d. All of the above

3. Imagine you want to persuade your friends to paint a mural with you. What would you want to know about them that could help you make a persuasive argument?

4. Explain how knowing more about your audience can improve your persuasive writing.

The Writing Process

Plan

Why you are writing and who will read your work are the two critical issues to explore before anything else. Digging into these two concepts more deeply will help you focus your thoughts.

Use the following scenario for exercises 5 through 10.

Your boss announces that your company will give raises to workers who have shown improvements in performance over the last year. Each employee who would like to be considered for a raise is required to submit a written document explaining why he or she should receive a raise.

---

5. What is the purpose: to persuade, inform, narrate, or explain?

6. What does your audience already **Know**?

7. What does your audience **Expect**?

8. What do **You Share** with your audience?

9. Describe your purpose and audience.

10. Based on your purpose and audience, how would you approach this writing task?

11. Write a paragraph based on the following purpose, audience, and topic.

    Purpose: To persuade   **Audience:** Supervisor   **Topic:** A raise

12. Write a paragraph based on the following purpose, audience, and topic.

    Purpose: To narrate   **Audience:** Your friends   **Topic:** A raise

13. Explain how the differences in purpose and audience affected your writing in exercises 11 and 12.

14. Describe an audience or reader who might read your writing in your everyday life.

    a. What does your audience already **Know**?

    b. What does your audience **Expect**?

    c. What do **You Share** with your audience?

IMPACT for Writing Requirements

In a classroom, writing prompts give specific instructions. Real-world writing tasks also have requirements. The IMPACT strategy helps you understand the purpose of a writing task. Imagine you are responding to the following job listing.

> *IMPACT*
> - **Identify** keywords.
> - **Make** a list of what to address.
> - **Propose** Approaches.
> - **Choose** a direction.
> - **Think** and proceed.

A busy dental office is seeking a friendly front office receptionist to join our team. We are a growing family dental practice and take pride in providing high quality care. Successful applicants must be able to answer a multi-line phone system and verify insurance eligibility. Requirements: typing 45 wpm or more, strong computer skills, exceptional customer service skills, and the ability to handle busy situations with a smile. Experience with DentalPoint software is preferred. To apply, please send résumé and cover letter to humanresources@abcdental.com. Include relevant experience and skills, and explain why you are interested in this position and consider yourself a good fit for our team.

I Identify Keywords

Keywords are important words that tell you about the writing task. If you have a paper copy of the prompt, you can use a pen or highlighter to identify keywords in the prompt. If the prompt is on a computer, you can note keywords. Identifying keywords will help you narrow your focus and use appropriate vocabulary in your response.

? **1.** Write down keywords in the prompt.

Keywords in the prompt include "busy," "dental," "friendly," "receptionist," "family," "multi-line phone system," "verify insurance eligibility," "45 wpm," "computer skills," "customer service," "smile," "DentalPoint," "résumé," "cover letter," "relevant experience and skills," "explain," and "good fit."

M Make a List of Separate Ideas or Parts to Address

A writing task may have more than one element or part. Create a list of requirements to make sure you understand the full task.

? **2.** Make a list of the things you must do when responding to this ad.

To apply for the job, you must:

- Email your résumé and a cover letter to humanresources@abcdental.com.

- Show relevant experience and skills.

- Explain why you're interested in the position.

- Explain why you think you are a good fit.

P A ***Propose Approaches***

Develop two or more different ways to respond to the writing task. This will help you be more thoughtful in your approach and address the prompt or requirements.

? **3.** Develop two or more approaches to the job posting.

Two approaches might be:

- Write a letter focusing on your past experience, mentioning relevant skills. Include a brief ending mentioning why you would make a great team member.

- Write a letter focusing on your relevant skills, relating them to your experience and explaining how they would make you a great team member.

C ***Choose the Best Direction***

Review the prompt or instructions. Choose the approach that best addresses the purpose of the writing task.

? **4.** Choose an approach to develop for your response.

Both responses address experience, skills, and why you would be a good team member. The ad focuses on important skills instead of experience, so focusing on skills is a good choice. You might note when you review the prompt that you should also mention why you are interested in the position.

T ***Think and Proceed***

You have started a response with IMPACT. Consider the best route forward to complete your planning. As you draft and evaluate, go back and review the prompt. Make sure that your response reflects the requirements of the writing task.

Practice It!

Use this passage and prompt to complete the following exercises.

Postal Service Considering Dropping Saturday Delivery

To restore the United States Postal Service (USPS) to financial stability, the USPS must reduce costs and generate new income. The USPS cannot meet its cost reduction goals without changing its delivery schedule to Monday through Friday only. Delaying these changes increases the potential that the USPS may become a burden to the American taxpayer.

Source: United States Postal Service, http://about.usps.com/news/national-releases/2013/pr13_0410bogstatement.htm

Write a letter to the Postal Service explaining why the USPS should or should not reduce its delivery service to five days a week. This assignment asks you to take a stand. You have an opportunity to convince the Postal Service whether Saturday mail service should continue or be discontinued. Write at least three paragraphs explaining your position. Include advantages and disadvantages of your recommendations and explain the impact it would have on rural and urban postal customers.

 1. Identify keywords in the prompt.

 2. Make a list of separate ideas or parts of the prompt to address.

    a. Write a list of parts of the prompt to address.

    b. Looking for verbs in the prompt can help you make identify what you need to do or address. Explain why.

> **Build Your Writing Skills**
>
> When you **Propose Approaches,** try to think of creative ideas. A variety of approaches can clear your mind, clarify your opinion, or identify issues to address. The important thing is to develop multiple options and keep your mind open to new ideas.

3. Propose two or more approaches to the prompt.

 4. Choose an approach by reviewing the prompt. Explain your reasons for your choice.

 5. Write a response to the prompt based on your chosen approach.

Check **Your Skills**

Complete the following exercises about purpose and audience.

 1. Examine the following writing prompt.

Write an essay directed to the College Scholarship Foundation Selection Board describing your current accomplishments, as well as your educational and career goals. In your response, explain how a $1,500 scholarship would help you reach your goals.

a. Write a paragraph describing the purpose and audience for this writing task using KEYS.

b. Use IMPACT to evaluate the prompt and decide on an approach.

c. Write a response for this writing task.

2. Examine the following writing prompt.

Choose an important historic event from any time period and explain its impact on today's world and on your life. In your response, explain multiple ramifications of the event.

   a. Write a paragraph describing the purpose and audience for this writing task using KEYS.

   b. Use IMPACT to evaluate the prompt and decide on an approach.

   c. Write a response for this writing task.

> *Remember the Concept*
>
> **KEYS:**
> - What does the audience **Know?**
> - What does the audience **Expect?**
> - What do **You Share** with the audience?
>
> **IMPACT:**
> - **Identify** keywords.
> - **Make** a list of what to address.
> - **Propose Approaches.**
> - **Choose** a direction.
> - **Think** and proceed.

Reading and Thinking
for Writing

Connections

Have you ever...

- Found it difficult to get started on a writing task?

- Worked in a group to improve a workplace procedure?

- Written a research paper or a summary of an article?

Getting started on a writing task can seem difficult. You have many options. That's why an important part of planning is reading and thinking to determine what you need to write. Writing is a creative act, and sometimes finding a focus can seem overwhelming. Reading and brainstorming can help you find a general focus, as well as identify details to develop your writing.

Two important tasks help you get started writing: reading and thinking. Reading gives you information and content for your writing. If you need more information for your writing, you will need to read. Approach the reading with your writing task in mind. Your goal is to find specific information or ideas for your writing.

Thinking is just as important as reading. You will think about what you read and about your topic. One technique to help you think is brainstorming. A good brainstorming strategy to start with is **idea clustering**. It is flexible, includes visual cues, and prevents you from editing while you are generating ideas. Also known as mind-mapping, idea clustering is a way to gather your ideas without judging them and to create a path for later organization.

Read

Think

Write

Reading for Writing

Many writing tasks involve reading and researching. You may need to evaluate written materials, look for evidence about a topic, or summarize materials. When you read for a writing task, you are reading for a specific purpose.

Beach erosion is a chronic problem along most open-ocean shores of the United States. Coastal populations continue to grow, and community infrastructures are threatened by erosion, This leads to increased demand for accurate information regarding past and present shoreline changes. There is also need for a comprehensive analysis of shoreline movement that is regionally consistent. To meet these national needs, the Coastal and Marine Geology Program of the U.S. Geological Survey (USGS) is conducting an analysis of historical shoreline changes along open-ocean sandy shores of the conterminous United States and parts of Alaska and Hawaii.

Adapted from "National Assessment of Shoreline Change Project," U.S. Geologic Survey, http://coastal.er.usgs.gov/shoreline-change/

Identify Your Reading Purpose

Prepare to read by examining your writing task. What is your goal? What do you need to accomplish by reading?

? 1. Imagine your goal is to write a research paper about beach erosion. You need to decide on a narrower topic. Describe your goal in reading this passage.

Your goal is to define your topic. You might want to find specific issues and sources of information regarding beach erosion.

Skim and Scan

Skim and scan to prepare for reading. If you want to understand the whole text or find important sections, skim to familiarize yourself with the text and get an overview. If you're looking for one particular piece of information, scan for the information you need.

? 2. Skim the passage. What is the central idea?

The central idea is that the U.S. Geologic Survey formed the Coastal and Marine Geology Program to study and provide accurate information about beach erosion.

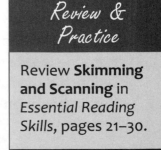

Review & Practice

Review **Skimming and Scanning** in *Essential Reading Skills*, pages 21–30.

Read and Take Notes

As you read, keep your purpose in mind. Take notes of important elements that you will need for your writing and of your thoughts about the reading. Highlight, underline, or write down passages that you will want to quote or paraphrase.

?   **3.** Note three things from the passage that might help you define a research paper topic.

You might note "community infrastructures are threatened by erosion," "there is an increased demand for accurate information," and "analysis of historic shoreline changes."

Evaluate the Reading

After you read, take a moment to evaluate what you've read. Look through your notes. What are your main thoughts? What are important details? How does the reading connect with your writing task?

?   **4.** Based on the passage, what are two possible research paper topics?

You might have many ideas for research topics based on this passage. One possible topic is the potential costs of erosion to a local community on a regional shoreline. Another topic could be the accuracy of existing information about erosion in a particular area.

Develop Your Ideas

Using the text, develop your ideas for your writing task. This may involve brainstorming, additional reading, outlining, synthesizing multiple readings, and other prewriting. As you plan, draft, and evaluate your writing, don't hesitate to go back to the reading to refresh your memory or find additional passages you want to discuss.

?   **5.** What next steps would you take to develop your research paper topic?

A good next step for a research paper is more reading. You might plan to find sources of information for potential topics, skim to get an overview, and use that information to narrow down your ideas to one topic.

Practice It!

Use the following prompt and passage for exercises 1 through 4.

Read the following passage. Write a response explaining whether you agree or disagree with the author and why.

High school is a difficult time. There are many important things going on: growing responsibilities, difficulties at home, choices about the future, finding one's identity. At this critical time, it is important that young people stay focused on their studies. Success in high school means success in the future. Coed schools add distractions and make it more difficult to keep students focused. Growing awareness of the opposite sex is natural. The desire to meet and interact with the opposite sex is healthy. Keeping these interactions out of schools, however, will help focus students on their studies. Separate high schools for young men and women are definitely a benefit to our youth.

1. Describe your goal in reading the passage.

2. Skim the passage. What is its central idea?

3. Read the passage and take notes for your response.

4. Write a response based on your reading.

Use the following prompt and passage for exercises 5 through 8.

Read the following passage. Write a response applying the concept of freedom of speech to the argument in the passage.

Criticizing the President of the United States is a delicate matter. We don't want to blindly agree with everything the country does. On the other hand, angry, overstated responses to the president's actions are negative for everyone. People tend to criticize presidents they don't like in the strongest terms, while calling on patriotism to stop others from criticizing presidents on the other side of the aisle. We should, instead, criticize the president only calmly and reasonably. Don't rail against the president's actions. Prepare your arguments thoughtfully and respond respectfully.

⭐ **5.** Describe your goal in reading the passage.

⭐ **6.** Skim the passage. What is its central idea?

⭐⭐ **7.** Read the passage and take notes for your response.

⭐⭐⭐ **8.** Write a response based on your reading.

Idea Clustering

When you plan a writing task, brainstorming can help you think of and develop ideas. One method of brainstorming is **idea clustering**. Idea clustering can help you think of creative, original, and unusual ideas.

Imagine that an entertainment blog asks you to contribute an article. "Anything goes," the blog editor tells you. You must define an article topic.

Center the Topic

The first step is simple: write one word or phrase that defines your topic in the center of a blank sheet of paper (in this case, "Entertainment"). For idea clustering, do not use a computer. Thinking about formatting your ideas will distract you from thinking about the topic.

Surround Your Topic with Ideas

In five to ten minutes, quickly write ideas, words, and phrases that you associate with your topic all over the page. Use any size or style of writing, and don't worry about repeating. Include verbs, nouns, adjectives, attitudes, emotions—anything. Silly thoughts are allowed!

? **1.** Take five minutes to surround the topic "Entertainment" with ideas.

Entertainment

Your idea cluster might look something like this:

Novels   Ender's Game   Movies   TV Games
Vonnegut   movies from novels   candy   Expensive   Comedy
Tolkein   popcorn   passive
          Johnny Carson   **Entertainment**   Theme songs
Active   Dancing   Radio   fun   Concerts
performing   Riding   Songs   Music
                                            Pandora

Connect Related Ideas

After time is up, look at your ideas, and draw lines between related ideas. As you draw, you will begin to see your ideas cluster together. There may be one idea that is not related to as many other ideas, and another idea related to most.

?   **2.** On your idea cluster, draw lines to connect related ideas.

Your idea cluster might look something like this:

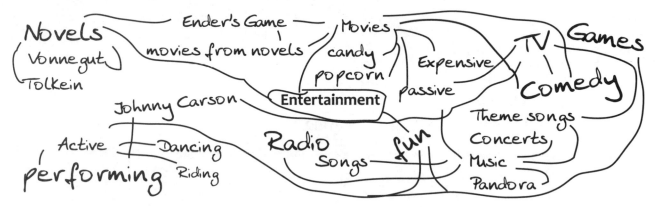

Describe the Relationships

Using a different pen or pencil, make notes on your thinking. Circle or add major categories. Describe relationships between concepts, or make notes on questions and ideas. Examine your finished idea cluster to identify ideas for your writing.

?   **3.** Add notes to your idea cluster describing categories, relationships, and questions.

Your idea cluster might look something like this:

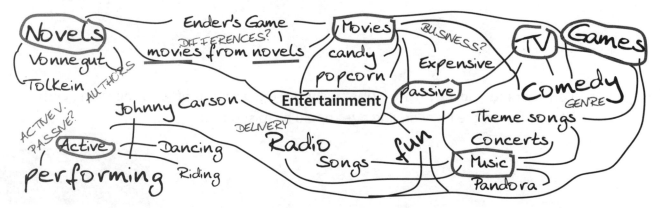

In this idea cluster, the difference between active and passive entertainment is interesting and may be a good choice for further exploration.

When you write, you might use many ideas from your idea cluster, or you might use only one. In some circumstances, you might not use any of the ideas in your finished work. The goal is to generate ideas to start developing your writing.

Complete the following exercises using idea clustering.

 1. Imagine that you need to write a response either agreeing or disagreeing with the statement that the legal driving age should be raised to 18.

    a. Surround the following topic with ideas.

Driving

    b. On your idea cluster, draw lines to connect related ideas.

    c. Add notes to your idea cluster describing categories, relationships, and questions.

 2. What insights or ideas did you gain from the idea cluster about driving?

3. Based on your idea cluster, write a brief response either agreeing or disagreeing with the statement that the legal driving age should be raised to 18.

Build Your Writing Skills

Don't censor or edit yourself when making an idea cluster. Write down all your ideas.

4. Imagine that you need to write an explanation of the term "hypothesis" and its importance in science. If you need more information, first research the term.

    a. Surround the following topic with ideas.

                                              Hypothesis

    b. On your idea cluster, draw lines to connect related ideas.

    c. Add notes to your idea cluster describing categories, relationships, and questions.

 5. How is idea clustering helpful to your writing?

 **6.** Based on your idea cluster, write a brief response explaining the term "hypothesis" and its importance in science.

Build Your Writing Skills

You can make more than one idea cluster for a writing task. Use an idea cluster when you need to generate new ideas.

7. Imagine that you need to write an explanation of the following quotation.

> The only maxim of a free government ought to be to trust no man living with power to endanger the public liberty.
>
> —*John Adams*

Source: John Adams, Notes for an oration at Braintree, 1772

a. Surround the following topic with ideas.

Power and Liberty

b. On your idea cluster, draw lines to connect related ideas.

c. Add notes to your idea cluster describing categories, relationships, and questions.

 8. How did the idea cluster help you understand the quotation?

Build Your Writing Skills

If you feel you're not generating enough ideas to begin writing, try sleeping on it. Start another idea cluster the next day.

 9. Based on your idea cluster, write a brief response explaining the quotation.

Check **Your Skills**

Use the following passage for exercises 1 through 3.

Observers Serve Vital Role for Fisheries

Observers are independent field biologists who are deployed aboard commercial fishing boats and at-sea processing facilities, and their work is vital to NOAA's mission of ensuring the economic and ecological sustainability of U.S. fisheries. Vessels operating in the West Coast Groundfish Trawl Catch Share Program are required to carry a certified observer on all fishing trips. In other fisheries along the West Coast, observers are assigned to fishing trips at random.

While at sea, observers collect a wide range of information. For example, they monitor and record catch data, particularly any discards (the unused catch that is returned to the sea) and endangered or threatened species caught. Observers also collect species data, including diversity of catch, condition of fish caught, seabird sightings, and any marine mammal interactions with fishing operations. In addition, they gather biological data, such as sex, fish lengths, and weight.

Adapted from "Observers serve vital role for fisheries," Northwest Fisheries Science Center, NOAA Fisheries, available at http://www.nwfsc.noaa.gov/news/features/observer/index.cfm

 1. Imagine that you must make a presentation about a career option for biologists. You have chosen to make a presentation about observers on commercial fishing boats. Read the passage and make notes for writing your presentation.

2. Make an idea cluster to help you prepare to write your presentation about observers on commercial fishing boats.

3. Based on your notes and your idea cluster, write an introduction for your presentation about a career as an observer on commercial fishing boats.

Remember the Concept

To read for writing:

- Identify your reading purpose.
- Skim and scan.
- Read and take notes.
- Evaluate the reading.
- Develop your ideas.

Create an **idea cluster** to brainstorm ideas.

Choosing an Organizational Structure

Connections

Have you ever...

- Trained a new co-worker to follow a company process?

- Tried to convince a friend to see a particular movie?

- Skipped a step in a recipe?

If you have, you've had to give organization to your thoughts, speech, and actions. Organizing your ideas is critical to being understood. Without organization, your coworkers will be confused, your arguments unpersuasive, and your cakes less than delicious. Organizing your ideas before you begin drafting will help you achieve your writing goal more quickly and effectively.

If you are packing a suitcase to capacity, it helps to think ahead and to use some trial and error. You need to fit everything in place in a logical way. Choosing an organizational structure is similar. The **RE-PAC** strategy helps you use your planning to find the best organizational structure for your writing through examining the needs of your writing task and trying out organizational ideas. To **RE-PAC:**

- **R**emember your purpose and audience.

- **E**valuate your ideas and prewriting.

- **P**ick two possible organizational structures.

- **A**rrange your prewriting into a beginning, middle, and ending.

- **C**ompare and choose the best organizational structure.

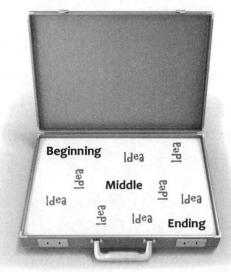

RE-PAC Your Ideas

Finding the best organizational strategy for your writing involves making some decisions. How do you decide which organizational structure is best?

Imagine your city is voting to decide whether or not to install speed bumps on a street in your neighborhood. The street is residential, and residents are concerned about fast cars passing. You have been asked to write an opinion piece for the local newspaper taking a stand on the issue.

Remember Purpose and Audience

Define your purpose and audience in order to focus your writing and give you a direction. Purpose and audience affect which organizational structure you will use.

? 1. What is your purpose and audience for this writing task?

In the case of this opinion piece, your purpose is to persuade other voters to vote with you about the installation of speed bumps in your neighborhood. Your audience is undecided voters who read the local paper.

Evaluate Your Ideas and Prewriting

Before choosing your organizational structure, it helps to have ideas and prewriting that you want to organize. Review your ideas and see how they logically fit together.

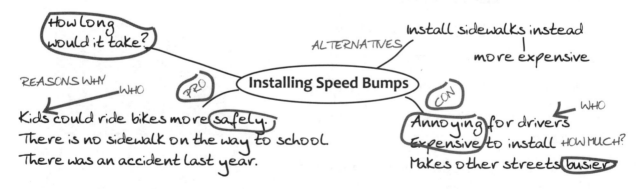

? 2. Evaluate the idea cluster. How do the ideas logically fit together?

You might group the pros of speedbumps together and contrast the cons. You can contrast who benefits and the type of benefits.

Pick Two Possible Organizational Structures

Based on your prewriting and ideas, what is a good organizational structure? Pick two potential structures. Use the following chart of organizational structures to make your choice.

Structure	What Is It?	Keywords
Descriptive	Describes what something is like	looks like, smells like, sounds like, feels like, adjectives
Chronological	Organizes information by time, in the order things happened	first, second, next, last, then, later, finally
Statement and Support	Gives an idea, then gives details to support it	for example, one reason, shows it's true
Comparison	Compares similarities and differences of two or more things	similarity, difference, like, unlike, as well, also
Cause and Effect	Shows reasons things happen; may be several causes or effects	cause, effect, as a result, because, consequently
Problem and Solution	Presents a problem and a proposed solution	problem, solution, solve, address the problem

3. Choose two organizational structures that might work for your purpose and audience. Why did you choose these structures?

You might select "Problem and Solution" because speed bumps are meant to solve a problem. You might also choose "Comparison" because you can compare the pros and cons of speed bumps.

Arrange Prewriting into a Beginning, Middle, and Ending

Organize your ideas into a beginning, middle, and ending for each organizational structure you're considering. You don't need to write complete sentences or include all of the details. Get an overview of the structure. Once you have charted a beginning, middle, and ending for each structure, ask, "How well does this order of ideas advance my purpose?"

? **4.** Complete the following chart to evaluate the potential organizational structures.

Purpose: _____   Audience: _____

Structure	Beginning	Middle	Ending	Does It Advance My Purpose?
Comparison				
Problem and Solution				

Your organizational chart might look like this:

Purpose: Persuade to install speed bumps   Audience: Undecided voters

Structure	Beginning	Middle	Ending	Does It Advance My Purpose?
Comparison	Establish pros and cons	Differences: focus on kids and safety vs. drivers and costs	Comparison: building speed bumps is worth it	Yes, somewhat
Problem and Solution	Problem: no sidewalk, direct route, accident, fast drivers	Solution: kids more safe	Even though: expensive, other streets busier	Yes, well

Compare and Choose the Best Structure

Compare how your ideas fit into the two organizational structures. Which works better for your purpose?

? **5.** Which structure best fits your purpose? Why did you choose this structure?

You might choose the problem and solution structure. Details from the cluster fit well, and the issue is better defined as a problem that needs a solution than a comparison between pros and cons. A problem and solution structure might be more compelling.

Use the following prompt to complete exercises 1 through 4.

Write a letter to the editor for your local paper either in favor of or opposing allowing children to own and use mobile phones.

1. Identify the purpose and audience for this writing task.

2. Create an idea cluster to help you complete this writing task.

3. Use the following chart to compare two organizational structures for this writing task.

Purpose: **Audience:**

Structure	Beginning	Middle	Ending	Does It Advance My Purpose?

4. Choose one organizational structure for this task. Explain your reasons for your choice.

Use the following prompt to complete exercises 5 through 8.

The most common states of matter are solid (such as iron), liquid (such as milk), and gas (such as oxygen). The state of matter depends on the surrounding temperature and pressure, and matter can change states. For example, melting iron at high temperatures results in a liquid (molten iron). Write one paragraph explaining the concept of states of matter, using water as an example.

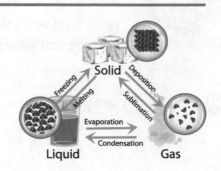

★ **5.** Identify the purpose and audience for this writing task.

★★ **6.** Create an idea cluster to help you complete this writing task.

★★ **7.** Use the following chart to compare two organizational structures for this writing task.

Purpose: **Audience:**

Structure	Beginning	Middle	Ending	Does It Advance My Purpose?

★★ **8.** Choose one organizational structure for this task. Explain your reasons for your choice.

Check Your Skills

Use the following prompt and passage for exercises 1 and 2.

Compare and evaluate the following online reviews of a local restaurant, Annie's Diner. Would you eat at the restaurant? Why or why not?

 I really enjoyed this restaurant. The portions were large, and the price was less than $10 per person. I went with four other people, and while one person's potatoes were undercooked, we all enjoyed our meal. I'll go back again to see if the food is always this good!

 Don't waste your time going to Annie's Diner. I had the lobster special, which was more expensive than anything on the menu. I hated the sauce, and that spoiled the whole lobster for me. Then I ordered chocolate cake for dessert. It was stale. I wouldn't ever go back there.

---

 1. Use the **RE-PAC** strategy to choose one organizational structure for this task. Explain your reasons for your choice.

 2. Respond to the prompt, using the organizational structure you chose in exercise 1.

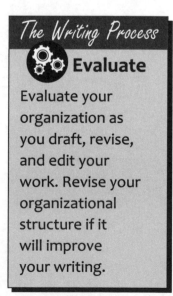

The Writing Process

Evaluate

Evaluate your organization as you draft, revise, and edit your work. Revise your organizational structure if it will improve your writing.

Use the following prompt and passage for exercises 3 and 4.

Read and reflect on the following quotation. Explain its meaning, using a modern-day example from your life or your knowledge of current events to illustrate the author's meaning.

United we stand, divided we fall. Let us not split into factions which must destroy that union upon which our existence hangs. Let us preserve our strength for the French, the English, the Germans, or whoever else shall dare invade our territory, and not exhaust it in civil commotions and intestine wars.

—*Patrick Henry*

Source: William Wirt Henry, *Patrick Henry: Life, Correspondences and Speeches,* 1891

 3. Use the **RE-PAC** strategy to choose one organizational structure for this task. Explain your reasons for your choice.

 4. Respond to the prompt, using the organizational structure you chose in exercise 3.

> *Remember the Concept*
>
> Use your ideas and planning to select an organizational structure that will work well for your purpose. Compare two possible structures to make the best choice.

FOCUS
Draft

Drafting is the process of choosing your words and writing your sentences. When you draft, it is important to continue to evaluate and plan. From your planning materials, you will begin to write sentences and paragraphs that will fit together into your organizational structure. The better your planning is, the easier it will be to draft your work.

Organization is important in writing a successful draft. Every written work has a beginning, middle, and ending. In a non-fiction work of medium length, such as a letter, memo, extended response, paper, blog post, or article, the beginning is usually an **introductory paragraph** or **introduction**. The introduction presents an overview of your central idea to the reader and makes the reader interested in what you have to say. The middle consists of **body paragraphs**. The **body** presents details that support your central idea. The ending is typically a **concluding paragraph** or **conclusion**. The conclusion reminds your reader of important ideas and leaves your reader with final thoughts about the topic. Essentially, you draw your reader in, present your detailed thoughts, and release your reader. You can visualize this basic structure graphically:

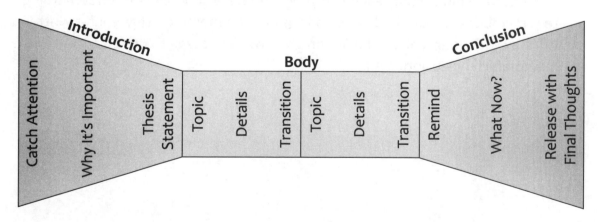

Your draft does not have to be perfect. In fact, count on the fact that your first draft won't be perfect. No first draft is perfect. However, it is important to get words on the page. Once you have a draft, you can evaluate, revise, and edit until you're satisfied with your work.

Draft in stages to make the writing process easier and more successful. Start by drafting a thesis statement of your central idea. A central idea will focus your work. Then, draft paragraphs for the introduction (the beginning), body (the middle), and the conclusion (the ending). Once all the pieces are in place, you can evaluate, revise, and edit.

This section provides lessons in drafting your work.

- **Developing a Thesis Statement**
  A thesis statement defines your central idea and gives your reader an overview of your work. Learn a strategy for drafting a thesis statement that clearly communicates your ideas.

- **Drafting the Introduction**
  Your introduction captures the reader's attention and identifies what you are attempting in your writing. The introduction is your reader's first impression. This lesson will give you a strategy to write an interesting introduction that makes your writing relevant to your reader.

- **Drafting Body Paragraphs**
  The body of your writing is the middle. The majority of your details and specifics are in the body, so it must be clear and logical. This lesson will help you organize and draft body paragraphs.

- **Drafting the Conclusion**
  The conclusion of your writing is the last impression you give your reader. Your conclusion reminds your readers of your central idea and gives them something to remember and ponder. If your conclusion is memorable, what you've written will stay with your reader. This lesson gives you a strategy to draft a strong and memorable conclusion.

Developing a
Thesis Statement

Connections

Have you ever...

- Found yourself saying, "I guess what I mean is..."?

- Listened to a speech that began, "Tonight I will explain four reasons why..."?

- Wanted to read a magazine article because the premise was intriguing?

A thesis statement is the statement of a central idea. In a speech, an article, or a discussion, it is important to make your central idea clear. A thesis statement gives your reader clues about what to expect in your writing. Having a strong and concise thesis statement will keep your writing organized and clear.

A thesis statement helps your reader focus on what you are saying. If you have a strong thesis statement, your reader does not need to spend energy wondering, "What is the point?" In an extended response, a short answer, a paper, or another short work, a thesis statement can usually be one sentence that states your message and the main supporting ideas by which you will explain it.

You can think of a thesis statement as a map that tells the destination and important landmarks along the way. In this lesson, you will learn to develop a thesis statement by answering two questions about your writing:

- What is your destination?

- How will you get there?

Developing a Thesis Map

To write a thesis, review your planning. You should know your purpose, audience, and organizational structure. From this information, identify:

- What is your destination? Identify your central idea.

- How will you get there? Identify your organization and main support.

A concise thesis statement is one sentence long, combining the "what" with the "how." Your core message will be precise. You will give enough information to get the reader interested, but not so much information that the reader thinks there's no need to keep reading. The thesis you write will depend on the purpose of your essay.

If your purpose is to:	Then your thesis should:
Persuade	State your claim (what you want your audience to believe) and a brief description of your evidence or reasons.
Inform	State the central message or topic and a few core details or major ideas you will present.
Narrate	State the message of the story or reason to tell the story and a main event or circumstance.
Explain	State the topic and key information required for understanding the explanation or the reason the explanation is important.

Imagine that you plan to write a local news article about a recent fundraiser at a community center. The event included an auction followed by a buffet dinner and then a swim party in the community pool. Afterwards, a local band performed a concert. Over 250 people attended, and the event raised $24,000, exceeding the goal. You have information about the menu, the music, and the prizes and winners for the auction, as well as statements from participants about the events of the evening.

What Is the Destination?

First, identify your central idea. Your central idea is the core of your thesis statement.

? **1.** Identify the central idea of the news article.

The purpose of the article is to inform. The central idea might be that the fundraiser was entertaining and successful.

Developing a Thesis Statement

How Will You Get There?

The second part of your thesis gives a clue to the essay's organization and content. Identify key supporting ideas and how they will be organized in your writing.

? 2. Imagine that you plan to write a chronological article about the fundraiser. What key chronological details would you include in your thesis?

Your thesis might note major events: the auction, dinner, swimming, and concert. Present them in chronological order, as you will in the essay. If you give a list of supporting ideas, your reader will expect them to occur in the essay in the same order as in the thesis.

Write the Thesis Statement

In one sentence, combine your central idea with core details that give your reader an idea of your organizational structure.

? 3. Write a thesis statement for this informative, chronological article.

Your thesis statement might read:

> The events of last Friday's entertaining and successful fundraiser included an auction, a dinner, a swim party, and a concert.

Although this example thesis contains a list of events, a thesis does not need a list of points in your writing. Many effective thesis statements give an overview of your approach:

> Last Friday's fundraiser was successful because of its well-planned, entertaining events.

Review Your Thesis Statement

When you are done developing your thesis statement, review what you have written. Does it communicate clearly to the reader? Is it easy to understand? Does it fit with your ideas?

? 4. Review your thesis statement. Revise and edit it if necessary.

Complete the following exercises about developing a thesis statement.

 1. How is a thesis statement similar to a map?

 2. How does the purpose of a writing task affect the thesis statement?

    a. The purpose defines what the writer will tell the reader.

    b. The purpose determines whether the thesis will be at the beginning or the ending.

    c. The thesis should be determined before the purpose.

    d. The purpose and the thesis are the same.

3. How does the organizational structure affect the thesis?

    a. The organization is determined by the structure of the thesis.

    b. The organization helps determine the content and order of the thesis.

    c. The thesis has nothing to do with the organizational structure.

    d. Organization is not determined until the end of a writing task.

4. The thesis statements below are not complete. Revise them to complete the thesis statements.

    a. I will discuss the history of computers.

    What is missing from this thesis statement?

    Write an improved thesis statement.

    b. Creativity is important to good writing.

    What is missing from this thesis statement?

    Write an improved thesis statement.

5. Complete the following unfinished thesis statements.

    a. The happiest surprise I have ever received . . .

    b. Hand-washing is important . . .

    c. Every four years, when voters elect a new president . . .

    d. Unpaid internships and apprenticeships should . . .

    e. I would like to be remembered . . .

 6. Imagine you are writing a review of a movie you have recently seen.

    a. What is the destination? Identify the central idea.

    b. How will you get there? Identify main supporting ideas, based on your organizational structure.

    c. Write a thesis statement for this writing task.

The Writing Process

✏ **Draft**

Draft your thesis first. This will help you stay on task—and on time—as you draft.

7. Imagine you must apply the following quotation to a modern event.

> …you should never let things get out of hand in order to avoid war. You don't avoid such a war, you merely postpone it, to your own disadvantage.
>
> —*Niccolò Machiavelli*

Source: Niccolò Machiavelli, *The Prince*, 1513

    a. What is the destination? Identify the central idea.

    b. How will you get there? Identify main supporting ideas, based on your organizational structure.

    c. Write a thesis statement for this writing task.

 8. Imagine you are writing a letter to the editor arguing either for or against allowing smoking in public bars and restaurants.

    a. What is the destination? Identify the central idea.

    b. How will you get there? Identify main supporting ideas, based on your organizational structure.

    c. Write a thesis statement for this writing task.

The Writing Process

Evaluate

After completing your draft, reread your thesis statement. You may need to revise it to better describe the finished work.

Check **Your Skills**

Use the following passage for exercises 1 and 2.

Young people who get tattoos are often criticized. How will they get jobs? How will they feel about their tattoos as they age? A tattoo, though, is an artistic statement. It marks you with an image or phrase that is important to you at a particular time in your life. The tattoo reflects your past self. We all carry our pasts with us into the future. Why not carry our pasts externally, as tattoos? Why not remember, and display, who we were and what we valued? We all make permanent decisions as young people: what college to attend, who to date, whether to marry. Honestly, a tattoo is less damaging and consequential than a bad relationship or poor career choice. Tattoos do not affect your skills and abilities. They only express the person you once were.

 1. Imagine you must write a response either agreeing or disagreeing with the argument in the passage. Write a thesis statement for your response.

 2. Imagine you must write a response applying the First Amendment, shown below, to the argument in the passage. Write a thesis statement for your response.

Amendment I

Congress shall make no law respecting an establishment of religion, or prohibiting the free exercise thereof; or abridging the freedom of speech, or of the press; or the right of the people peaceably to assemble, and to petition the Government for a redress of grievances.

Source: U.S. Bill of Rights, 1791, available at http://www.archives.gov/exhibits/charters/bill_of_rights_transcript.html

Use the following passage for exercise 3.

How Fossil Fuels Were Formed

Contrary to what many people believe, fossil fuels are not the remains of dead dinosaurs. In fact, most of the fossil fuels we find today were formed millions of years before the first dinosaurs. Fossil fuels, however, were once alive. They were formed from prehistoric plants and animals that lived hundreds of millions of years ago.

Think about what the Earth must have looked like 300 million years or so ago. The land masses we live on today were just forming. There were swamps and bogs everywhere. The climate was warmer. Ancient trees and plants grew everywhere. Strange looking animals walked on the land, and weird looking fish swam in the rivers and seas. Tiny one-celled organisms called protoplankton floated in the ocean.

When these ancient living things died, they decomposed and became buried under layers and layers of mud, rock, and sand. Eventually, hundreds and sometimes thousands of feet of earth covered them. In some areas, the decomposing materials were covered by ancient seas, and then the seas dried up and receded.

During the millions of years that passed, the dead plants and animals slowly decomposed into organic materials and formed fossil fuels. Different types of fossil fuels were formed depending on what combination of animal and plant debris was present, how long the material was buried, and what conditions of temperature and pressure existed when they were decomposing.

Source: U.S. Department of Energy, adapted from "How Fossil Fuels were Formed," available at: http://www.fossil.energy.gov/education/energylessons/coal/gen_howformed.html

 3. Based on the passage, write a thesis statement for an article explaining why there is a limited amount of fossil fuel, particularly oil, in the Earth.

> *Remember the Concept*
>
> To write a thesis statement, ask:
>
> - What is the destination?
> - How will I get there?

Drafting an Introduction

Have you ever...

- Heard an audience react to the first line of a speech?
- Walked into class late and had a hard time understanding?
- Been hooked on a story from the first sentence?

An introduction is your first impression of a written work. A strong introduction doesn't just tell your readers what you plan to say. It makes them want to keep reading. Your introduction is the way you attract your reader's attention and let them know what to expect.

Grabbing a person's attention can be tricky, but that is exactly what an introduction should do. The introduction convinces the reader to care about your message.

The effectiveness of your introduction is dependent on your ability to generate original ideas. In this lesson, you will learn a strategy to generate interesting ideas and use them to draft your introduction. How can you generate ideas that grab a reader's attention? You will draft your introduction with a...

Hook, Line, and Sinker

Your **hook** is an interesting beginning to catch attention. Your **line** gives the reader a reason why your topic is important or interesting, and your **sinker** is your thesis statement that explains your central idea.

Learn It!

Catch—Hook, Line, and Sinker

Your introduction has the big job of catching, and holding, the interest of your readers. Your introduction should catch your reader's attention...

Hook, Line, and Sinker

Imagine you are writing an article about vacations. You have already narrowed your topic to "vacation options on a budget." You have already written the thesis, "Many great, low-cost vacations are available, such as camping, volunteering at a vacation destination, visiting relatives, or touring your city as an outsider would."

Hook

A hook grabs your reader's attention. It can be a humorous or surprising statement, a quotation, an interesting fact, an anecdote, an example, a word picture, or a question. Review your planning, and make a list of possible hooks. Then, choose and draft a short hook that fits the tone of your writing.

? 1. Make a list of statements, quotations, facts, anecdotes, examples, word pictures, and questions you might use as a hook for an article about vacations on a budget.

? 2. Choose an idea with an appropriate tone, and draft a short hook for your article.

Your list could include a description of a camping trip and a quotation about traveling. Questions might include "Who is coming with me?" and "What is my vacation budget?" A surprising statement could be, "The best vacations are the cheapest." You might decide on the hook:

Who is coming with me? We'll have a great budget vacation!

Line

Next, brainstorm for a "line." Answer the following questions:

- Why is my topic important?
- Why is what I'm writing interesting?

Build Your Writing Skills

A **word picture** is a descriptive passage that focuses on conveying an image. Describe the sights, sounds, smells, feels, or tastes of a particular event.

After you answer the questions, draft a line that explains why the reader should care about what you're writing.

? **3.** Draft a line that explains why the reader should care about your article about budget vacations.

You might write:

> Everyone enjoys getting away for a vacation, but affording your dream vacation can be a problem.

Sinker

Your "sinker" is your thesis statement. This is a brief, but specific, description of what you will say and how you will say it. It is often the last sentence of the introduction. Your thesis statement should include your central idea and an indication of your main supporting ideas and organizational structure. The thesis statement for this article is:

> Many great, low-cost vacations are available, such as camping, volunteering at a vacation destination, visiting relatives, or touring your city as an outsider would.

Hook, Line, and Sinker

Put your hook, line, and sinker together to draft your introduction. Add transitions to make sure your introduction reads smoothly and makes sense.

? **4.** Draft an introduction to the article.

You might write:

> Who is coming with me? We're going to have a great budget vacation! Everyone enjoys getting away for a vacation, but affording your dream vacation can be a problem. With a little bit of creativity, even a cheap vacation can be thrilling. Many great, low-cost vacations are available, such as camping, volunteering at a vacation destination, visiting relatives, or touring your city as an outsider would.

Complete the following exercises about drafting an introduction.

 1. Imagine you are writing a presentation about Washington, D.C. for a class. Use the thesis statement, "When in Washington, D.C., tourists should visit essential political sites such as the White House, as well as cultural sites such as the Smithsonian Institution."

a. Brainstorm for a hook.

What quotation might interest your audience in traveling to Washington, D.C.?

What fact might interest your audience?

What anecdote or description might interest your audience?

What is a surprising statement that might interest your audience?

What questions could you ask to interest your audience?

b. Brainstorm for a line.

Why is traveling to Washington, D.C. important?

Why is traveling to Washington, D.C. interesting?

2. Imagine that you must write a proposal to increase employee retention at your workplace. Your customer service department has a high turnover which causes high training costs and decreased productivity. Two potential methods of employee retention have been proposed. You must choose one of the following options to recommend in your proposal.

Employee exit surveys show that 68% of employees who leave are looking for career advancement. A group at your workplace proposes a career development program that will help train and select employees for upper management.

Another group proposes that increased worker compensation is the better approach to retention. This group suggests increased benefits combined with salary increases linked to length of service. The total costs are approximately the same as the career development program.

   a. Draft a **hook:** a beginning statement to interest your reader.

   b. Draft a **line:** a reason why your reader should care about your topic.

   c. Draft a **sinker:** a thesis statement.

   d. Draft an introductory paragraph.

3. Imagine you are writing an analysis of the following quotation to explain its meaning and relevance to the modern world.

> In every political society, parties are unavoidable. A difference of interests, real or supposed, is the most natural and fruitful source of them. The great object should be to combat the evil: 1. By establishing a political equality among all. 2. By withholding unnecessary opportunities from a few, to increase the inequality of property, by an immoderate, and especially an unmerited, accumulation of riches. 3. By the silent operation of laws, which, without violating the rights of property, reduce extreme wealth towards a state of mediocrity, and raise extreme indigence towards a state of comfort. 4. By abstaining from measures which operate differently on different interests, and particularly such as favor one interest at the expense of another. 5. By making one party a check on the other, so far as the existence of parties cannot be prevented, nor their views accommodated.
>
> —*James Madison*

Source: *Papers of James Madison,* "On Parties," 1792

    a. Draft a **hook**: a beginning statement to interest your reader.

    b. Draft a **line**: a reason why your reader should care about your topic.

    c. Draft a **sinker**: a thesis statement.

    d. Draft an introductory paragraph.

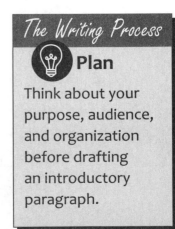

The Writing Process

💡 **Plan**

Think about your purpose, audience, and organization before drafting an introductory paragraph.

Check **Your Skills**

Use the Hook, Line, and Sinker strategy to draft introductions for the following exercises.

 1. Draft an introduction for an editorial agreeing or disagreeing with the following passage and analyzing the argument in the passage.

The Second Amendment guarantees the right to gun ownership: "A well regulated Militia, being necessary to the security of a free State, the right of the people to keep and bear Arms, shall not be infringed." However, this amendment was written in a time when warfare, crime, and society were much different than today. Today, we must judge the best laws by scientific investigation and our values as a society. Gun ownership contributes to suicide rates, accidental deaths, and violent crimes. We no longer need a militia of private citizens. Instead, we need fair and consistent gun regulation.

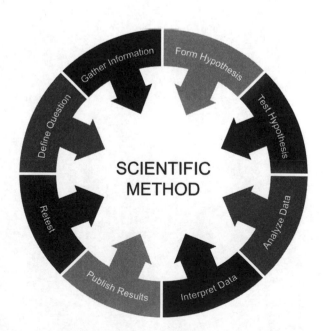

2. Draft an introduction for a presentation that explains the scientific method and its importance in scientific experimentation.

3. Draft an introduction for an analysis and comparison of the arguments in the following two passages. In your thesis statement, clearly state which argument is stronger.

Beauty contests are pointless and insulting to women. Despite attempts to include talent and personality events, pageants are still focused on women's bodies and faces. They parade women in skimpy bathing suits and evening dresses. The takeaway is that women are valued for their looks. It is a poor message for our society.

Pageant contests are well-intentioned and harmless. They present the whole person: looks, personality, and talents. Contestants must answer questions intelligently and conduct themselves well in multiple circumstances. As private events, there is nothing wrong with adult pageants. In fact, pageant winners receive scholarships and help with charity events and fundraising. The net result is positive for society.

Remember the Concept

Draft an Introduction with a Hook, Line, and Sinker.

- **Hook:** Grab attention.

- **Line:** Explain why it's important.

- **Sinker:** Present your thesis statement.

Drafting Body Paragraphs

Have you ever...

- Read an article to find details about an event?

- Looked for a particular passage in a book?

- Been skeptical about an argument until you read the detailed evidence supporting it?

Body paragraphs are the middle of your writing, where you explain details and give specifics. The details of your writing are essential. They explain and defend what you are trying to say.

Body paragraphs provide a logical progression of supporting ideas and details. They consist of ideas, explanations, reasons, evidence, narration, and information. They are the blocks, or steps, between your starting point and your destination. Each body paragraph connects to what precedes it and what follows it.

The number of body paragraphs you write will depend on your writing task. A short email or short answer might be one paragraph, with a beginning, middle, and ending that aren't divided into separate paragraphs. A paper or article might have one or two body paragraphs, or it might have ten pages' worth. The writing task and your own ideas will determine how many body paragraphs you need.

Just like a larger writing task, a body paragraph has a beginning, middle, and ending. Paragraphs can have many types of structures, but one good organization has:

- An introduction to the paragraph's topic.

- A middle that provides specific details.

- A conclusion and transition to the next paragraph.

Building Body Paragraph Blocks

Body paragraphs fit together like blocks, connected by transitions. Each paragraph has a beginning, middle, and ending. It discusses details of a topic that is related to your central idea.

People speak in "topic–detail" form in everyday encounters:

At the bank: "I'd like to cash this check. Please make it in fives and tens. Do you need to see my ID?"

At home: "I'm so tired. I think I'll go to bed early. Work really wiped me out today."

With friends: "That movie was amazing! The ending was unexpected, and I was surprised to find out she was guilty. I'll have to see the sequel when it's released."

In each case, the first sentence tells the topic, and the rest go into detail, elaborate, or support the first sentence.

Imagine you are writing an editorial supporting free subway transport for all citizens in your city. Write a body paragraph based on the thesis, "Providing free subway transportation within the city would decrease pollution and lessen congestion, providing a better future for our city."

Write an Introductory Topic Sentence

Write a sentence telling the topic of the paragraph. You don't need a one-to-one ratio of paragraphs for each idea in the thesis statement. Some ideas need more development, and different writing tasks will require more or less detail. You do need a topic or idea to hold your paragraph together. Determine what you will write about for each paragraph.

1. Write a topic sentence for a body paragraph supporting the thesis statement.

You might write:

Free subway fare would encourage more riders, thereby decreasing pollution.

This sentences links back to the thesis statement and introduces pollution as a topic.

Write Detail Sentences

The middle of your paragraph will have sentences that give details about the topic. These sentences are sometimes called "supporting sentences." They provide details that expand on the topic, prove it, or add to it.

?   **2.** Write two to four detail sentences about free subway passes reducing pollution.

You might write:

> With more people riding the subway, our city would have fewer cars producing pollution. Increased ridership would not cause a significant increase in the amount of energy required for subways to run, so each additional rider represents much less pollution in the air.

Write a Transitional Sentence to Connect to the Next Paragraph

Since paragraphs are part of a larger work, they often need transitions at the beginning or ending. At the end of a paragraph, a transition sentence can create an ending that shows how one idea is connected to the next. This keeps your reader interested in reading. We are used to hearing transitional sentences in our everyday lives.

> In the conference room: "Next on our agenda, we will discuss..."

> At home: "Now that you've finished your homework, it's time to clean your room."

The following list contains some transitional devices that you can use in your writing:

Above all	As a result	Also	Especially	As well as
However	In addition	Similarly	On the other hand	

The Writing Process

✏ **Draft**

If you're not sure how to transition to the next paragraph, write all of your paragraphs and then come back to add transitional sentences or phrases. Transitions can go at the beginning or end of paragraphs, as well as at the beginning or end of sentences within the paragraph.

?   **3.** Imagine that the next paragraph will discuss reducing congestion. Write a transitional sentence to end the paragraph.

You might write:

> Of course, a reduction of cars on the road has additional benefits.

Using what you know about topic sentences, detail sentences, and transitions, complete the following exercises.

 1. The following sentences of a paragraph are out of order. Label each sentence as T (topic sentence), D (detail sentence), or C (concluding or transitional sentence).

_____ Historical fiction tells an imaginary story that takes place in the "real" past.

_____ In either case, the reader can expect both truth and surprises.

_____ Events and people from that time may affect the characters' lives, but the main characters or plot elements themselves are fictional.

_____ Fiction and non-fiction are distinctly different genres of writing; however, historical fiction and creative non-fiction don't fit easily into the definitions of fiction as "not true" or non-fiction as "true."

_____ Creative non-fiction retells actual events and depicts actual people, but with fictional elements added to enhance the drama of the story.

 2. Rewrite the paragraph in the order you consider most effective.

3. Rewrite the following paragraph in the most effective order. Delete sentences that don't belong.

Using this as a fundraiser, the space program can advance other missions without overburdening the average citizen with increased taxes. Opportunities to orbit the earth are rare; however, there are some who have the financial means and willingness to pay a million dollars or more for the privilege of orbiting the earth. NASA should allow privately chartered launches into orbit for those willing to pay for them. While there is a market for spaceflight, NASA should move quickly to tap into it. NASA would need to make sure its "customers" were physically able to withstand the rigors and stresses of spaceflight, but this expense could be added to the cost of one ticket.

4. Imagine that you must write a proposal to increase employee retention at your workplace. Your customer service department has a high turnover which causes high training costs and decreased productivity. Two potential methods of employee retention have been proposed. You must choose one of the following options to recommend in your proposal.

Employee exit surveys show that 68% of employees who leave are looking for career advancement. A group at your workplace proposes a career development program that will help train and select employees for upper management.

Another group proposes that increased worker compensation is the better approach to retention. This group suggests increased benefits combined with salary increases linked to length of service. The total costs are approximately the same as the career development program.

a. Write a topic sentence for a body paragraph in your proposal.

b. Write three to five detail sentences for the body paragraph.

c. Write a transitional concluding sentence for the body paragraph.

d. Review and revise your whole paragraph.

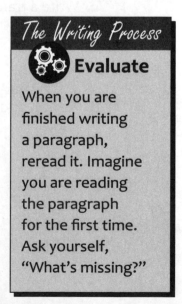

The Writing Process

Evaluate

When you are finished writing a paragraph, reread it. Imagine you are reading the paragraph for the first time. Ask yourself, "What's missing?"

5. Imagine you are writing an analysis of the following quotation to explain its meaning and relevance to the modern world.

In every political society, parties are unavoidable. A difference of interests, real or supposed, is the most natural and fruitful source of them. The great object should be to combat the evil: 1. By establishing a political equality among all. 2. By withholding unnecessary opportunities from a few, to increase the inequality of property, by an immoderate, and especially an unmerited, accumulation of riches. 3. By the silent operation of laws, which, without violating the rights of property, reduce extreme wealth towards a state of mediocrity, and raise extreme indigence towards a state of comfort. 4. By abstaining from measures which operate differently on different interests, and particularly such as favor one interest at the expense of another. 5. By making one party a check on the other, so far as the existence of parties cannot be prevented, nor their views accommodated.

—*James Madison*

Source: *Papers of James Madison*, "On Parties," 1792

a. Write a topic sentence for a body paragraph in your analysis.

b. Write four to six detail sentences for the body paragraph.

c. Write a transitional concluding sentence for the body paragraph.

d. Review and revise your whole paragraph.

Build Your Writing Skills

Once you are finished writing detail sentences, reread. Do you need more support? What other details would add to your writing?

Check **Your Skills**

Draft body paragraphs for the following writing tasks.

 1. Draft body paragraphs for an editorial agreeing or disagreeing with the following passage and analyzing the argument in the passage.

> The Second Amendment guarantees the right to gun ownership: "A well regulated Militia, being necessary to the security of a free State, the right of the people to keep and bear Arms, shall not be infringed." However, this amendment was written in a time when warfare, crime, and society were much different than today. Today, we must judge the best laws by scientific investigation and our values as a society. Gun ownership contributes to suicide rates, accidental deaths, and violent crimes. We no longer need a militia of private citizens. Instead, we need fair and consistent gun regulation.

 2. Draft body paragraphs for a presentation that explains the scientific method and its importance in scientific experimentation.

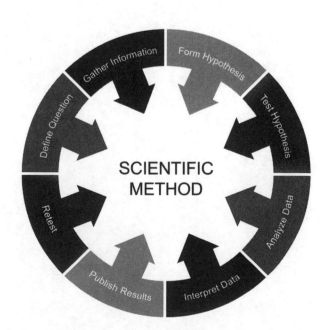

3. Draft body paragraphs for an analysis and comparison of the arguments in the following two passages. In your body paragraphs, show which argument is stronger.

Beauty contests are pointless and insulting to women. Despite attempts to include talent and personality events, pageants are still focused on women's bodies and faces. They parade women in skimpy bathing suits and evening dresses. The takeaway is that women are valued for their looks. It is a poor message for our society.

Pageant contests are well-intentioned and harmless. They present the whole person: looks, personality, and talents. Contestants must answer questions intelligently and conduct themselves well in multiple circumstances. As private events, there is nothing wrong with adult pageants. In fact, pageant winners receive scholarships and help with charity events and fundraising. The net result is positive for society.

Remember the Concept

To create strong paragraphs, write topic, detail, and transitional sentences.

Drafting a Conclusion

Have you ever...

- Walked out of a movie theater with the last scene resonating in your mind?

- Had a good idea because of the end of an article?

- Remembered the last line of a book?

Your conclusion is the last impression that you leave with the reader. A good conclusion will help the reader remember your central idea and give the reader ideas for thought.

A good conclusion reminds the reader of your central idea, but it does not simply repeat what you have already stated. Making a conclusion fresh and memorable is sometimes difficult. However, you can create a striking conclusion by expanding on your central idea and applying it to a bigger picture:

- How does this central idea apply to bigger-picture issues in the world?

- How does this central idea apply outside the scope of the writing task?

- What is a new way to think about this central idea?

- What is important to remember about this central idea?

The conclusion pulls your reader from the details of your paragraphs back into the larger world, hopefully having changed him or her in some way. Your conclusion should be composed carefully, because it is the last chance you have to affect your reader.

Writing a Memorable Conclusion

Learn It!

Your conclusion may be read last, but it is definitely not "least." A strong conclusion can help readers remember your writing and can inspire them to action or ideas. Use a three-step process to form a strong and memorable conclusion.

Remind   What Now?   Let Go

Imagine you are writing the article about vacations discussed in the lesson on Drafting the Introduction. You have narrowed your topic to "vacation options on a budget," and you have written the thesis, "Many great, low-cost vacations are available, such as camping, volunteering at a vacation destination, visiting relatives, or touring your city as an outsider would."

Remind

First, remind the reader of your central idea. What are the main takeaways that you want your reader to remember? What is the one thing you hope your reader remembers from your writing? You don't want to restate the thesis word for word, but you do want to remind the reader of important ideas.

?   1. What important concepts do you want the reader to remember about budget vacations?

You might answer:

> Planning ahead is key to enjoying a vacation on a budget. There are many options for fabulous but inexpensive vacations.

What Now?

Next, relate your idea to a bigger picture. How do your ideas apply to the world in a bigger way? What does your central idea make you wonder or realize? What should the reader do differently, if anything, with the knowledge from your writing? Answering these questions can help you develop suggestions for your reader to change their actions moving forward.

?   2. How could you relate your central idea to a bigger picture?

Your ideas may include that enjoyment, fun, and relaxation are the true focus of a vacation or that a "cookie-cutter" vacation with no imagination and a huge budget won't necessarily be fun. You might realize that what's advertised isn't necessarily best, and that people should look beyond the obvious to find meaningful experiences.

Let Go

It's time to release the reader. What can you say at the very end that reflects your attitude about the subject? Your last sentence should have a deliberate tone to convey your attitude. Let readers know how to feel as they exit the essay. Are you excited? Inspired? Thoughtful?

?   **3.** Write an ending sentence, setting a final tone for your article.

You might choose to "let go" on an encouraging and motivational note:

> The most important advice is to find a vacation that you will enjoy.

Put It All Together

Put together your reminder of your central idea, your connection to a bigger picture, and your ending that sets a tone. Add transitions or additional details if they are needed.

?   **4.** Write a conclusion for the article.

You might write:

> There are many options for fabulous but inexpensive vacations, as long as you plan ahead. Don't be limited by the "cookie-cutter" vacations that are advertised. It's important to look beyond what's obvious to find the vacation that's right for you. The most important advice, whatever your budget, is to find a vacation that you will enjoy. After all, that's the point of a vacation!

Complete the following exercises about drafting a conclusion.

 1. Imagine you are writing a presentation about Washington, D.C. for a class. Use the thesis statement, "When in Washington, D.C., tourists should visit essential political sites such as the White House, as well as cultural sites such as the Smithsonian Institution."

a. **Remind:** Brainstorm important ideas to remind your reader.

What are the main takeaways that you want your reader to remember?

What is the one thing you hope your reader remembers from your writing?

How can you restate your central idea in a new way?

b. **What Now?** Brainstorm connections between your central idea and a bigger picture.

How do your ideas apply to the world in a bigger way?

What does your central idea make you wonder or realize?

What should the reader do differently, if anything, with the knowledge from your writing?

c. **Let Go:** What tone do you want to convey in your final words?

2. Imagine that you must write a proposal to increase employee retention at your workplace. Your customer service department has a high turnover which causes high training costs and decreased productivity. Two potential methods of employee retention have been proposed. You must choose one of the following options to recommend in your proposal.

Employee exit surveys show that 68% of employees who leave are looking for career advancement. A group at your workplace proposes a career development program that will help train and select employees for upper management.

Another group proposes that increased worker compensation is the better approach to retention. This group suggests increased benefits combined with salary increases linked to length of service. The total costs are approximately the same as the career development program.

    a. For your conclusion, draft a reminder of your important ideas.

    b. Draft a connection between your central idea and a bigger picture.

    c. Draft a final sentence that conveys your attitude to your reader.

    d. Draft your concluding paragraph.

3. Imagine you are writing an analysis of the following quotation to explain its meaning and relevance to the modern world.

In every political society, parties are unavoidable. A difference of interests, real or supposed, is the most natural and fruitful source of them. The great object should be to combat the evil: 1. By establishing a political equality among all. 2. By withholding unnecessary opportunities from a few, to increase the inequality of property, by an immoderate, and especially an unmerited, accumulation of riches. 3. By the silent operation of laws, which, without violating the rights of property, reduce extreme wealth towards a state of mediocrity, and raise extreme indigence towards a state of comfort. 4. By abstaining from measures which operate differently on different interests, and particularly such as favor one interest at the expense of another. 5. By making one party a check on the other, so far as the existence of parties cannot be prevented, nor their views accommodated.

—*James Madison*

Source: *Papers of James Madison*, "On Parties," 1792

a. For your conclusion, draft a reminder of your important ideas.

b. Draft a connection between your central idea and a bigger picture.

c. Draft a final sentence that conveys your attitude to your reader.

d. Draft your concluding paragraph.

Check **Your Skills**

Draft conclusions for the following writing tasks.

1. Draft a conclusion for an editorial agreeing or disagreeing with the following passage and analyzing the argument in the passage.

> The Second Amendment guarantees the right to gun ownership: "A well regulated Militia, being necessary to the security of a free State, the right of the people to keep and bear Arms, shall not be infringed." However, this amendment was written in a time when warfare, crime, and society were much different than today. Today, we must judge the best laws by scientific investigation and our values as a society. Gun ownership contributes to suicide rates, accidental deaths, and violent crimes. We no longer need a militia of private citizens. Instead, we need fair and consistent gun regulation.

2. Draft a conclusion for a presentation that explains the scientific method and its importance in scientific experimentation.

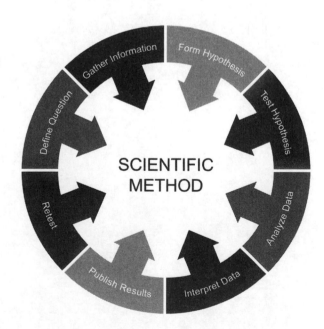

3. Draft a conclusion for an analysis and comparison of the arguments in the following two passages. In your conclusion, clearly state which argument is stronger.

Beauty contests are pointless and insulting to women. Despite attempts to include talent and personality events, pageants are still focused on women's bodies and faces. They parade women in skimpy bathing suits and evening dresses. The takeaway is that women are valued for their looks. It is a poor message for our society.

Pageant contests are well-intentioned and harmless. They present the whole person: looks, personality, and talents. Contestants must answer questions intelligently and conduct themselves well in multiple circumstances. As private events, there is nothing wrong with adult pageants. In fact, pageant winners receive scholarships and help with charity events and fundraising. The net result is positive for society.

> **Remember the Concept**
>
> In your conclusion:
>
> - **Remind**
>   What should your reader remember?
>
> - **What Now?**
>   How do your ideas relate to a bigger picture?
>
> - **Let Go**
>   What is your attitude or tone?

FOCUS
Evaluate

Evaluating your writing is an essential part of successful communication. When you evaluate what you write, you can identify weaknesses and strengths. Evaluation leads you to revise and edit your work until you are satisfied with the result.

This section will introduce you to methods of revising and editing, as well as several important aspects of writing to evaluate, revise, and edit.

- **Revising and Editing**
  Revising and editing are the ways that you improve your work. This lesson will give you an overview of processes for revising and editing.

- **Reading Critically**
  Reading your own work can sometimes be difficult. This lesson gives you a strategy to step back from your work and read it critically to identify areas for improvement.

- **Language and Word Choice**
  Your choice of words is the way you convey meaning to your reader. This lesson will help you make good choices in your language and improve your communication.

- **Voice and Tone**
  An author's voice and tone tells you about the author's personality and attitude. Tone and voice are strongly related to the author's purpose and audience. This lesson will give you strategies to assess and tailor your voice and tone as a writer.

- **Unity and Cohesion**

  A strong central idea and good organization will help you improve the unity and cohesion of your writing. This lesson will give you tools to evaluate your writing's unity and cohesion and to improve your organization.

- **Fluidity**

  Fluidity is the flow of your writing. In this lesson, you will learn to evaluate your use of varying sentence structures and transitions to improve fluidity.

- **Clarity**

  Clarity is essential to good writing; it means that your writing is clear and easy to understand. This lesson will provide a strategy to help you evaluate and improve the clarity of your writing.

Revising and Editing

Have you ever...

- Thought of a better response after an argument?

- Accidentally sent an email with spelling mistakes?

- Found missing words in a newspaper article or blog?

A draft of a written work will always have messy spots because writing can always be improved. That is why writers revise and edit their work. When you take the time to evaluate your work, you can improve it immensely.

Revising your work means making fundamental or major changes. You might reorganize what you've written, add new content, or eliminate sections. A major revision might mean changing your central idea or starting over from scratch.

Editing your work means making relatively minor changes. You might change a sentence to make it clearer, correct errors, remove unnecessary phrases, or choose more evocative words. Editing is a way to polish your work.

You can compare revising and editing to renovating a home for sale. If you want to sell a home at a profit, you need to prepare the property. Both the physical structure and the interior decor need to be repaired and improved.

Preparing writing for an audience demands renovation as well. The foundation, or structure, of written work needs to be solid. The interior decoration, or style, needs to be attractive. Before you present written work to an audience, both structure and style should be in tip-top condition.

Revising with POSE

To revise, get an overview of your writing. Is it working? Is it focused? Does it fulfill its purpose? Does it give enough relevant detail and support? Evaluate your **POSE**:

- **P**urpose
- **O**rganization
- **S**pecifics
- **E**ffectiveness

Imagine you are evaluating your classmate's response to the prompt, "Explain the process of oxidation using a specific example." Your classmate wrote the following paragraph.

Everyone knows that rust forms when iron is exposed to water. You know that this oxidation is the result of an electrochemical process that ultimately leads to unprotected iron becoming rust. During the extraction of iron from its ore, iron oxide reacts with carbon monoxide. The iron oxide loses oxygen molecules, resulting in iron. The carbon monoxide gains oxygen molecules, resulting in carbon dioxide. When one substance is oxidized, another substance loses oxygen, a process called reduction.

Purpose

Ask, does the work fulfill its purpose? If the writing strays from its purpose or writing task, make revisions.

? **1.** Does this paragraph fulfill the writing task? What revisions would you suggest?

The writing prompt asks the writer to explain the process of oxidation and to use a specific example. Although the paragraph uses specific examples (extracting iron from its ore and the formation of rust), it never defines oxidation. Adding a clear definition of oxidation would be a helpful revision.

Organization

Ask, is the work effectively organized? Does the writing have a logical, effective organization with a beginning, middle, and ending? If not, revision is needed.

?   **2.** Is the paragraph well organized? What revisions would you suggest?

The paragraph is not very logically organized. It lacks a strong central idea: a single, clearly stated definition of oxidation. You might begin with a definition of oxidation and then present the specific example illustrating oxidation. The portion that discusses rust could be used as an ending or conclusion.

Specifics

Ask, does the work contain enough specific, appropriate details to support the ideas and fulfill the task? If not, details may need to be researched, elaborated, or added.

?   **3.** Does the paragraph contain enough specific details? What revisions would you suggest?

The paragraph includes details and specifics about examples of oxidation. The definition of oxidation is the main missing piece.

Effectiveness

Ask, is the writing effective? Does the overall writing have the correct tone for its purpose? Is the response successful? If not, revision is needed.

?   **4.** Is the writing successful in content and tone? What revisions would you suggest?

The tone at the beginning of the paragraph ("everyone knows" and "you know") is overly informal. You might revise the paragraph to create a more formal tone.

A revised paragraph might read:

> Oxidation is a chemical reaction that causes a substance to gain oxygen. When one substance is oxidized, another substance loses oxygen, a process called reduction. One example of oxidation and reduction occurs during the extraction of iron from ore. In this process, iron oxide reacts with carbon monoxide. The iron oxide loses oxygen molecules, resulting in iron. The carbon monoxide gains oxygen molecules, resulting in carbon dioxide. The most common type of oxidation that people recognize is rust formation on iron exposed to water. This oxidation is the result of an electrochemical process that ultimately leads to unprotected iron gaining oxygen molecules and becoming iron oxide, or rust.

Use the following scenario and passage for exercises 1 through 5.

Imagine you are evaluating your classmate's response to the prompt, "Explain the following quotation by John F. Kennedy. 'Only an educated and informed people will be a free people.'" Your classmate wrote the following response.

Freedom is important. Consider this example: a person has a curable ailment. Two treatments are available. One is nothing more than a placebo in a fancy bottle. The other is a proven cure. If the person lacks information and education to make a choice, that person can be manipulated by the company selling the placebo. The person can make a choice, but it is not an informed choice. Freedom is what you have when you have education and information.

Source of Quotation: John F. Kennedy, remarks at the 90th Anniversary Convocation of Vanderbilt University, 1963

1. **Purpose:** Does the response fulfill the writing task? What revisions would you suggest?

2. **Organization:** Is the response well organized? What revisions would you suggest?

3. **Details:** Does the response contain appropriate details? What revisions would you suggest?

4. **Effectiveness:** Is the response successful in content and tone? What revisions would you suggest?

5. On a computer or a separate sheet of paper, revise the paragraph.

Use the following scenario and passage for exercises 6 through 10.

Imagine you are evaluating your classmate's response to the prompt, "Take a side on the issue of whether salaried employees should receive overtime pay. Defend your position." Your classmate wrote the following response.

> Yes, everyone should get overtime pay. You deserve money for your work and your time, right? Why shouldn't you get extra money if you work extra time? Companies always want to pay as little as possible. But every company gets benefits from your time and energy. That's what they're buying from you, right? It's important to have laws that make the company pay for your overtime, even if you earn a salary.

6. Purpose: Does the response fulfill the writing task? What revisions would you suggest?

7. Organization: Is the response well organized? What revisions would you suggest?

8. Details: Does the response contain enough appropriate details? What revisions would you suggest?

9. Effectiveness: Is the response successful in content and tone? What revisions would you suggest?

10. On a computer or a separate sheet of paper, revise the paragraph.

Editing with FREE

When you edit, you are checking for clarity and correcting mistakes. It can be difficult to find your own errors. The **FREE** process helps you edit one sentence at a time.

- **Focus:** Focus on one sentence.

- **Read:** Read aloud to see if it makes sense and sounds right.

- **Errors:** Check for common errors.

- **Evaluate:** Does the edited sentence work? Is it correct?

Focus

The first step is to focus on one single sentence. Narrowing your focus makes it easier to edit your work. By focusing on just one sentence, you can pay attention to each word as well as the intended meaning of the sentence.

Focus on the following sentence.

For the benefit of making good decisions when you seek to try balancing you're budget, you must prioritize the importance of items in the budget.

Read

Read the sentence aloud to check if it sounds natural. We are used to hearing spoken language. Reading aloud will help you check if what you've written sounds right. You can catch awkward language, wrong words, or bad sentence structure.

If you are in a classroom or test-taking situation, try reading the sentence quietly to yourself or try to "hear" the words silently in your head.

? **1.** Read the sentence aloud. Correct any errors or problems that you notice.

You might notice that the sentence sounds wordy and unnecessarily long. The beginning of the sentence could be much simpler. You might edit it to read:

To make good decisions when you balance you're budget, you must prioritize the importance of items in the budget.

Errors

Check the sentence for common errors, such as commonly confused words like "their," "there," and "they're," or "your" and "you're." Many of these errors are difficult to find by reading aloud. Words such as "their" and "there" sound the same.

Everyone has common mistakes that they make when they write. Keep a diary of mistakes that you commonly make so you can check for them in your writing.

?   **2.** Check the sentence for common errors and correct them.

> **Review & Practice**
>
> Learn more about finding and correcting common errors on pages 245–278.

You might notice that "you're" is the wrong word. The contraction "you're" means "you are." The correct word is the possessive "your." You should edit the sentence to read:

> To make good decisions when you balance your budget, you must prioritize the importance of items in the budget.

Evaluate

Evaluate your corrected sentence. Are you satisfied with its clarity and accuracy?

?   **3.** Evaluate the edited sentence. Make any additional improvements or corrections.

When you evaluate the edited sentence, you might notice that "prioritize the importance of" is redundant. You can eliminate the phrase "the importance of." Your final sentence might read:

> To make good decisions when you balance your budget, you must prioritize items in the budget.

> **The Writing Process**
>
>  **Draft**
>
> As you draft, watch for common errors that you make in your writing. The habit of checking for common errors will improve your writing over time.

Practice It!

Edit the following passage in exercises 1 through 15.

In the novel *War and Peace*, Leo Tolstoy write, "I cannot conceive of a man not being free unless he is dead." He describes is a particular kind of freedom: a personal, inner freedom. Every person has freedom of though and freedom within the confines of there situation. A person in jail can chose to read, study, and improve themselves; a person who is in a wheelchair can choose to train themselves thoroughly and become an athlete.

1. **Focus:** Write down the first sentence that you will evaluate and edit.

2. **Read:** Read the sentence aloud. What errors or problems do you notice?

3. **Errors:** Are there any common errors in the sentence?

4. **Evaluate:** Make corrections and evaluate the edited sentence.

5. How did your editing improve the sentence?

6. **Focus:** Write down the next sentence that you will evaluate and edit.

7. **Read:** Read the sentence aloud. What errors or problems do you notice?

8. **Errors:** Are there any common errors in the sentence?

9. **Evaluate:** Make corrections and evaluate the edited sentence.

10. **Focus:** Write down the next sentence that you will evaluate and edit.

11. **Read:** Read the sentence aloud. What errors or problems do you notice?

12. **Errors:** Are there any common errors in the sentence?

13. **Evaluate:** Make corrections and evaluate the edited sentence.

14. **Focus:** Write down the next sentence that you will evaluate and edit.

15. **Read:** Read the sentence aloud. What errors or problems do you notice?

16. **Errors:** Are there any common errors in the sentence?

17. **Evaluate:** Make corrections and evaluate the edited sentence.

18. How did your editing improve the paragraph as a whole?

Check Your Skills

Use the following scenario and passage for exercises 1 and 2.

Imagine you are evaluating your classmate's response to the prompt, "Explain and critique the quotation by John Quincy Adams, 'Individual liberty is individual power, and as the power of a community is a mass compounded of individual powers, the nation which enjoys the most freedom must necessarily be in proportion to its numbers the most powerful nation.'" Your classmate wrote the following response.

It is difficult to define freedom. John Quincy Adams has defines the power of a nation as the freedom of each of the people, combined. The more freedom the people have, the more powerful the nation is as a group. He is talking about the amount of freedom allowed politically by the government to each citizen. The problem with this definition of a nation's power is that the people do not always act together and combine there individual power. People often struggle against each other. Perhaps Adams believes that this struggle ultimately results in better decisions and laws, and therefore the nation becomes more powerful.

Source of Quotation: John Quincy Adams, Letter to James Lloyd, 1822

 1. Evaluate the paragraph. What are its strengths and weaknesses?

 2. Revise and edit the paragraph.

Use the following passage for exercises 3 and 4.

Imagine you are evaluating your friend's letter to the editor before she sends it in to the local newspaper. Your friend wrote the following paragraph.

The 1999 National Gambling Impact Study found that "the high-speed instant gratification of Internet games and the high level of privacy they offer may exacerbate problem and pathological gambling." Gambling at home over the Internet is really harmful. Online gambling is a serious problem. Gambling is illegal in our state, many people spend countless hours and dollars gambling online. This leads to gambling addiction and money flowing out of our state, likely overseas. Our state needs to make it a priority too limit the availability of online gambling and to increase education and outreach for gambling addiction.

---

 3. Evaluate the paragraph. What are its strengths and weaknesses?

 4. Revise and edit the paragraph.

Remember the Concept

To revise your work, review its:

- **Purpose**
- **Organization**
- **Specifics**
- **Effectiveness**

To edit your work:

- **Focus** on a sentence.
- **Read** it aloud.
- Check for **Errors.**
- **Evaluate** the edited sentence.

Reading Critically

Have you ever...

- Read your writing the next day and found errors?

- Helped a friend by reading his or her story?

- Realized that an email you sent didn't express what you were trying to say?

Having a friend, instructor, or classmate read your work gives you a new perspective on what you've written. However, it's not always an option. Stepping back and reading what you've written with fresh eyes can help you evaluate your writing in a similar way. **Reading critically** means to read from a new perspective so that you can evaluate and analyze what you've written.

When you evaluate your own work, think about how you would evaluate someone else's text. You can use any reading strategies that you know. Reading your work critically will help you answer questions about your writing. How effective is your writing? What will a reader understand from reading your work?

One strategy you can use to read critically is **PAAR**:

- **Preview:** What can you understand about your writing by previewing it? Skim to see if you can quickly identify main ideas.

- **Annotate:** Read through your work and make notes. Underline important ideas and significant words. Note questions in the margins. Ask questions: What does this mean? What does this support?

- **Analyze:** Write a critical analysis of what you've read.

- **Revise:** Use your analysis to revise your writing.

Reading Your Writing Critically

When you read critically to evaluate your writing, you put aside your identity as the author and become a reader. Approach your writing as you might approach a newspaper article, short story, or blog post that you want to analyze.

Imagine you have written the following paragraph for a science paper.

Tardigrades are tiny, eight-legged animals that live in water. Even if they are denied food and water for a decade, tardigrades can rehydrate. Tardigrades can survive a broad range of extreme temperatures, and they can live under pressure approximately six times greater than the deepest ocean trenches. These tiny creatures withstand hundreds of times the amount of ionizing radiation that would kill a person and can even live in the vacuum of space. Tardigrades are strange and interesting animals, even though they are small.

Preview

Skim your writing to identify the central and supporting ideas. Have you communicated your intended message? What would a reader understand by skimming your work?

? 1. Skim the paragraph. What is the central idea?

Based on skimming, you might decide that the central idea is to describe tardigrades. However, a closer reading shows that the paragraph focuses on tardigrades' ability to survive in extreme conditions. You might revise the paragraph to make the central idea clearer.

Annotate

Read your writing. Annotate by underlining and highlighting and by noting important ideas, significant words, and questions you have about the writing. What would a reader note and wonder about your work?

? 2. Read and annotate the paragraph. Below, note important ideas, significant words, and questions about the response.

The important idea is that tardigrades can survive in extreme conditions. You might wonder whether a rehydrated tardigrade has any ill effects or problems. The passage notes that the tardigrade can survive in a wide range of temperatures, but you might wonder exactly what that range of temperatures is.

Analyze

Analyze what you have read by identifying strengths and weaknesses.

?　**3.** What are the strengths and weaknesses of the response?

One of the strengths of this passage is that it gives a number of details about extreme circumstances that the tardigrade can withstand. One weakness is that the central idea is not clear at the beginning or end of the paragraph.

Revise

Have you communicated clearly? Have you discovered new ideas or questions through your critical reading? Revise your work based on your critical reading.

?　**4.** Based on your critical reading, revise the response.

You might revise the paragraph in this way:

> The tiny, eight-legged, water-dwelling animals known as tardigrades are able to live in extreme conditions. Even if they are denied food and water for a decade, tardigrades can rehydrate and function normally. Tardigrades can survive temperatures between almost absolute zero and hotter than the boiling point of water, and they can live under pressure approximately six times greater than the deepest ocean trenches. These tiny creatures withstand hundreds of times the amount of ionizing radiation that would kill a person and can even live in the vacuum of space. Tardigrades show the versatility of life on Earth and its ability to survive severe circumstances.

Build Your Writing Skills

Challenge yourself to improve your writing. What idea could be clearer? What information or details could be added? What unnecessary information could be deleted?

Practice It!

Imagine you are evaluating your response to the prompt, "Are video games good, bad, or neutral for society? Write a response that supports your position with evidence." You wrote the following draft.

Video games have both benefits and drawbacks. One of the benefits of video games is that they give inexpensive enjoyment, but a more important benefit is that video games can improve skills. Some video games for children are designed to be educational. A study by the Max Planck Institute for Human Development and Charité University Medicine St. Hedwig-Krankenhaus showed that video gaming causes increases in the brain regions responsible for spatial orientation, memory formation, strategic planning, and fine motor skills. Still, violent video games are controversial. Some want to ban violent video games, but from the evidence, it is unclear whether video game violence causes violent behavior.

★ 1. **Preview:** Skim the response. What is the central idea?

★★ 2. **Annotate:** Read and annotate the response. Below, note important ideas, significant words, and questions about the response.

★★ 3. **Analyze:** What are the strengths and weaknesses of the response?

★★ 4. **Revise:** Based on your critical reading, revise the response.

★★★ 5. Research and write your own response to the prompt, and then read critically to revise your response. Use a computer or a separate sheet of paper.

Use the following scenario and passage for exercises 6 through 10.

Imagine you are evaluating a memo you are writing to remind employees about the company's internal promotion policy. You wrote the following draft.

Our company's policy is to promote from within whenever possible. We strive to make opportunities for growth available for all employees. If you are interested in promotion opportunities, please take the time to log in to your employee account and update your skills and experience. From your employee account, you will also find job listings of available positions on our website. Apply to any open positions through your employee account. If you have any questions about how to advance in the company, send me an email at human_resources@trc.com. Don't forget to update your skills and experience on the website and browse job opportunities.

6. **Preview:** Skim the response. What is the central idea?

7. **Annotate:** Read and annotate the response. Below, note important ideas, significant words, and questions about the response.

8. **Analyze:** What are the strengths and weaknesses of the response?

9. **Revise:** Based on your critical reading, revise the response.

10. Write a business memo describing a workplace policy, and then read critically to revise your memo. Use a computer or a separate sheet of paper.

Use the following scenario and passage for exercises 11 through 15.

Imagine you are evaluating your response to the prompt, "Explain the following quotation by Frederick Douglass. 'Those who profess to favor freedom, and yet depreciate agitation, are men who want crops without plowing up the ground.'" You wrote the following draft of your response.

The quotation by Frederick Douglass uses growing crops as a metaphor for freedom. In this metaphor, freedom is the crop being grown. Agitation, such as protests, is the field being plowed. The ground must be torn up in order to grow the crops; similarly, voices must protest, be heard, and create debate in order to have freedom. Douglass's metaphor is similar to the idiom, "You can't make an omelet without breaking a few eggs." Agitation may be unsettling, but it is necessary to maintain freedom.

Source of quotation: Frederick Douglass, an address on West India Emancipation, 1857

★ **11. Preview:** Skim the response. What is the central idea?

★★ **12. Annotate:** Read and annotate the response. Below, note important ideas, significant words, and questions about the response.

★★ **13. Analyze:** What are the strengths and weaknesses of the response?

★★ **14. Revise:** Based on your critical reading, revise the response.

★★ **15.** Write your own response to the prompt, and then read critically to revise your response. Use a computer or a separate sheet of paper.

Check **Your Skills**

Use the following scenario and passage for exercises 1 through 3.

Imagine you are evaluating a cover letter you are writing for a job application. So far, you have drafted the following paragraph.

My skills and experience fit well with the requirements of the project manager position. The job listing mentions that the job requires someone who can handle deadlines well, who works well with clients, and who can prioritize and organize work. My experience in a busy retail store has prepared me well. Every day, I must prioritize to organize the store and perform my duties, while providing excellent customer service to clients. While working this demanding job, I have earned an associate's degree in business, where I developed my computer skills and understanding of business. I have learned to manage my time to fulfill all of my duties.

 1. Read critically and revise the paragraph.

 2. Draft an original paragraph, explaining your qualifications for the position.

 3. Read critically and revise your draft.

Use the questions on page 329 to evaluate your response.

Use the following scenario and passage for exercises 4 through 6.

Imagine you are evaluating your response to the prompt, "Do voter ID laws help or hinder democracy? Write a response, supporting your position with evidence." You wrote the following draft of your response.

Voter ID laws require identification from voters. Proponents state that these laws prevent voter fraud by identifying people who show up to the polls. Opponents say that this type of voter fraud is minimal at best and that the true effect of voter ID laws is to suppress voting among minorities and the poor. Support is strongest for the opposing argument; voter ID laws ultimately hinder democracy. There is no evidence for widespread polling-place fraud. However, a report by the U.S. Election Assistance Commission found that there was statistically significant correlation between voter ID laws and reduced turnout.[1] Voter ID laws likely have a minor effect, but the effect on turnout likely outweighs the effect on fraud.

---

[1]Source: United States Election Assistance Commission, "Best Practices to Improve Voter Identification Requirements," available at http://www.eac.gov/assets/1/workflow_staging/Page/62.PDF

 4. Read critically and revise the response.

 5. Draft an original response to the prompt.

 6. Read critically and revise your draft.

> ### Remember the Concept
>
> Read critically to evaluate your writing.
>
> - **Preview**
> - **Annotate**
> - **Analyze**
> - **Revise**

Use the questions on page 329 to evaluate your response.

Language and Word Choice

Connections

Have you ever...

- Noticed something different in a large poster when you stood closer to it?

- Watched a show on a high-definition television?

- Listened to a friend retell an event and felt like you were there with him?

If you have, then you have noticed the impact that specific, unique details can make. Details help us picture places and events in our minds and understand more fully what we read.

When writers repeat the same nouns and verbs again and again, they communicate nothing new. To solve this problem, be aware of your choice in words and the language you use. To keep readers interested, use words that communicate well: **SCVIDs**.

What are SCVIDs? They are:

- **Specific:** "Young, brown-eyed girl" is more specific than "child."

- **Concrete:** "She sparkled in her gown" is more concrete than "She looked pretty."

- **Vivid:** "Brilliant scarlet" is more vivid than "red."

- **Imaginative:** "Hope was no longer elusive" is more imaginative than "He saw light at the end of the tunnel."

- **Details:** "Skyscraper" is more detailed than "building."

SCVIDs are the details that make your writing understandable, interesting, and unique. They are often not the words that come to your mind first, but words that come to mind with some thought.

Using SCVIDs

Incorporate SCVIDs into each stage of the writing process. To use SCVIDs effectively, you need to have them "on the tip of your tongue." When you plan, make a list of SCVIDs. When you draft, use your SCVIDs. Finally, when you evaluate, edit using SCVIDs.

List — Use — Edit

Imagine you are writing a blog post about the New Deal to honor President Franklin D. Roosevelt's birthday. When brainstorming, you wrote down "jobs," "financial regulations," and "economy." If you use these three descriptors again and again in your writing, chances are that your reader will lose interest without learning much about the New Deal.

Plan: Make a List of SCVIDs Using Your Five Senses

Using SCVIDs does not just mean adding adjectives. You will also choose more descriptive nouns and verbs. Notice the difference between these two sentences:

Last weekend, I visited my mother.
Last Friday, I drove to my mother's farm in Springfield.

You learn more by reading the second sentence because it contains specific details. Now imagine the impact that SCVIDs can make in an entire letter or blog post. When you plan, make a list of SCVIDs that relate to your topic, including nouns, verbs, and adjectives. Use words for all five senses. What do you see, hear, taste, touch, and smell? Also include SCVIDs for abstract ideas such as love, trust, or denial.

1. Make a list of SCVIDs for the words "jobs" and "economy."

One possible list of SCVIDs might include:

Jobs: employment, effort, sweat, public works program, building infrastructure, occupations, farmers, agricultural workers, construction workers, livelihood

Economy: recovery, Great Depression, relief, devastation, poverty, wealth

Draft: Use the SCVIDs to Write Your Draft

Reference the list of SCVIDs as you begin to write your draft.

? **2.** Draft a paragraph including your SCVIDs for the words "jobs" and "economy."

You might write:

> President Franklin D. Roosevelt made the New Deal, a group of laws and executive orders to encourage economic recovery. The New Deal made employment, including a public works program that helped revitalize the country's infrastructure. Construction workers made and repaired roads and buildings.

You may not use all of the words from your list of SCVIDs, but the list will help you use a greater variety of more specific words.

Evaluate: Edit Using the SCVIDs

When revising and editing your work, read each paragraph and ask yourself where details can be more specific, concrete, vivid, and imaginative. To help you evaluate your language, circle all nouns and adjectives in your writing. Replace or remove the repeated, vague, and non-descriptive ones. Then, underline all verbs, and replace the repeated and non-specific verbs. Look out for overused verbs such as "be," "do," "look," "see," and "say."

? **3.** Review and edit your paragraph, using SCVIDs.

The words "roads" and "buildings" are vague. The verb "made" is overused and unspecific. You could edit the paragraph this way:

> President Franklin D. Roosevelt implemented the New Deal, a group of laws and executive orders to encourage economic recovery. The New Deal created employment, including a public works program that helped revitalize the country's infrastructure. Construction workers built and repaired bridges, highways, post offices, airports, court houses, and other public structures.

> **Build Your Writing Skills**
>
> Avoid relying on the thesaurus feature in word processing software. Using SCVIDs is not about using big words, but about using the best descriptive words.

Use your knowledge of SCVIDs to complete the following exercises.

1. Write a list of SCVIDs for each of the following words:

   quiet _____

   nice _____

   say _____

   fast _____

   person _____

Use the following sentence to complete exercises 2 through 5.

Chlorophyll is crucial for photosynthesis because it allows plants to absorb energy from light.

2. Write a list of SCVIDs you could use to draft a paragraph on this topic.

3. Draft a paragraph using some or all of the SCVIDs from exercise 2.

4. Circle all nouns and adjectives in your paragraph. Are they the best choice of words? Rewrite your paragraph, replacing ineffective words with SCVIDs.

Build Your Writing Skills

The SCVIDs you choose will depend on your audience. For example, you would use different SCVIDs to explain the causes of war to an 11-year-old than you would writing about war for a 30-year-old.

5. Underline all the verbs in your paragraph. Rewrite your paragraph, replacing ineffective, vague verbs with stronger, more specific verbs.

6. How can using SCVIDs improve the writing that you do every day?

Use the following prompt and passage to complete exercises 7 through 10.

Read and respond to the following letter to the editor. In your response, evaluate the author's argument, explaining its strengths and weaknesses.

> I have just learned that a popular coffee-maker company is planning to use DRM (digital rights management) software in new coffee makers. This technology will prevent consumers from using other companies' single-serve coffee products in the coffee makers. I've already run into this problem with ink for my inkjet printer! I cannot choose a store brand of ink for my printer because a computer chip in the printer will reject the lower-cost ink. In my opinion, this type of action kills competition. Allowing companies to use DRM software is against the free market. It takes away consumer choice. This type of action should be illegal, because it ultimately harms the free market and consumers.

7. Write a list of SCVIDs to respond to the prompt.

The Writing Process

Evaluate

When you edit, it can be helpful to have a friend circle the verbs in your draft. Remember that each sentence must have at least one verb.

---

8. Draft a paragraph using some or all of the SCVIDs from exercise 7.

 9. Circle all nouns and adjectives in your response. Rewrite your response, replacing them with more specific, concrete, vivid, and imaginative details.

 10. Underline all verbs in your response. Rewrite your response, including more descriptive verbs.

Build Your Writing Skills

As you develop a list of SCVIDs, try to imagine yourself surrounded by and inside the situation and describe what you see, hear, smell, taste, feel, and think.

Check Your Skills

Complete the following exercises about SCVIDs.

★★ **1.** Choose SCVIDs to complete the paragraph.

The road **(a.)** _____ up the mountain like a soft-serve yogurt cone. At the top, a group of students gathered, **(b.)** _____ together and then breaking into smaller groups. Every few minutes, one student would run to another group and quickly run back. The last cloud **(c.)** _____, and the students looked around themselves. The view spread in front of them, a picnic blanket landscape: a **(d.)** _____ patchwork of greens and yellows. The hum of student activity rose until the mountaintop was almost **(e.)** _____. Then there was a sudden "Fwhoop!" as a glider slid into the air. Another opened, then a third; red, orange, and pink, they circled the students. Applause rang out as the three gliders circled overhead then drifted back down, following the swirl of the road around the mountain. The students **(f.)** _____ their success. As design teams, they had successfully launched their first hang gliders.

★★ **2.** Develop a list of SCVIDs about how clouds form. Rewrite the paragraph below using SCVIDs from your list.

The air around us always contains some water. When the air is near the ground, the water present is typically in the form of water vapor, an invisible gas. Warm air, including water vapor, from near the ground rises up away from the ground. When the air rises away from the warm ground, the air cools. The cool air cannot hold as much water vapor. This causes some water to condense onto small particles. A small water droplet forms around each particle. The droplets come together into clouds. A similar process causes fog to form on very cold days.

3. Develop a list of SCVIDs that describe a historic event. Draft a description of the event using your SCVIDs. Edit your response as necessary to be as descriptive as possible.

Write your answer below or type your response on a computer. Take approximately 25 minutes to respond.

 4. Develop a list of SCVIDs to explain a procedure or process. Draft an explanation of the procedure of process using your SCVIDs. Edit your response as necessary to be as descriptive as possible.

Write your answer below or type your response on a computer. Take approximately 25 minutes to respond.

*Remember
the Concept*

Write using SCVIDs.

- When you plan, list SCVIDs.

- When you draft, use SCVIDs.

- When you evaluate, edit with SCVIDs.

Use the questions on page 329 to evaluate your response.

Voice and Tone

Have you ever...

- Felt uncomfortably overdressed or underdressed for an event or meeting?

- Explained a work procedure to a new co-worker and later explained it to a friend?

- Watched a confident speaker on stage?

In different circumstances, we speak, dress, and act differently. We tailor our language to an audience. In written communication, an author creates an impression through **voice** and **tone**. Together, the author's voice and tone show the author's personality and attitude. Purpose and audience play an important role in the author's language choices and in the voice and tone of the final work.

Your **voice** is the way that you present your personality when you write. What message and image do you communicate? How do you show your character in your writing? What can the reader infer about you as a person?

Your **tone** shows your attitude. How do you feel about your topic? How do you feel about your audience? Your tone can be angry or annoyed; pleased or joking; serious or businesslike. Tone is often dictated by your purpose and audience. You will use a different tone in a memo to a client than in a letter to your son.

Your voice and tone develop a relationship with the reader. Through voice and tone, you express yourself and your attitudes.

Developing a Voice

Your voice expresses your personality and develops a relationship with the reader. By evaluating your writing, you can develop a more confident, active voice.

Imagine that you are a manager of a client service department. You are writing a memo to employees about setting client expectations. You have written the following paragraph.

The reason that clients complain is mostly because their expectations aren't met. You probably deal with unhappy clients every day. Clients complain a lot of the time when they don't receive the service they think they deserve. Every client's contract is limited; it sets limits on services and time frames for responses. We can't really expect our clients to always read and understand their contracts, though. It's often too late once the client is unhappy to explain our policies. So, I'd like to ask you to have a client expectations call with every new client. In the call, try to explain the client's contract and what their employees can expect from our service department. If clients understand what to expect, they likely won't be disappointed.

Define Your Relationship to Your Audience

Are you a peer or colleague writing to someone of similar authority? Are you an expert writing to learners? Are you a learner writing to teacher? Are you a friend to your reader? Define your relationship to your audience to help find your voice.

?   1. In this memo, what is your relationship to the audience?

In this scenario, you are a manager writing to employees. As a manager knowledgeable about client expectations, you are an expert on the topic. The goal is for readers to learn from the memo.

Read Your Work Aloud

Read your work aloud to evaluate your voice. What is your relationship to the topic? What would a stranger think of you as a writer? Write a list of adjectives to describe yourself as an author.

? 2. Read the passage aloud. Write a list of adjectives to describe yourself as an author, based on the passage.

You might describe the author as tentative, friendly, and casual. These adjectives don't fit well with the author's relationship to the audience.

Check for Confidence

Be confident in your statements. Give reasons for your opinions and evidence for your facts. When evaluating your writing, look for unconfident words like "maybe," "might," or "almost."

? 3. Review the passage. What words or phrases could be changed to make the writing more confident?

You might identify the following words that seem unconfident: "mostly," "you probably," "a lot of the time," "really," "always," "often," "like to ask," "try," and "likely."

Revise and Edit

Based on your evaluation of voice, revise and edit your work. Choose adjectives that should describe you as a writer. Then, use words and phrasing to convey that impression.

? 4. Revise and edit the passage to improve the author's voice.

The author should be an expert and a businesslike authority. You might write:

> The company receives client complaints because client expectations aren't met. Clients complain when they don't receive the service they believe they deserve. Every client's contract sets limits on services and time frames for responses. This company can't expect clients to read and understand their contracts on their own. Once the client is unhappy, it is too late to explain company policies. To solve this problem, representatives will conduct a client expectations call with every new client. In the call, representatives will explain the client's contract and what the client's employees can expect from the service department. If clients understand what to expect, they will not be disappointed.

Use the following scenario and passage for exercises 1 through 5.

Imagine that for a science exam you wrote the following draft to respond to the prompt, "You may have heard that we are made of 'stardust' or 'star stuff.' Explain the science behind this claim."

It's amazing! We're made of stardust! Did you know that every chemical element on Earth was formed in a star? In the core of every star, nuclear fusion reactions are happening. These reactions created elements all around us, including carbon and iron. I recall hydrogen and helium formed quickly after the Big Bang, and then stars formed as gravity drew particles together. As clouds of gas and dust became denser, they became hotter, eventually becoming stars. At the core of stars, hydrogen and helium fused to become heavier elements. Since the carbon formed in the heart of stars is the basis of life on Earth, it is said that we are formed of stardust.

---

1. What is the author's relationship to the audience?

2. Read the passage aloud. Write a list of adjectives to describe the author.

3. Review the passage. What words or phrases could be changed to make the writing more confident?

4. Revise and edit the passage to improve the author's voice.

5. Research and write your own response to the prompt, and then evaluate and revise your voice. Use a computer or a separate sheet of paper.

Use the following scenario and passage for exercises 6 through 10.

Imagine you are writing a presentation for your daughter's seventh grade class about the attack on Pearl Harbor. You have drafted the following paragraph.

> President Franklin Roosevelt called December 7, 1941 "a date which will live in infamy." On this date, the Japanese military launched a surprise attack on the U.S. base at Pearl Harbor in Hawaii. Many American lives were lost. Before the attack, the U.S. was uninvolved in World War II. However, the Japanese were worried that the U.S. military could interfere with the war in Asia, so they attacked to destroy U.S. forces in the Pacific. The attack seems to have backfired because it led to the U.S. joining World War II and ultimately defeating the Germans and Japanese.

6. What is the author's relationship to the audience?

7. Read the passage aloud. Write a list of adjectives to describe the author.

8. Review the passage. What words or phrases could be changed to make the writing more confident?

9. Revise and edit the passage to improve the author's voice.

10. Research and write a brief presentation about Pearl Harbor, and then evaluate and revise your voice. Use a computer or a separate sheet of paper.

Developing Tone

Tone is the emotion created in a piece of writing by the attitudes the author has toward the reader and the subject. Word choice, voice, structure, and rhythm all contribute to tone.

Imagine that you need to write a positive, friendly response to a client's irritated complaint. You have written the following paragraph.

I understand from your email that you claim you didn't receive the check shipped to you overnight on March 2. However, I have tracked the package with the delivery service, and they state that it was delivered as addressed on March 3. The problem is that you entered the wrong address in your account, so the error is yours. The check was delivered to the address in our database. I have spoken with the delivery service, and the recipients at the incorrect address returned the package. It is currently on the way back to our offices, but unfortunately will not arrive until Monday. When the package arrives, we will ship it to the correct address. In the future, please check your address for important deliveries.

Identify Your Desired Tone

Your tone is linked to your purpose and audience. What impression do you want to give the reader? What attitude or emotion do you want to convey in your writing?

? 1. What would be an appropriate tone for this passage? Why?

Since the goal is to write a positive, friendly business letter that appeases the client, an appropriate tone would be businesslike, positive, friendly, and helpful.

Read the Writing Aloud

Read your work and evaluate the tone. Write down a list of your own adjectives to describe the author's attitude. Are there variations in the tone? Are they appropriate?

? 2. Read the passage aloud. Write down adjectives to describe the passage's tone.

You might say that the tone is businesslike, critical, or condescending. While the passage is sometimes businesslike and conveys relevant information, the tone is not friendly or helpful. It is often critical of the client, which might make the client more upset.

Identify Words that Convey Tone

Find words in the text that convey tone. What attitude or emotion do the words show?

? **3.** Find words or phrases in the passage that show the author's tone.

You might note phrases such as "you claim," "you entered the wrong address," "the error is yours," and "In the future, please check your address." These phrases have a critical tone.

Revise to Improve Tone

Revise the passage to clarify the tone and remove misleading words or phrases that convey the wrong tone.

? **4.** Revise and edit the passage to improve the author's tone.

You might write:

> I understand from your email that you never received the check shipped to you overnight on March 2. I apologize for the delay. I have tracked the package with the delivery service, and they state that it was delivered as addressed on March 3. Unfortunately, your address was entered incorrectly in your account information, and the package was delivered to this incorrect address. The good news is that I have spoken with the delivery service, and the recipients returned the package. It is currently on the way back to our offices, and we will ship it to the correct address immediately when we receive it on Monday. Please let me know if there is anything else I can do to help.

Use the following scenario and passage for exercises 1 through 5.

Imagine you are writing an email to a friend to explain why you support unions for fast food workers. You have written the following paragraph.

The argument that unions are "anti-capitalism" is patently ridiculous. Unions are a part of the free market, because the free market is obviously based on free actions by individuals. If individuals can't act freely, where is the free market? Anyone would realize that workers joining together in a union is clearly a natural market reaction to unfair wages and working conditions! Objecting to unions because they are "anti-capitalism" is like saying that the free market only applies to companies! Next you'll say that individuals can't negotiate for salary increases because it's "anti-capitalism"!

⭐ 1. What would be an appropriate tone for this passage? Why?

⭐ 2. Read the passage aloud. Write down adjectives that describe the tone throughout the passage.

⭐ 3. Find words or phrases in the passage that show the author's tone.

⭐⭐ 4. Revise and edit the passage to improve the author's tone.

⭐⭐ 5. Research and write your own argument for or against unionizing fast food workers, and then evaluate and revise your tone. Use a computer or a separate sheet of paper.

Use the following scenario and passage for exercises 6 through 10.

Imagine you plan to speak at a town meeting about your concerns about young people using e-cigarettes. You have written the following paragraph.

E-cigarettes are a new technology. We know that smoking cigarettes is harmful, but is smoking an e-cigarette really safe? The theory is, I think, that an e-cigarette only gives off water vapor, not smoke. It still delivers nicotine, though, doesn't it? There's not really a lot of evidence about the effects of e-cigarettes because the technology is so new. I think it's better to be cautious and discourage young people from smoking e-cigarettes until we know the possible effects.

6. What would be an appropriate tone for this passage? Why?

7. Read the passage aloud. Write down adjectives that describe the tone throughout the passage.

8. Find words or phrases in the passage that show the author's tone.

9. Revise and edit the passage to improve the author's tone.

10. Research and write your own paragraph giving a clear position about e-cigarettes. Evaluate and revise your tone. Use a computer or a separate sheet of paper.

Use the following scenario and passage for exercises 11 through 15.

Imagine you are writing a passage for your company handbook explaining what the term "stakeholders" means. You have written the following paragraph.

The concept of a stakeholder is clearly essential. A stakeholder is any person or entity who is affected by a policy or action. Don't think that a stakeholder is just a customer or employee. You're thinking too narrowly. Stakeholders can be investors, bosses, coworkers, suppliers, or members of the community. Anyone our company affects might be a stakeholder in a decision. Whenever you write a proposal, report, or memo, keep in mind who the stakeholders are. The more thoughtful we are about stakeholders, the better our policies will be.

⭐ **11.** What would be an appropriate tone for this passage? Why?

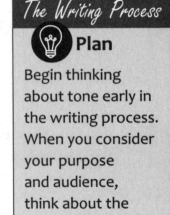

The Writing Process

💡 **Plan**

Begin thinking about tone early in the writing process. When you consider your purpose and audience, think about the appropriate tone.

⭐ **12.** Read the passage aloud. Write down adjectives that describe the tone throughout the passage.

⭐ **13.** Find words or phrases in the passage that show the author's tone.

⭐⭐ **14.** Revise and edit the passage to improve the author's tone.

⭐⭐⭐ **15.** Research and write your own explanation of the term "stakeholders," and then evaluate and revise your tone. Use a computer or a separate sheet of paper.

Check Your Skills

Complete the following exercises about voice and tone.

1. Fill in the blanks with the word(s) that most accurately reflect the voice and tone of the rest of the passage.

Ever since *Jurassic Park*, popular culture has been entranced with the idea of recreating extinct species. Today, this **(a.)** _____ possibility might actually become feasible! Don't worry, scientists can't bring back dinosaurs. There is another extinct animal, though, that scientists believe they can clone: the woolly mammoth. Can you imagine seeing a(n) **(b.)** _____ mammoth at a zoo? In a few dozen years, it may not be so far-fetched. Scientists have found **(c.)** _____ well-preserved blood from a woolly mammoth. This blood may be used to create stem cells and clone a mammoth. This **(d.)** _____ process is called "de-extinction"—bringing back a(n) **(e.)** _____ species.

Use the following passage for exercises 2 and 3.

Free trade agreements are a controversial topic. A free trade agreement allows for trade without restriction between a group of countries. Tariffs, or taxes on imported goods, are eliminated, as are other restrictions on trade. Some argue that the free market should be expanded internationally. Others warn that free trade agreements can cost jobs in wealthy countries and inhibit development in poorer countries.

Those in favor of free trade agreements argue that free trade promotes competition and economic development by expanding the free market. When a group of countries have a free trade agreement, they create a stronger joint economy. Since tariffs are eliminated, prices are lowered for consumers.

Those opposing free trade agreements say that jobs will move to countries with lower wages and standards of living. The economies of wealthier countries will suffer due to job loss. Meanwhile, less economically developed countries will not be able to develop small industries; these young industries will not be able to compete with big industries from wealthy nations.

Should trade be free, without tariffs or restrictions? When are tariffs helpful, and when are they a hindrance to economic growth?

2. Read the passage, which gives arguments for and against free trade agreements. In your response, analyze both positions to determine which one is best supported. Use specific evidence from the passage to support your claim. Take approximately 25 minutes to respond.

 3. Describe and evaluate your voice and tone in your response, using specific examples from the response.

> *Remember the Concept*
>
> **Evaluate Voice**
>
> • Define your relationship with your audience.
>
> • Read your work aloud.
>
> • Check for confidence in your work.
>
> **Evaluate Tone**
>
> • Identify the desired tone.
>
> • Read your work aloud.
>
> • Identify words that convey tone.

Use the questions on page 329 to evaluate your response.

Unity and Cohesion

Connections

Have you ever...

- Looked for information in a brochure and found it missing?

- Heard a speech in which the presenter drifted off topic?

- Put together a list of strong examples in order to prove a point?

When you speak, you hope to be understood. Writing aims for the same goal. A reader is likely to become confused if the written communication drifts off topic, employs irrelevant examples, or uses vague words. In contrast, writing is powerful when ideas build progressively into a unified whole. This integrated wholeness is **unity** and **cohesion**.

You can use visual images to understand the principle of unity and cohesion. Envision:

- A map of the United States where all the states fit together.

- A completed jigsaw puzzle where each piece becomes part of the whole.

- A dancer who moves gracefully and never takes an awkward step.

- A home interior where the wall colors, pictures, and furniture create a pleasing blend.

Unity and cohesion are achieved when ideas, materials, or actions come together to create a smooth and seamless result.

Evaluate Unity with TOS

Make sure that your ideas fit together in a logical way and connect with your central idea. Evaluate your writing with a **TOS** organizer.

Imagine you are a customer service representative at an insurance company. You need to write an annual self-assessment report for your employee review. You have written the following paragraph.

> I am a hard worker who provides excellent customer service and values my job. This year, I have done significant professional development training to improve my skills. Some of the department meetings I have attended seem to lack focus, but I diligently fulfill my functions. I have found that I provide valuable suggestions to proposed policies and activities. I have strong survey ratings among clients and success in renewing customer contracts. I have a track record of achievement at the company, and I hope to continue improving my skills and my value to the firm.

Target Your Purpose

Start by focusing on your purpose. Review your writing. What is your central idea? The central idea will keep your writing unified.

1. Write the central idea of the paragraph in the TOS organizer.

Target Your Purpose (Central Idea)	
Ordered Elements	**Specific Relationships**

The central idea is found in the first sentence. You could restate the idea, "I am a hard-working and successful employee."

Order Elements and Specify Relationships

To evaluate the unity of a written work, identify the elements in the writing. What are main details or supporting ideas? Write down these elements in order and specify their relationships with the central idea. This will help you identify elements that are out of place.

2. Write the elements and relationships of the paragraph in the TOS organizer.

Target Your Purpose (Central Idea)	
I am a hard-working and successful employee.	
Ordered Elements	**Specific Relationships**

The paragraph discusses professional development, which shows improved skills. Then, it mentions unfocused meetings, which lacks a relationship. Next, it mentions providing valuable suggestions, which shows success as an employee and good skills. Finally, it mentions strong survey ratings and renewed contracts. These also show success and good customer service. It ends with a conclusion: having a good track record and continuing to improve.

Evaluate and Revise

Evaluate the ordered elements and relationships. Can they be reordered in a better way? What elements don't support the central idea? Revise the work.

3. Evaluate the ordered elements. Using a computer or separate sheet of paper, revise the paragraph to improve unity and cohesion.

Target Your Purpose (Central Idea)	
I am a hard-working and successful employee.	
Ordered Elements	**Specific Relationships**
professional development	improved skills
unfocused meetings	no relationship
providing valuable suggestions	success as employee, due to skills
survey ratings and renewed contracts	success and good customer service
good track record, continued improvement	conclusion and summary

You might write:

> I am a hard worker who provides excellent customer service and values my job. This year, I have done significant professional development training to improve my skills. My improved skills allow me to provide valuable suggestions to proposed policies and activities. I have strong survey ratings among clients and success in renewing customer contracts, which shows my strong customer service skills. I have a track record of achievement at the company, and I hope to continue improving my skills and my value to the firm.

Use the following scenario and passage for exercises 1 through 3.

Imagine you are writing a blog post commemorating the purchase of Alaska in 1867. You have written the following paragraph.

The $7.2 million purchase of Alaska from Russia on March 30, 1867 was widely criticized, but ultimately beneficial. Secretary of State William H. Seward was criticized for buying the large, mostly unexplored land, and critics called the deal "Seward's folly." Alaska increased the size of the U.S. by about 20 percent, though. Seward barely convinced the Senate to approve the purchase, a decision that passed by only one vote. However, gold was discovered in Alaska in the 1880s and 1890s, bringing an influx of people. Today, Alaska's petroleum pipeline provides a profitable mineral resource. On January 3, 1959, under President Eisenhower, Alaska became the 49th state.

---

 1. Complete the TOS organizer.

Target Your Purpose (Central Idea)	
Ordered Elements	**Specific Relationships**

 2. Evaluate the ordered elements and relationships. What improvements can you make by reordering, adding, or removing elements?

 3. Revise the paragraph to improve unity and cohesion.

Use the following scenario and passage for exercises 4 through 6.

Imagine you are writing a grant application for a project to provide solar power to rural areas around the world. You have written the following paragraph.

Solar power can change a rural village. In developed nations, solar power is increasingly popular. In an area without access to infrastructure, solar power provides energy for cooking, water purification, and drip irrigation. Use of solar power in sub-Saharan Africa has increased in recent years. The availability of solar energy increases food security and allows economic development. In addition, solar power is environmentally friendly. Ultimately, solar power can help eliminate poverty in rural areas with little access to technology.

 4. Complete the TOS organizer.

Target Your Purpose (Central Idea)	
Ordered Elements	**Specific Relationships**

 5. Evaluate the ordered elements and relationships. What improvements can you make by reordering, adding, or removing elements?

 6. Revise the paragraph to improve unity and cohesion.

Use the following scenario and passage for exercises 7 through 9.

Imagine you are writing a letter to the editor about the need for a third political party. You have written the following paragraph.

Partisanship does nothing but prevent progress. A political party is a group with similar interests. When there are only two parties in a political system, an impasse is inevitable. Historically, the U.S. has usually had only two major parties. The two parties have no reason to compromise. Imagine taking a vote between two people on opposite sides of an issue. No progress is made. The Republicans and the Democrats are currently the two political parties dominating the U.S. government. A third party is needed to "break the tie." In a system with three political parties, compromise works. Two parties can join together to compromise and create a majority. Still, the existence of political parties is inevitable.

---

7. Complete the TOS organizer.

Target Your Purpose (Central Idea)	
Ordered Elements	**Specific Relationships**

8. Evaluate the ordered elements and relationships. What improvements can you make by reordering, adding, or removing elements?

9. Revise the paragraph to improve unity and cohesion.

> *The Writing Process*
> ✏ **Draft**
> Keep your purpose, audience, and central idea in mind as you write. This will help you avoid drifting off topic or straying in your focus.

Check Your Skills

Use your understanding of unity and cohesion to complete the following exercises.

 1. Imagine that you have the necessary credentials for this job listing and want to apply for the following job.

The Adams Morgan Community Center in Washington, D.C. has an opening for a community event organizer. A bachelor's degree in social work or a related field is desired. The position requires a self-starter who can manage a budget, work with community members, and plan community-building events from start to finish. To apply for this position, send a cover letter and résumé to Amelia Holmes at aholmes@adams-morgan.com.

---

   a. Write a cover letter below or type your response on a computer. Take approximately 25 minutes to respond.

   b. Evaluate your cover letter with a TOS organizer. Explain how your cover letter shows unity and cohesion.

> ### Build Your Writing Skills
>
> Offer direct support of the central idea. If an example is out of sync with the central idea, get rid of it. Your examples need to tie back directly to your purpose.

Use the questions on page 329 to evaluate your response.

2. Read the following passage, and write a cohesive response that evaluates the unity and cohesion of the passage. Identify at least three areas that could be improved and suggestions for improvement. Include multiple pieces of evidence from the passage to support your answer.

Community service is an important part of K–12 education. Young people learn to think about more than themselves and develop empathy for others. Students are exposed to areas of community life unfamiliar to them, such as elder care programs and parks in need of cleanup. Some students think community service is a waste of time because they are not interested in their assignments. Students gain new experiences, which sometimes lead to career pathways. Community service is a necessary part of school for many students.

> ### Remember the Concept
>
> Use a TOS organizer to evaluate unity and cohesion.
>
> - Target the central idea.
> - Order elements.
> - Specify relationships.

Use the questions on page 329 to evaluate your response.

Fluidity

Connections

Have you ever...

- Become caught up in reading a book or article?

- Noticed that some writing seems almost musical?

- Had to stop and think because a sentence didn't seem to connect with what you just read?

When you hear the word "fluids," what comes to mind? You probably think of liquids such as water or juice. What's the connection between the fluids we drink and the **fluidity** we strive toward as writers? When you pour juice into a glass, the liquid flows in a steady, unbroken stream. The same principle applies to writing. Writers want their writing to unfold as naturally and smoothly as water filling a cup or a river flowing to the sea.

Think about synonyms for the word "fluid": flowing, continuous, rolling, smooth. All these words evoke images of uninterrupted processes. Writers create this effect by taking care to connect ideas smoothly, without gaps or missing connections. Fluid writing:

- Connects ideas in a logical order.

- Explains relationships and connections.

- Uses transition words, phrases, and sentences.

- Varies sentence structure, using combined sentences when appropriate.

Evaluating and improving the fluidity of your writing will make it easier to read and help keep the attention of the reader.

Learn It!

Creating Fluidity: Find and Fill Gaps to Create Flow

There are many ways to create fluidity in your writing. Two important strategies are using transitions and varying sentence structure.

Imagine you are writing an account of Earth Day events for your community college newspaper. You have written the following paragraph.

> The Ecology 101 class completed a community service project at a local park in celebration of Earth Day. The class picked up garbage at the park. Students painted park benches. Students cleaned playground equipment. The class planted flowers around trees and benches. The Ecology class achieved a lot during the day, improving the experience of the park.

Find the Gaps

Where is the writing choppy or jumping from one topic to another? Read your text aloud to help you hear where the text has bumpy spots. Find the gaps that are preventing fluidity.

?   **1.** Identify three or more places in the passage where you could improve fluidity.

You might choose the ends of any of the first five sentences. At the end of the first sentence, the writer shifts from a central idea to a supporting detail. The writer could signal this shift with a transition. Sentences two through five sound choppy and repetitive. They need a fix.

Add Transitions

Evaluate where transitions can improve the fluidity, and choose transitions to add to the text. Transitions can clarify relationships including time, location, and logical order. A transition can be a word, a phrase, or an explanatory connecting sentence. Here are a few example transition words and phrases that can help bring fluidity to your writing.

Time	Location	Logical Order
later, during, soon, while, before, after, now, next, eventually, today, tomorrow, in the evening	to the right, to the left, up, down, alongside, beside, inside, outside, below, above, in the back	first, second, third, also, moreover, furthermore, as a result, consequently, at the same time, similarly

? **2.** Choose two transitions to add to the passage.

You could include transitions to show how the events are related in time. You might change the second sentence to read, "The project began with garbage collection throughout the park." The phrase "the project began" locates this event in time. You might change the fifth sentence to read, "In the afternoon, the class planted flowers around trees and benches."

Vary Sentence Structure

Varied sentence structure adds to fluidity. If your sentences sound choppy, it may be due to short sentences that begin with similar subjects. Adding transitional words can help vary sentence structure, as can combining short sentences.

? **3.** Identify two sentences that would become more fluid if they were joined. Write them as one combined sentence.

The sentences "Students painted park benches. Students cleaned playground equipment" sound choppy. Both sentences begin with "students" followed by a verb. Try joining the sentences in a few ways, looking for logical relationships between the ideas:

- Students painted park benches and cleaned playground equipment.

- After painting the park benches, students cleaned playground equipment.

- To improve the park's appearance, students painted benches and cleaned playground equipment.

Final Review

Once you've revised for fluidity, reread the passage to evaluate fluidity.

? **4.** Review the revised passage and make any additional changes to improve fluidity.

The Ecology 101 class completed a community service project at a local park in celebration of Earth Day. The project began with garbage collection throughout the park. To improve the park's appearance, students painted benches and cleaned playground equipment. In the afternoon, the class planted flowers around trees and benches. The Ecology class achieved a lot during the day, improving the experience of the park.

Edit the following passage in exercises 1 through 4.

A School Notice from the Health Office

Teachers should follow the following procedures. These procedures apply when an elementary child feels sick during the school day. Children should get a hall pass from the teacher to see the nurse. Children should have a buddy accompany them to the nurse in case of faintness. The nurse will write a health report. The nurse will send the health report to the teacher. The teacher should make sure the health report goes home to the parent or guardian that afternoon.

1. Read the passage aloud. Where do you hear choppiness and find gaps?

2. Choose sentences that could be improved with transitions, and rewrite those sentences with transitions.

3. Choose sentences where you could vary the sentence structure to add fluidity. Rewrite those sentences.

4. Review the paragraph. In the space below, write the revised, more fluid, paragraph.

> **Build Your Writing Skills**
>
> Sentences can be short and choppy, but they can also be too long and tangled. Try to make your sentences clear and logically connected.

Use the following scenario and passage for exercises 5 through 8.

Imagine that you are writing a paragraph on social upheaval in the 1960s for a social studies exam. You have written the following draft.

The 1960s was a time of great change in American culture. The Civil Rights Movement came to a climax. It was led by Dr. Martin Luther King. Women began to agitate for their rights. Gloria Steinem headed the newly formed National Organization of Women (NOW). College students began to agitate against the conservative norms of their parents. College students launched what is now called the "Sexual Revolution." The 1960s changed the course of the twentieth century.

---

5. Read the passage aloud. Where do you hear choppiness and find gaps?

6. Choose sentences that could be improved with transitions, and rewrite those sentences with transitions.

7. Choose sentences where you could vary the sentence structure to add fluidity. Rewrite those sentences.

8. Review the paragraph. In the space below, write the revised, more fluid, paragraph.

★ 9. Practice your skills creating fluidity by combining the following short sentences.

a. We tested two groups. We found no significant difference in the results.

b. The election was close. The election resulted in a victory for the incumbant.

c. New breakthroughs in cancer research appear in the media every day. New breakthroughs in cancer research take years to develop into usable therapies.

★ 10. Improve the fluidity of the following short sentences by either adding transitions or varying sentence structure.

a. The council meeting lasted ten hours. Dozens of people spoke.

b. Extreme weather events can be costly and deadly. Extreme weather events may occur more frequently in the future.

c. School shootings are traumatic for communities. The causes of school shootings are controversial.

★★ 11. Describe a political issue that you find important. Review your response by finding gaps, adding transitions, varying sentence structure, and reviewing fluidity. Type your response on a computer or use a separate sheet of paper.

★★ 12. Imagine that you are peer editing a friend's paper and find her style choppy. What advice would you give your friend?

Build Your Writing Skills

Let your ears be your guide. If sentences sound choppy, think about using transitions to smooth out the connections between sentences.

Check Your Skills

Using your understanding of fluidity, complete the following exercise.

1. Complete the paragraph below by adding appropriate transitions.

   Abraham Lincoln was assassinated at Ford Theater in 1865. **(a.)** _____
   the assassin, John Wilkes Booth, learned that General Grant and Lincoln were to attend
   a play at the theater that night. **(b.)** _____ his information about General
   Grant was incorrect. Only the Lincolns attended the event. **(c.)** _____
   the Lincolns arrived late to the theater and were seated in the Presidential Box. **(d.)**
   _____ Booth, a well-known actor at the time, walked into the theater
   and gained entry to the box. **(e.)** _____ Booth shot Lincoln at point-blank
   range at a moment when the audience filled the theater with laughter.

2. Choose the most fluid sentence(s).

   a. Velocity is a measurement of an object's speed. Nevertheless, velocity is a
      measurement of an object's direction of movement.

   b. Velocity is a measurement of an object's speed. Velocity is also a measurement of
      an object's direction of movement.

   c. Velocity is a measurement of an object's speed and direction of movement.

   d. Velocity is a measurement of an object's speed. However, velocity measures an
      object's direction of movement.

3. Choose the most fluid sentence(s).

   a. The new law is confusing, and the law's language is meant to deceive readers.

   b. The new law is confusing. The law's language is meant to deceive readers.

   c. The new law is confusing because its language is meant to deceive readers.

   d. The language of the law is confusing. The language is meant to deceive readers.

4. Use the following information to write a description of the origin of the Manhattan
   Project. Use fluidity strategies to enhance the flow of your writing.

   - In 1939, Germans made advancements toward developing an atomic bomb.

   - Scientists Albert Einstein and Enrico Fermi warned the president of the dangers of
     Germany developing an atomic weapon.

   - President Roosevelt agreed to start American research into atomic weapons.

   - The American effort to build an atomic bomb was named the Manhattan Project.

   Type your response on a computer or use a separate sheet of paper.

Use the following passage for exercises 5 and 6.

Organ donation is a good idea. The donor loses nothing and can save or greatly improve a life. Unfortunately, our current system of opting in to organ donation is flawed. Many people don't think about their organ donor status. They don't take the trouble to check a box or put a sticker on their driver's license to become a donor. Under an opt-out model, where every citizen is automatically an organ donor unless they indicate otherwise, many more citizens donate organs. In Germany's opt-in system, only 12% of people are organ donors. In nearby Austria, which has an opt-out system, more than 99% of people are organ donors. An opt-out system saves lives with no down side. Anyone who does not want to be an organ donor can easily opt out of organ donation.

---

 5. Write an evaluation of the argument given in the passage. Is it a strong or weak argument? Support your evaluation with evidence from the passage.

 6. Evaluate the fluidity of your response to the previous exercise. Explain how your response achieves fluidity, providing specific examples from the response.

> *Remember the Concept*
>
> To make your writing more fluid:
>
> - Find gaps.
> - Add transitions.
> - Vary sentence structure.
> - Review.

Use the questions on page 329 to evaluate your response.

Clarity

Connections

Have you ever…

- Asked for driving directions and become even more confused by what you were told?

- Had an "ah-ha" moment when you understood a concept for the first time?

- Listened to a speech and been dazzled by its focused, powerful message?

Clarity is important in your writing. When your writing is clear, you are communicating your message. Your reader can understand your meaning. Writers often know what they are trying to say but have difficulty communicating clearly.

Think of your writing as a window. The reader looks through the window to see your meaning. If the window is not clear, your reader will not be able to see. A clean, clear window makes your message visible to all. To write with clarity:

- Know what you want to say. The clearer you understand your own meaning, the clearer your writing will be.

- Keep your writing organized and connected to your central idea.

- Understand what your audience knows and doesn't know. Start from your audience's existing knowledge and add new information.

- Use simple, direct phrasing that is easy for the reader to understand.

Using POP to Clarify Writing

To make your writing clearer, evaluate the **POP**:

Purpose — Order — Phrasing

Imagine you are giving a presentation to your son's fourth grade class. You have written the following explanation of this quotation from the Declaration of Independence: "That to secure these rights, Governments are instituted among Men, deriving their just powers from the consent of the governed."

A government is an agreement about how a society will live together. The word "instituted" means created something. The quote tells the purpose of government and the way the government gets its power and it is to make sure people's rights are upheld and from the agreement of the people. The founding fathers defined the purpose of government so that they could explain their reasons for rejecting the British colonial government.

Purpose

To write clearly, know what you want to say. Does your writing have a clear message, purpose, or central idea? Does each sentence have a purpose?

? 1. Evaluate the purpose of the paragraph. What could you revise or edit to clarify the purpose?

The writing task has a clear purpose: to explain the quotation, "That to secure these rights, Governments are instituted among Men, deriving their just powers from the consent of the governed." However, the purpose is not clear in the paragraph. It needs a clearly stated central idea. You might write, "The quotation from the Declaration of Independence defines the purpose of government and the origin of government's power."

Order

Think about the organization of your work. Are ideas in a logical order? Do you start with what the reader knows and then introduce new ideas? Do you provide transitions and explanations that support your meaning?

? **2.** Evaluate the order of the paragraph. What could you revise or edit to clarify the order?

The order seems disjointed. The explanation of "instituted" isn't linked to the central idea. You might want to think about what the reader knows. Start with the reader's knowledge, and introduce new ideas. For example:

Known	New
The quotation from the Declaration…	…defines government's purpose and origin.
The purpose of government…	… is to uphold rights.
The origin of government…	…is the agreement of the people.

The central idea introduces the ideas of the purpose and origin of government. The following sentences begin by referencing these ideas, since now the reader knows about them.

Phrasing

Some sentences are confusingly worded. Look for elements that might confuse readers:

- Is the sentence too long or awkward?
- Are there confusing strings of words or mismatched groups of words?
- Is it clear what pronouns, adjectives, adverbs, and phrases reference?
- Do the words you chose convey the right meaning?

? **3.** Evaluate the phrasing of the paragraph. What could you revise or edit to clarify the phrasing?

One sentence that's very confusing is, "The quote tells the purpose of government and the way the government gets its power and it is to make sure people's rights are upheld and from the agreement of the people." This sentence is long, and it's unclear what "it" references. The final revision might read:

> The quotation from the Declaration of Independence defines the purpose of government and the origin of government's power. According to the quote, the purpose of government is to uphold the rights of the people and to "secure these rights." The origin of government's power is the "consent of the governed," which means the agreement of the people. The founding fathers defined the purpose of government in the Declaration of Independence so that they could explain their reasons for rejecting the British colonial government.

Use the following scenario and passage for exercises 1 through 4.

Imagine that you are writing a letter to the editor about copyright law reform. You have written the following paragraph.

Copyright law needs reform. You can't sing "Happy Birthday" at a restaurant without paying a fee. Music industry organizations threaten to sue bar owners for unauthorized performances by cover bands. They will threaten a lawsuit against anyone for any use of a song. Online videos can get taken down because it's playing in the background. When there is a problem is when it should get changed, so the law is the problem. Defining clearly harmless uses of copyrighted material, the music industry and other large industries won't be able to take advantage of small businesses and individuals.

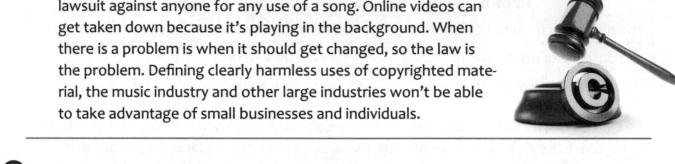

1. Evaluate the purpose of the paragraph. What could you revise or edit to clarify the purpose?

2. Evaluate the order of the paragraph. What could you revise or edit to clarify the order?

3. Evaluate the phrasing of the paragraph. What could you revise or edit to clarify the phrasing?

4. Revise the paragraph, with clear purpose, order, and phrasing.

Use the following scenario and passage for exercises 5 through 8.

Imagine that you are taking a science exam. You must explain the causes and effects of antibiotic-resistant bacteria. You have written the following paragraph.

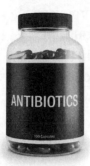

Antibiotic resistance is a public health problem. Widespread use of antibiotics has caused drug-resistant bacteria to develop making these difficult to treat. Antibiotics may be overprescribed, used excessively in farm animals, and misused, particularly by people not taking the full course of antibiotics. These all contribute to the development of drug resistance in bacteria. In some cases these become so resistant that modern medicine has no effective treatment. When these spread, they cause dangerous infections.

5. Evaluate the purpose of the paragraph. What could you revise or edit to clarify the purpose?

6. Evaluate the order of the paragraph. What could you revise or edit to clarify the order?

7. Evaluate the phrasing of the paragraph. What could you revise or edit to clarify the phrasing?

8. Revise the paragraph, with clear purpose, order, and phrasing.

Use the following scenario and passage for exercises 9 through 12.

Imagine that you are documenting how to customize invoices in the software your company makes. You have written the following paragraph.

Invoices are generated using a template, and the template file is called invoice.tpl, which is found in the "templates" folder, which is in the folder "TT Accounting." You can modify the logo by replacing or editing the logo.jpg file that is in the "images" folder in the "TT Accounting" folder, or you can modify it by opening and editing the invoice.tpl file. To open it, go to the templates tab and choose it. Once you have opened the file, you can modify the template text and save it, and you can also change the fields that are used on the invoice.

---

9. Evaluate the purpose of the paragraph. What could you revise or edit to clarify the purpose?

10. Evaluate the order of the paragraph. What could you revise or edit to clarify the order?

11. Evaluate the phrasing of the paragraph. What could you revise or edit to clarify the phrasing?

12. Revise the paragraph, with clear purpose, order, and phrasing.

Check Your Skills

Use your knowledge of clarity to complete the following exercises.

1. Choose the best revision to clarify the following sentence.

    There are many scams perpetrated via email, and one of the most common is phishing, where fake emails are sent supposedly from banks or other institutions.

    a. There are many scams perpetrated via email. One of the most common is phishing, where scammers send fake emails supposedly from banks or other institutions.
    b. Many scams perpetrated via email, one is phishing, where fake emails are sent supposedly from banks and other institutions.
    c. Phishing means fake emails, a common email scam, supposedly from banks.
    d. One common email scam is phishing. In a phishing scam, criminals send fake emails, supposedly from banks or other institutions.

2. Choose the best revision to clarify the following sentence.

    The hospital visiting hours are not open in the evening after 6:00 P.M.

    a. The hospital visiting hours are closed in the evening after 6:00 P.M.
    b. After 6:00 P.M., the hospital visiting hours are not open in the evening.
    c. The hospital visiting hours end at 6:00 P.M.
    d. After 6:00 P.M., the hospital visiting hours are not open.

3. Choose the best revision to clarify the following sentence.

    Going to the office in the morning, the weather was cold and rainy.

    a. Going to the office in the morning, and the weather was cold and rainy.
    b. Going to the office in the morning. The weather was cold and rainy.
    c. As I was going to the office in the morning, the weather was cold and rainy.
    d. The weather, going to the office in the morning, was cold and rainy.

4. Choose the best revision to clarify the following sentence.

    Because of the way TV shows portray families, they are often promoting stereotypes.

    a. Because of their portrayals of families, TV shows often promote stereotypes.
    b. Because of the way TV shows portray families, stereotypes are often promoted.
    c. Because of the way TV shows portray, families are often promoting stereotypes.
    d. Because of the way TV shows portray families, it is often promoting stereotypes.

Use the following passage for exercises 5 and 6.

Home schooling is a controversial topic. Proponents of home schooling say that it allows parents to control their child's education. Parents can choose a curriculum tailored to their children, beliefs, and lifestyle. Home schooling provides personalized instruction that advocates say is more successful than public or private schools, especially for children with special needs. However, opponents say that there is a lack of quality control in home schooling. While some parents may provide good instruction, others may teach incorrectly or even neglect teaching altogether. Additionally, opponents raise concerns that home-schooled children may not learn social skills or experience a wide variety of viewpoints.

 5. Write an evaluation of the arguments given in the passage. Which position is best supported? Support your evaluation with evidence from the passage.

 6. Evaluate the clarity of your response to the previous exercise. Explain how your response achieves clarity, providing specific examples from the response.

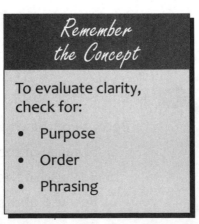

Remember the Concept

To evaluate clarity, check for:

- Purpose
- Order
- Phrasing

Use the questions on page 329 to evaluate your response.

FOCUS
Submit

Submitting your work is a final step in the writing process. The requirements for submitting your work depend on its method of publication. Publishing software has its own features for checking and submitting your work. Individuals or organizations also have specific requirements for how a document should look and be submitted.

- Are you sending a book outline to a potential publisher? The publisher will have formatting and submission guidelines.

- Are you sending a letter to a company? You will format it as a business letter and stamp and address it according to postal guidelines.

- Are you submitting a brochure to a printer using an online brochure builder? You will use the printer's online software to check and submit your work.

- Are you submitting a paper to a professor? You will need to follow a style for your paper's format and bibliography. You may need to email a specific type of file, submit your paper online, or hand in a printed paper.

- Are you writing a blog post? The software will give you a way to preview how your post will look before hitting the "submit" button.

No matter what final form your work will take, you should proofread before finalizing your writing. Proofreading is a final check for errors, such as spelling, grammar, or formatting errors. The proofreading step gives you a last chance to make sure your work presents a good impression through high quality and a lack of basic mistakes.

This section has two lessons about finalizing your work.

- **Proofreading**
  Learn a strategy to carefully check for and correct errors in your work. Proofreading is similar to editing, but more limited because it is a final check before publishing. By the time you proofread, you should consider your writing complete and ready to publish.

- **Publishing**
  The process of publishing depends on your writing's purpose. Each publisher has special requirements. This lesson gives you an overview of the publishing process to help you publish many types of writing.

Proofreading

Connections

Have you ever...

- Noticed a spelling error in a newspaper or magazine?

- Spellchecked a document but still ended up with an error, such as "form" instead of "from"?

- Realized that you accidentally left a word out of a sentence?

Proofreading offers writers a last chance to correct and polish their work. Proofreading is like a final cleaning that writers give to their work. Like microscopic dust, the errors that writers sweep from their work during proofreading are typically small. Small errors often turn up in writing and can be hard to detect. Proofreading offers a final sweep and polish to make a document shine.

Grammar, punctuation, and spelling—the types of errors writers usually check for when they proofread—are referred to as **language mechanics**. To understand this term, think about the work performed by an automobile mechanic or equipment repairman. Mechanics fix the nuts, bolts, and other small parts that keep machines operating. Language mechanics are the nuts and bolts that help your writing communicate.

Written texts need tune-ups, so writers proofread their work to correct technical errors in grammar, punctuation, and spelling. Proofreaders are on the look-out for small errors, such as incorrect words, missing words, incorrect capitalization, sentence fragments, missing commas, or awkward phrasing.

Proofreading: The Language Microscope

Proofreading involves looking at sentences under a microscope. As a proofreader, you will check the clarity of each sentence, the accuracy of each word, and the correctness of each punctuation mark. While you proofread, you will need to check a dictionary, thesaurus, or grammar book or website when you are unsure about a word, phrase, or sentence. While proofreading demands careful observation, it improves your writing and your language skills. Use the following passage to practice your proofreading skills.

You can easily conserve water, in the bathroom, during a drought. Avoid flushing the toilet unnecessarily. If you need dispose of a tissue, throw it in the trash instead of the toilet. Instead of taking a bath, take a short shower. Turn off the water when you dont need it. You can even use a bucket to catch the excess water. Use this waste water to water plants in the garden, similarly, when your brushing your teeth, don't leave the water running. A few simple steps can save a lot of water

Apply the Microscope: Slow Down and Look Closely

Proofreading is done slowly. You are more likely to discover small errors if you observe your writing slowly and carefully. Here are three techniques for "slow motion" reading:

- Try reading your text aloud, word by word, without rushing.

- Try placing a ruler or sheet of paper beneath the sentence you are examining to focus on one line and read each word.

- Try reading backwards, from right to left, to find errors.

? 1. Use each "slow motion" reading method described above to proofread the passage. Find at least three errors.

You might notice a missing period on the last sentence, a missing apostrophe on the word "don't" in the fifth sentence, and the missing word "to" in the phrase "you need to dispose."

Look through the Microscope: Hunt Down Usage Errors

Learn common errors so that you can find them in your final draft. You can start by using the following list of errors, but the best strategy is to keep a diary of your own common errors. Most writers make the same mistakes consistently.

Common Errors	
Word Mishaps	commonly confused words, misspellings, using the wrong word, incorrect capitalization, confusing or wrong pronouns, missing words
Sentence Mishaps	fragments, run-ons, incorrect subject-verb agreement, illogical shifts, awkward structure
Punctuation Mishaps	comma splices, forgotten apostrophes, commas where they're not needed, missing periods

? **2.** Use the list of common errors to find at least two additional errors in the passage.

You might find the following additional errors: two unnecessary commas in the first sentence, a comma splice between "in the garden" and "similarly," and "your brushing" instead of "you're brushing."

Exit the Microscope: One Last Look

As you correct errors, look nearby for other errors. Errors often happen in groups. Also check for mistakes you might make when correcting errors: deleting too much, making the change in the wrong place, or making a typo.

? **3.** Correct the errors in the passage. In the space below, write the corrected passage.

The final corrected passage might read:

> You can easily conserve water in the bathroom during a drought. Avoid flushing the toilet unnecessarily. If you need to dispose of a tissue, throw it in the trash instead of the toilet. Instead of taking a bath, take a short shower. Turn off the water when you don't need it. You can even use a bucket to catch the excess water. Use this waste water to water plants in the garden. Similarly, when you're brushing your teeth, don't leave the water running. A few simple steps can save a lot of water.

Practice It!

Researchers carefully designs scientific experiments, every experiment has **variables**, elements that can change. For example, if you are testing the permanence of a new die, one variable might be the amount of of dye and another might be the amount of light that hits the dye. The best experiments control the circumstances so that only one variable effects the results. Experiments usually contain a control group and a treatment group, two groups which are as similar as possible. The treatment group is effected by the variable being studied. The control group is not affected by the variable being studied, it shows the affects of other variables on the experiment.

1. Proofread the paragraph by reading it aloud. What errors did you find, and how would you correct them?

2. Proofread the paragraph using a piece of paper or ruler to isolate each line. What additional errors did you find, and how would you correct them?

3. Proofread the paragraph by reading the passage backwards, word by word. What additional errors did you find, and how would you correct them?

4. Based on the errors in the paragraph, what types of errors would you advise the writer to look for when proofreading?

Technology Tip

Spellchecking can help you eliminate errors, but don't rely on spellcheckers alone.

Proofread the following passage in exercises 5 through 8.

The ability to prioritize is essential for career success. Whenever you're are bombarded with a list of task. You need to evaluate, order, and schedule. Frist, evaluate each task. What is the urgency: high or low? What is the amount of effort or time needed to complete the task: high or low? Order tasks with urgent, low-effort tasks first. Than, brake up high-effort tasks into smaller tasks. In between these smaller tasks. Complete low-urgency, low-effort tasks. Schedule time for the high-effort tasks in order of urgency. Prioritizing well will decrease you're stress and increase your effectiveness.

5. Proofread the paragraph by reading it aloud. What errors did you find, and how would you correct them?

6. Proofread the paragraph using a piece of paper or ruler to isolate each line. What additional errors did you find, and how would you correct them?

7. Proofread the paragraph by reading the passage backwards, word by word. What additional errors did you find, and how would you correct them?

8. Based on the errors in the paragraph, what types of errors would you advise the writer to look for when proofreading?

9. List four types of errors you commonly make in your writing. What is the best way to catch these particular errors?

 10. What method of proofreading do you find most helpful? Why?

 11. Imagine your friend was marked down 10% on a college paper for spelling and punctuation errors. What advice would you give your friend to avoid this situation in the future?

 12. What are the potential consequences of a spelling error on a job résumé or cover letter? Why is proofreading especially important in job applications?

Build Your Writing Skills

Any time your mind questions a writing detail—a comma, word spelling, or grammar issue—check it! When in doubt, go to a reference source for an answer.

Check Your Skills

Use your knowledge of proofreading to complete the following exercises.

1. Circle the errors in the following sentences.

   Their are many possible ways to reform immigration laws. Because the availability of illegal jobs encourages immigration. One important reform is to crack down on employers who higher illegal immigrants, especially at lower then minimum wages.

2. Circle the errors in the following sentences.

   Though interpretation of the U.S. Constitution, the Supreme Court determines what can or can't be law. Supreme Court decisions have lead too integrating schools, overturning abortion laws, and enforcing Miranda rights. Those who disagree with court rulings often criticize "activist judges," on on the other hand, the majority of lawmakers and voters may not respect the inherent rights of the minority.

3. Circle the errors in the following sentences.

   I have supporting my family for two years with out a college degree. This experience have taught me the value of hard work, persistence, and planning. It has also shown me the value of education. I plan too put my hard work, persistence, and planning skills work to help me succeed in college.

4. Which is the best correction to the following sentence?

   Birds' have adapted lightweight, strong bones to withstand the stress of flying.
   a. Replace **Birds'** with **Bird's**
   b. Replace **Birds'** with **Birds**
   c. Replace **to** with **too**
   d. Replace **to** with **two**

5. Which is the best correction to the following sentence?

   The New Deal consisting of domestic programs that created jobs, reformed the financial system, and boosted the economy.
   a. Replace **that** with **who**
   b. Replace **that** with **than**
   c. Replace **consisting** with **consisted**
   d. Replace **consisting** with **consists**

Use the following passage for exercise 6.

Based on our market research report, television advertising is not proving successful for our camping and outdoor gear marketing. Focus groups show that our target audience spends more time on teh Internet then watching television. Our advertising department is currently developing a a pilot Internet advertising program and the marketing department will presenting a plan for viral Internet marketing next week.

 6. Proofread the paragraph. What errors did you find, and how would you correct them?

Use the following passage for exercise 7.

Stay-at-home fathers are becoming more and more common in todays socity. Many fathers chose to stay at home because there partners have better jobs or because they cannot find work. In either case, a stay-at-home dad can be a grate benifit to the children.

 7. Proofread the paragraph. What errors did you find, and how would you correct them?

Remember the Concept

To proofread your work:

- Go slowly.
- Check for common errors.
- Check for nearby errors and problems caused by corrections.

Publishing

Connections

Have you ever...

- Sent a job application through email?

- Written a blog post or commented on an online article?

- Submitted a letter to the editor to a local paper?

Publishing means distributing your writing to your audience. A book is printed and distributed to stores. A blog post is published on the Internet where readers can access it. A letter is published by mailing it to the recipient. An email is published by hitting the "send" button. Whenever you write for an audience, you will publish your writing.

Today, more and more individuals are publishing their writing to a wide audience. The Internet has given people easier access to publication. Posting on a blog or social media site is an inexpensive, accessible way to publish your work.

Not all publishing reaches a wide audience, however. An email message or a college paper is usually meant for an audience of one. Hitting "send" or printing out your paper is still a type of publishing. Your final work will need to be formatted according to specific guidelines and sent to your audience by a specific method.

Written works are often published in the workplace. Memos are distributed to groups of coworkers. Proposals are sent to clients. Training materials are printed and used every day. Any work that is written for an audience will be published.

The Publishing Process

Publishing your work requires you to choose and understand a venue. You must understand and follow the publishing requirements of the venue.

Imagine you have created a spreadsheet for your department providing the schedule for a large TV marketing project. You need to send the spreadsheet to everyone in your department.

Identify the Publishing Venue

First, identify where and how you will publish your work. Often, you will know in advance how you intend to publish your writing. If it's a letter, you will mail it. If it's a blog post, you will publish it to your blog.

?   **1.** What venue would you use to publish your spreadsheet?

You might publish your spreadsheet by emailing it to your department. You could also print the spreadsheet and distribute it. If you used online spreadsheet software, you could email a link to the spreadsheet online.

Understand Publishing Requirements

Publishing a spreadsheet will have specific requirements. If you are unsure of the requirements, research your publishing venue. The following are possible venues:

- If you email a spreadsheet, you will need to write an email and attach the file.
- If you print a spreadsheet, you will need to choose printer settings and make copies.
- If you distribute an online spreadsheet, you will need to provide access to the spreadsheet and send a link to recipients.

?   **2.** If you email the spreadsheet, what publishing requirements will the email have?

This business email requires:

- Choosing your department members as recipients.
- Writing a brief, informative subject line.
- Writing a body with a greeting, email body, and signature.
- Attaching the spreadsheet.

Prepare the Text for Publication

To prepare the text for publication, you may need to format the text, add additional elements such as a bibliography or cover letter, and complete any other publishing requirements. How you prepare the text will depend on the requirements of your publishing venue.

3. Write an email to accompany the spreadsheet.

To marketingdepartment@jmco.com
Subject
Send  project-schedule.xlsx

The email should be direct and to the point. You might write:

To marketingdepartment@jmco.com
Subject TV Marketing Project Schedule
Greetings everyone,
I'm attaching the spreadsheet for our upcoming television marketing project schedule. Please let me know if you have any questions or concerns.
Thanks,
Margaret Collins
Send  project-schedule.xlsx

Publish

When your text is prepared, all you need to do is send or submit it. Check that you have followed all the requirements before publishing.

4. How would you publish your prepared email?

Since this is an email, you would publish it by hitting the "send" button. Before sending, make sure that you have the correct recipients, that the correct file is attached, and that your subject line is clear.

Use the following scenario for exercises 1 through 4.

Imagine you have written the following blog post for your company's blog. You have finished writing the post and want to publish it from your blog publishing software.

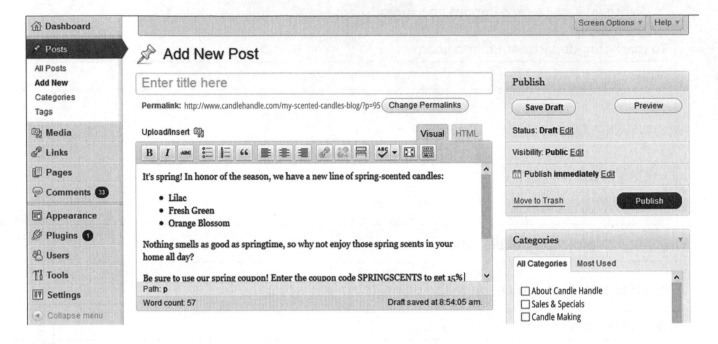

1. What is the venue you are using to publish the post?

2. Examine the interface. What are the publishing requirements for the post?

3. What steps should you take to prepare the post for publications? Write any missing elements.

4. What would you check before publishing? What step would you take to publish the post?

Use the following scenario and prompt for exercises 5 through 8.

Imagine you have written a college paper in response to the following prompt.

The U.S. Supreme Court decision of Marbury v. Madison (1803) established the doctrine of judicial review. Explain the majority decision and its effects on U.S. law. Format your paper using MLA style and submit it to my mailbox by 5:00 P.M. May 21.

★ **5.** What is the venue you are using to publish your paper?

★★ **6.** How can you determine the publishing requirements of the paper?

★★ **7.** Academic papers are formatted according to style guides. The most common guides are MLA (Modern Language Association) and APA (American Psycological Association). Style guides give specific requirements for formatting an academic paper. One requirement of MLA style is a "Works Cited" page where you list works you reference in your paper. On this page, works are listed in order by the author's last name.

A listing for a book follows the following general format:

Author's Last Name, Author's First Name. *Capitalize and Italicize the Book Title.* Editor (if there is one). Edition (if there is one). City Published: Publisher, Year.

Example:

Smith, Mary T., and John Jones. *A Guide to Learning MLA Style.* Ed. Tom Torrence. 3rd ed. New York: HarperCollins, 2001.

On a computer or on a separate sheet of paper, format and order the following listings for your "Works Cited" page.

American Law in Global Perspective: The Basics by George P. Fletcher and Steve Sheppard. Published in Oxford by Oxford University Press in 2004.

Constitutional Law, Fifth Edition, by Geoffrey R. Stone. Published in New York by Aspen Publishers in 2005.

Marbury v. Madison: The Origins and Legacy of Judicial Review by William E. Nelson. Published in Lawrence, KS by University Press of Kansas in 2000.

> *Writing Tip*
>
> If college is in your plans, become familiar with the MLA and APA styles for formatting academic papers.

8. What would you check before publishing? What step would you take to publish your paper?

9. Explain a time when you published your writing by delivering it to an audience. What publishing venue did you use? What were the publishing requirements, and how did you fulfill them?

10. Research the publishing requirements for sending a letter to the editor to your local newspaper. What steps do you need to take to send in a letter to the editor?

11. Write and send a letter to the editor to your local paper on an issue that is important to you. How difficult or easy was the publishing step? Why?

Check **Your Skills**

Use the following scenario and passage for exercises 1 and 2.

Imagine you are applying for the following job listing. You have written a résumé and a cover letter in a word processing program.

Mitch-Field Chemicals is seeking a research group assistant who can manage large projects and work well with a team. Experience in a research or academic environment is preferred. Send your cover letter and résumé as email attachments to Angela Lozano at hr@mitchfieldchemicals.com.

---

 1. Write an email to publish your résumé and cover letter.

To
Subject

Send

 2. What steps do you need to take to finalize and send your job application?

3. Describe the publishing process and how you will apply it in school, work, and other aspects of life.

Write your answer below or type your response on a computer. Take approximately 25 minutes to respond.

Remember the Concept

To publish your work, understand and follow the requirements.

- Identify the venue.
- Understand the requirements.
- Prepare the text.
- Publish.

Use the questions on page 329 to evaluate your response.

Organization

Organization is one of the most important elements of good writing. Developing well-organized writing will help you have a strong central idea, specific supporting details, and a compelling conclusion. Good organization helps you communicate well:

- You need a clear central idea so that you can develop an organization that supports your idea.

- You need strong evidence to show a logical progression of ideas and support your central idea.

- You need to explain your evidence and why it supports your central idea.

- You need a good conclusion to give your writing a satisfying ending.

The most basic elements of organization are a beginning, middle, and ending. Every paragraph, letter, email, paper, report, blog post, poem, or book you might write has a beginning, middle, and ending.

The beginning introduces your ideas. Like the first few minutes of a movie or book, it catches the reader's attention and sets up what will follow. What is your tone? What is your position? In a paper or academic response, the introduction should include a statement of your central idea: your thesis. Give any background or details that help you explain and set up your central idea.

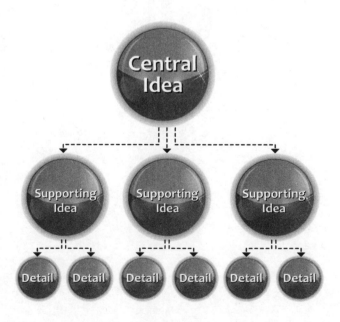

The middle is the main part of your writing. The middle contains the support for your central idea and explains your thinking. It is the longest part and often the most difficult to write. To be successful writing the middle, you need to develop good content. That means identifying enough supporting ideas and specific details to accomplish the goal of your writing task. Explain the connections between your ideas, and present them in a logical order.

The ending is your last chance to communicate with the reader. To leave your reader with a positive impression, you want a strong ending that provides a conclusion. Just like a bad ending can ruin a movie, a bad ending can leave a paper or academic response flat. The best conclusions give some new insight into the ideas the author presents, while restating the central idea in a new way. How does the central idea apply to a bigger picture? What is an unaddressed point or unanswered question?

This section will give you additional practice developing your organization for specific situations.

- **Organizing Short Answers**
  Apply techniques for organization to paragraph-length responses.

- **Organizing Extended Responses**
  Develop a good organization for longer academic and workplace responses.

- **Organizing Workplace Documents**
  Practice organizing reports, letters and emails, or other workplace documents.

Organizing Short Answers

Connections

Have you ever...

- Responded to a post on a blog?

- Described a process or event to a new hire?

- Decided how to reply to an email from a client?

Each of these tasks requires a short response. A short response is brief, but it still needs to be organized. If you're reading a recipe, you want clear directions. If you're reading an email, you want to understand the main point. When you write, organization helps you communicate clearly.

Short answers require analyzing an issue or question and then providing a brief but effective answer or comment in an appropriate tone. Because the response is shorter, every sentence should add to the meaning, purpose, and clarity of your communication.

A short answer typically replies to a question, prompt, or passage. In a college class or formal exam, you will have to write short answers to show your knowledge, typically in a limited time frame. With limited time, organization is especially important. Plan, draft, and evaluate to organize your writing:

- **Plan** a central idea and supporting details by examining materials and thinking through the task.

- **Draft** a well-organized response focused on your central idea.

- **Evaluate** whether the organization of your response communicates clearly and effectively.

Organizing a Short Answer Using the Writing Process

You should be able to write an effective short answer in about ten minutes. Your response may be one or more paragraphs and should have a beginning, middle, and ending. The key to good organization in a short response is to have a developed central idea with supporting details.

Read the following passage. Explain how the data from water samples supports or does not support the conclusion that *E. coli* bacteria levels are not affected by temperature or pH levels. Include multiple pieces of evidence from the passage to support your answer. Take approximately 10 minutes to respond.

Little Creek *E. coli* Bacteria Study

The Little Creek *E. coli* Bacteria Study is an effort to determine the source or sources of elevated *E. coli* levels in Little Creek, an important component of our city's watershed and a popular swimming hole during the summer months. Effects of ingesting *E. coli* include severe abdominal cramping, diarrhea, and seizures, but Little Creek's *E. coli* levels are within acceptable levels for recreation.

In June, July, August, and September, scientists measured temperature, pH, and levels of *E. coli* at four sites. The goal of the study was to learn whether temperature or pH were factors in raised levels of *E. coli.* Temperature was measured in degrees Fahrenheit. Warmer temperatures can encourage bacterial growth. The pH levels show acidity or basicity of the water. A pH level of less than seven signals basicity, a more ideal environment for bacteria growth.

Results indicate that neither temperature nor pH levels have triggered the high levels of *E. coli*. Water temperatures are expectedly higher in the hotter months of July and August, but *E. coli* levels during those months remain the same regardless of water temperature. Nor does the data point to pH levels as a cause of *E. coli*.

However, increased levels of *E. coli* were found at Site 4, the location where water from a farm irrigation ditch (FID) is released into Little Creek. The FID is uncovered and therefore an open target for chemical farm runoff, animal feces, and other toxins.

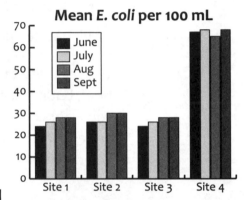

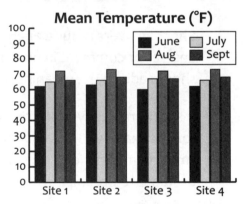

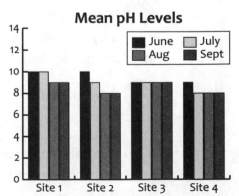

Plan

Focus on organization right away for a short answer. Examine the question and source materials. Identify two things:

- What is your central idea?

- What are supporting details?

Your central idea and details will drive the organization of your response.

? 1. Write a one-sentence central idea, and identify two to four details from the passage to support the central idea.

The exercise is asking you to show how the claim made in the report is either supported or not supported by the data. You will need to study the data in the charts and determine whether the claim made in the report is supported by this data. Since the data supports the claim, you might write:

> In the Little Creek *E. coli* Bacteria Study, the claim that *E. coli* levels are not affected by temperature or pH levels is supported by the data.

Since you examined the data to come to this conclusion, you should be able to identify details to support it.

> Levels of *E. coli* do not go up when the temperature rises in the hotter months of July and August. Site 2 is a good example.

> The pH levels do not drop below seven, which would create an environment to encourage bacterial growth.

> Site 4 has similar temperature and pH as other sites, but it has more bacteria.

Draft

Organize your response with a beginning, middle, and ending:

- Start with the central idea at the beginning.

- Fill the middle with details. Add specifics from the passage and make connections to the central idea.

- Add a conclusion at the end.

2. Draft your response using the following organizer.

Beginning:	*Your Central Idea*
Middle:	*Supporting Details and Connection to the Central Idea*
Ending:	*Conclusion*

You might write:

In the Little Creek *E. coli* Bacteria Study, the claim that *E. coli* levels are not affected by temperature or pH levels is supported by the data. The chart shows that levels of *E. coli* did not go up when the temperature rose in the hotter months of July and August. For example, at Site 2, the *E. coli* level was the same in June and July, while temperatures rose from the low to high 60s. The bacteria level rose in August, but stayed the same in September, although temperatures fell. Since high temperatures encourage bacterial growth, you might expect high temperature to correlate with higher bacterial levels. Since this wasn't the case, something else must have caused high levels of bacteria. There was a similar lack of correlation between pH and *E. coli*, according to the data. The pH never dropped below seven, a pH level that might encourage bacterial growth. Site 4 had high *E. coli* levels, but the pH remained at eight or nine. The pH and temperature at Site 4 were the same as or less than the other sites, but the bacteria level was consistently higher. Since the data shows that high *E. coli* levels were not caused by temperature or pH, they must have been caused by something else. The passage suggests that they were caused by runoff from a farm, which would be a good avenue for further study.

 ## Evaluate and Submit

Evaluate your organization as you draft. Does it make sense? Do you need transitions, more specific details, or connections to the central idea? Make changes to clarify your ideas and improve your organization. Continue to evaluate after you draft, until you are ready to submit your response.

? **3.** Revise your short answer to improve its organization.

Since you often have limited time to write a short response, evaluate as you plan and draft. When you're finished, do one last check for language errors, clarity, and transitions.

Practice It!

In a scientific study, a control group is a group that is not affected by the factor being studied. For example, in a study of how constant, strong light affects plant growth, a control group might receive normal light. This allows scientists to compare the experimental group, which has undergone a treatment, to the control group, which has received no treatment. Comparing an experimental group with a control group allows scientists to effectively test for an independent variable. Using a control group is especially necessary when there are complex factors that might affect the experiment. Administering a placebo is one example of using a control group. While one group receives a dose of medication, the other group receives a "fake dose," meant to have no effect. In this way, the experiment can account for complex factors—for example a flu that is going around or the body's natural ability to heal on its own—that might affect the experiment.

1. Explain how a control group could be used for a study on the effect of regular exercise on clinical depression. Discuss the importance of the control group for the larger study. Include multiple pieces of evidence from the passage to support your answer.

   a. Write a one-sentence central idea and identify two to four details from the passage to support the central idea.

The Writing Process

✏ **Draft**

Use specific details and connect them to your central idea.

b. Draft your response using the organizer. Evaluate as you draft and after you draft.

Beginning:	*Your Central Idea*

Middle:	*Supporting Details and Connection to the Central Idea*

Ending:	*Conclusion*

Use the following passage from an employee handbook for exercise 2.

Doscero Industries encourages an open environment where employees can voice their ideas and concerns. We believe that free communication leads to improvement of our processes and policies and prevents negative behavior on a systemic level. If an employee has a concern about ethics, that concern should be voiced to the employee's manager. Managers are responsible for maintaining a supportive environment for free communication of all concerns. If a concern involves the manager's performance directly, the employee should voice this concern to the manager's superior. Any reported instance of potentially unethical or questionable behaviors or policies will be investigated thoroughly. The company will act promptly to respond to improper behavior and will not tolerate any retaliation against employees who raise their concerns in good faith.

 2. Kara works for Doscero Industries. She notices that her manager distributes less work to his good friend, Kara's coworker Max. Explain what actions you would recommend Kara take based on the company policy. Include multiple pieces of evidence from the passage to support your answer.

    a. Write a one-sentence central idea and identify two to four details from the passage to support the central idea.

The Writing Process

💡 **Plan**

Read and understand the prompt and passage before you begin writing.

b. Draft your response using the organizer. Evaluate as you draft and after you draft.

Beginning: *Your Central Idea*

Middle: *Supporting Details and Connection to the Central Idea*

Ending: *Conclusion*

Check Your Skills

Use the following passage to write well-organized responses for exercises 1 and 2.

Amplified Greenhouse Effect Shifts North's Growing Seasons

Vegetation growth at Earth's northern latitudes increasingly resembles lusher latitudes to the south, according to a NASA-funded study based on a 30-year record of ground-based and satellite data sets.

"Higher northern latitudes are getting warmer. Arctic sea ice and the duration of snow cover are diminishing. The growing season is getting longer, and plants are growing more," said Ranga Myneni of Boston University's Department of Earth and Environment.

An amplified greenhouse effect is driving the changes, according to Myneni. Increased concentrations of heat-trapping gases, such as water vapor, carbon dioxide, and methane, cause Earth's surface, ocean, and lower atmosphere to warm. Warming reduces the extent of polar sea ice and snow cover, and, in turn, the darker ocean and land surfaces absorb more solar energy, thus further heating the air above them.

"This sets in motion a cycle of positive reinforcement between warming and loss of sea ice and snow cover, which we call the amplified greenhouse effect," Myneni said. "The greenhouse effect could be further amplified in the future as soils in the north thaw, releasing potentially significant amounts of carbon dioxide and methane."

However, researchers note that plant growth in the north may not continue on its current trajectory. The ramifications of an amplified greenhouse effect, such as frequent forest fires, outbreaks of pest infestations, and summertime droughts, may slow plant growth. Also, warmer temperatures alone in the boreal zone do not guarantee more plant growth, which also depends on the availability of water and sunlight.

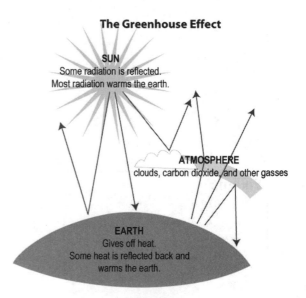

The Greenhouse Effect

SUN
Some radiation is reflected.
Most radiation warms the earth.

ATMOSPHERE
clouds, carbon dioxide, and other gasses

EARTH
Gives off heat.
Some heat is reflected back and
warms the earth.

Source: Adapted from "Amplified Greenhouse Effect Shifts North's Growing Seasons." Author: Kathryn Hansen. Production editor: Dr. Tony Phillips. Credit: Science@NASA.
http://science.nasa.gov/science-news/science-at-nasa/2013/10mar_greenhouseshift/

1. Describe and evaluate the arguments given in the article for why the amplified greenhouse effect may not mean a continued, steady increase in plant growth in the northern latitudes. Include multiple pieces of evidence from the passage to support your answer.

Write your answer below or type your response on a computer. Take approximately 10 minutes to respond.

 2. The greenhouse effect is projected to cause ice melt in the arctic and antarctic. Explain how the greenhouse effect would cause arctic and antarctic ice to melt. Include multiple pieces of evidence from the passage to support your answer.

Write your answer below or type your response on a computer. Take approximately 10 minutes to respond.

Technology Tip

When you write on a computer, you can write your central idea and details as a brief outline. Then fill in the connections, more details, and conclusions.

Use the questions on page 329 to evaluate your response.

Use the following passage to write a well-organized response for exercise 3.

A U.S. Senator has proposed a bill that would cut military spending by 10% over the next five years. Those supporting the bill argue that military spending of over $670 billion a year is unnecessary and unreasonable when Russia and China combined spend only around $150 billion annually on their militaries. Those arguing against the bill state that it is dangerous to national security to cut military spending. They point out that the Department of Defence budget is only approximately 17% of the U.S. budget and encourage budget cuts in other areas, especially the Department of Health and Human Services (including Medicare and Medicaid) and the Social Security Administration, which together total over 47% of the budget.

3. Write a short email to your U.S. Senator, explaining either your support for or opposition to the bill described in the passage. Include multiple pieces of evidence from the passage to support your answer.

Write your answer below or type your response on a computer. Take approximately 10 minutes to respond.

> ### Remember the Concept
>
> **Plan:** Identify a central idea and supporting details.
>
> **Draft:** Organize a paragraph with a beginning, middle, and ending.
>
> **Evaluate:** Evaluate your organization as your write.

Use the questions on page 329 to evaluate your response.

Organizing Extended Responses

Connections

Have you ever...

- Defended a decision you made for your company?

- Expressed your views about a local issue for your school?

- Analyzed news articles about a political controversy?

Good organization will help you communicate well about complex topics. At work or in college, you will need to write responses to reports, books, or memos. Many careers and degrees require independent research to investigate topics. In your personal life, you may need to respond to a letter from a company, write a blog post reviewing a movie, or exchange emails about a political issue.

In an **extended response** you analyze written material and present your ideas backed by evidence. On an exam, your time will often be limited. The writing process will help you evaluate the issue, gather evidence, formulate your conclusion, and organize your work.

Plan: Review materials, develop your central idea, find evidence, and begin organizing your ideas into an appropriate structure.

Draft: Write a response within a clear organizational structure, including a beginning, middle, and ending.

Evaluate: Review your writing for clarity, sense, and transitions. Make sure your organization communicates well and is easy to follow.

Submit: Make any final corrections, and submit your response.

An extended response should have good organization, well-developed ideas, and substantial details. Organization is essential to an effective response.

Developing an Organized Extended Response

A well-organized response has a clear beginning, middle, and ending. It contains supporting details clearly connected to the central idea. The organization is appropriate to the purpose, and there is a clear, logical progression of ideas.

Read the following passages and write an extended response in which you analyze both positions. Explain which position is best supported and why. Include multiple pieces of evidence from the passages to support your answer. Typing your response on a computer will give you the best practice. Your total writing time should be about 45 minutes.

Non-voters Are Not Participating in the Political Process

U.S. voter turnout has shrunk to abysmally low levels during the last three decades. In 1996, less than half the qualifying citizens bothered to cast votes for the President of the United States. After fighting to secure our independence and to obtain voting rights for minorities and women, it is a shame that our citizens have become so complacent. Folks, we are dropping the ball.

As the eminent philosopher John Stuart Mill said, "Political machinery does not act of itself. As it is first made, so it has to be worked, by men, and even by ordinary men. It needs, not their simple acquiescence, but their active participation." Voter participation is an example of active participation at the most fundamental level. It is the one act that every ordinary man can do. It happens only once or twice a year and does not require extensive traveling, public speaking engagements, or monetary investment. Without democratic participation, government fails. Our government doesn't simply keep running without maintenance and care. Wake up, non-voters! Without full voter participation our government is not complete, and we will continue to drop the ball.

Non-voting Is Action

I am writing in response to the article accusing non-voters of "dropping the ball." This narrow perception is so far from the truth that I wonder if the author has any idea at all about the nature of today's political climate. Today's U.S. voters are presented with a two-party system that is so rigid and heavily enforced that other parties have little to no chance of ever presenting their views to the general public, much less getting elected.

The result is a large group of voters who choose not to vote as a means of expressing their distaste for the consistently limited choice of candidates. By choosing not to vote, the citizen is proclaiming, "I don't like either of them." While this may not seem like John Stuart Mill's idea of "active participation," it is the only voting-booth-related action available to citizens who refuse to choose the lesser of two evils. Rather than blame non-voters for "dropping the ball," let's look at our disenfranchising political system.

 Plan

If you have 45 minutes to write an extended response, it helps to come to the task prepared with an organizational structure in mind. The most common organizational structure for this type of writing is a **Statement and Support** structure. Start by using and learning the **Statement and Support** graphic organizer.

An extended response is dependent on material that you must understand and analyze. Spend about 10 minutes of planning time purposefully reading. Identify important ideas, good or flawed arguments, and other details that will help you build a central idea.

?
1. Spend about 10 minutes filling out the graphic organizer with a central idea, supporting ideas, and evidence from the passages. You may expand the chart to include more supporting ideas.

Statement and Support

Central Idea:	Details or Explanation:
Supporting Idea:	Details and Evidence:
Supporting Idea:	Details and Evidence:
Conclusion:	Details or Explanation:

You might complete the organizer like this:

Central Idea:	Details or Explanation:
"Non-voters Are Not Participating in the Political Process" has a better argument.	Provides some facts and evidence, while the other is unsupported opinion.
Supporting Idea: "Not Participating" uses a logical argument that government doesn't work without voter participation and that it is not a huge task to vote.	**Details and Evidence:** "political machinery does not act of itself" Voting does affect government. "It happens only once or twice a year and does not require extensive traveling" True, though voting can sometimes be difficult.
Supporting Idea: "Non-voting Is Action" lacks support	**Details and Evidence:** "Other parties have little to no chance of … getting elected" is not always true. "Choose not to vote as a means of expressing their distaste" has no evidence. Is this really why?
Conclusion: The first is better supported but is calling people "complacent" helpful?	**Details or Explanation:** Voting can be made easier or mandated. Just calling people "complacent" doesn't help solve the problem.

 Draft

Your draft should include a beginning, middle, and ending:

- **Beginning:** Introduce your ideas. Include an interesting beginning, your central idea, and any details or explanation you need to introduce your ideas. You don't need to list all your supporting ideas. That's not interesting, and it doesn't set up your ideas for the reader. In fact, it can cause repetition in your writing and a lack of fluidity.

- **Middle:** Explain each of your supporting ideas, using details and evidence. Connect each idea clearly to your central idea. Restate ideas from the passage instead of relying on direct quotes. If you do use a direct quote, explain its significance.

- **Ending:** Connect your ideas to a larger picture, or draw additional conclusions about your central idea. What makes your central idea meaningful? What did you discover in the process of planning and drafting? What additional thoughts do you have? Sum up your ideas, but be careful not to be redundant.

2. Spend about 20 minutes drafting your extended response on a computer or separate sheet of paper.

Evaluate

Evaluate your organization as you write and after you complete your draft:

- Do you have logical transitions between ideas?

- Do you make connections between your arguments and evidence?

- Do you have evidence and details to support your ideas?

- Do you have a strong central idea supported by the organization?

 3. Spend about 10 minutes evaluating your organization and revising your work.

Submit

Submit

Take a final look over your extended response to make any final corrections. Then, submit your response. Here is a sample response:

> Why do some citizens choose not to vote? Are they dissatisfied or complacent? The article "Non-voters Are Not Participating in the Political Process" claims that non-voters are "dropping the ball." It presents a stronger case than the rebuttal article, which attributes a specific attitude to non-voters with little evidence.
>
> The author of the "Not Participating" article makes a logical argument that voter participation is necessary for a government to function properly. He or she quotes John Stuart Mill that government does not run itself. Voting does affect government policies and actions. The author also argues that voting is not difficult since it happens seldom and since polling booths are near every neighborhood. Though the author supports his or her idea with facts, voting can sometimes be difficult for those with no transportation, no child care, or difficulty getting off work.
>
> The rebuttal article claims that people choose not to vote because they are dissatisfied with the lack of choices in the two-party system. It claims that not voting is a form of active participation. The article makes a valid point that the two-party system forces out alternative opinions, but it overstates the idea that other parties can't get elected. Third-party candidates are elected in local elections, as governors, and as congressmen. However, the author's main point is that people don't vote due to disgust with the two-party system, and the article fails to give any evidence to support this statement. Is political dissatisfaction really the reason non-voters don't visit the polls?
>
> In truth, there are likely many types of non-voters. Understanding their reasoning requires sociological study which is lacking in both opinion articles. Though the article opposing non-voters is stronger, scolding non-voters for "dropping the ball" accomplishes little. Examining ideas such as mandatory voting, early voting, and voting by mail is a better way to attack the problem of voter non-participation.

Practice It!

Use the following passages for exercise 1.

I am certainly not an advocate for frequent and untried changes in laws and constitutions. I think moderate imperfections had better be borne with; because, when once known, we accommodate ourselves to them, and find practical means of correcting their ill effects. But I know also, that laws and institutions must go hand in hand with the progress of the human mind. As that becomes more developed, more enlightened, as new discoveries are made, new truths disclosed, and manners and opinions change with the change of circumstances, institutions must advance also, and keep pace with the times. We might as well require a man to wear still the coat which fitted him when a boy, as civilized society to remain ever under the regimen of their barbarous ancestors.

—*Thomas Jefferson*

Source: Thomas Jefferson, Letter to Samuel Kercheval, June 12, 1816. Available at
http://teachingamericanhistory.org/library/document/letter-to-samuel-kercheval/

The U.S. Supreme Court makes interpretations of our constitutional rights, but sometimes their interpretations are simply wrong. In its Citizens United ruling, the Court ruled that corporations as "associations of citizens" retain the right of free speech based on the First Amendment to the Constitution. Because of this ruling, corporations are allowed to spend unlimited amounts of money, often anonymously, to support politicians and political causes.

However, free speech is a human right. Corporations are inhuman, legal entities without inherent rights. Corporations exist to protect their owners and officers from liability from their businesses. Should they then be considered "associations of citizens" with rights to free speech? Citizens can support candidates. Corporations are not citizens. They do not vote. They cannot be jailed. They are self-interested in laws that will help them make money. That is why I support a constitutional amendment declaring that corporations do not have constitutional rights.

—*Alphonse Kittridge, Letter to the Editor*

1. In your response, develop an argument about how Mr. Kittridge's position reflects the enduring issue expressed in the excerpt from Thomas Jefferson. Analyze the strength of Mr. Kittridge's argument. Incorporate relevant and specific evidence from the passages and your own knowledge of the enduring issue to support your analysis. Type your response on a computer if possible or use a separate sheet of paper. Take up to 25 minutes to respond.

    a. Plan: Spend about five minutes filling out the graphic organizer with a central idea, supporting ideas, and evidence from the passages.

Statement and Support

Central Idea:	Details or Explanation:
Supporting Idea:	Details and Evidence:
Supporting Idea:	Details and Evidence:
Conclusion:	Details or Explanation:

    b. Draft: Spend about 15 minutes drafting your extended response on a computer or on a separate sheet of paper.

    c. Evaluate and Submit: Spend about five minutes evaluating your organization and revising your work before finalizing your extended response.

Use the following passage to complete exercise 2.

Zero-Tolerance Policies in Schools

Many schools have implemented "zero-tolerance" policies toward violence among students. These policies are often responses to school shootings and other extreme instances of school violence. Under zero-tolerance policies, any violence will result in suspension or expulsion. These polices have resulted in significant controversy.

The goal of zero-tolerance violence policies is to discourage violence by removing any violent students from the school. Proponents state that students cannot learn where there is the threat of violent behavior, and expelling all students who participate in violence is a strong deterrent. They argue that strong policies are needed in order to prevent disastrous violent events such as school shootings.

A zero-tolerance violence policy disallows students from making excuses and removes potentially biased administrative decisions based on conflicting reports from students, according to proponents. Even teacher reports can be unreliable, proponents say, since witness reports of what happened in violent situations is notoriously undependable. Zero-tolerance violence policies in schools discourage all violent behavior so that schools can maintain a safe environment for learning, proponents say.

However, zero-tolerance violence policies have come under criticism for their unconditional response to violent behavior. Students who are bullied or attacked must not defend themselves or they will face expulsion in many situations. In some instances, a student who is attacked is considered involved in a violent incident, whether or not he or she fights back.

Parents and students argue that expulsion is often unfair and unnecessary, and some parents object that they should have a say in the punishment of their sons and daughters. Instead of creating a violence-free, safe environment, opponents say, zero-tolerance policies create an insecure atmosphere where students fear they can be expelled by a twist of fate. Opponents are also concerned that expulsion does not deal with the problem of violent behavior; it merely removes violence from the school and pushes it into the community.

Debate over zero-tolerance violence policies continues as communities try to balance individual rights with the good of the school as a whole.

2. Read the passage, which gives arguments for and against zero-tolerance violence policies in schools. In your response, analyze both positions to determine which one is best supported. Use specific evidence from the passage to support your claim. Take approximately 45 minutes to respond.

a. **Plan:** Spend about 10 minutes filling out the graphic organizer with a central idea, supporting ideas, and evidence from the passages.

Statement and Support

Central Idea:	Details or Explanation:
Supporting Idea:	**Details and Evidence:**
Supporting Idea:	**Details and Evidence:**
Conclusion:	**Details or Explanation:**

b. **Draft:** Spend about 20 minutes drafting your extended response on a computer or on a separate sheet of paper.

c. **Evaluate and Submit:** Spend about 10 minutes evaluating your organization and revising your work before finalizing your extended response.

Check Your Skills

Use the following passage for exercises 1 and 2.

People use energy drinks to stay alert while driving, to stay up late and study, or as a morning or afternoon boost. These drinks cause an increase in energy often followed by a "crash." Energy drinks contain caffeine—sometimes as much as 184 milligrams—combined with sweeteners and other ingredients. Even if you've never been tempted to reach for an energy drink, you are probably familiar with the controversy over this relatively new addition to our beverage aisles.

Because of the extreme levels of caffeine and the resulting negative health effects, some consumers have proposed banning energy drinks or developing regulations to keep them away from children and expectant mothers. Proponents of a ban are especially concerned about the industry's penchant for marketing to children and teens, in some instances distributing free samples at youth sporting events.

In 2010, a high school football player in Missouri had a seizure and stopped breathing after consuming an energy drink. He now speaks against the use of energy drinks and works to get them removed from campuses. The symptoms that appear on the list of energy drink incidents documented by the Food and Drug Administration include convulsions, hypertension, loss of consciousness, anaphylactic shock, renal failure, and death. There have also been cases of fetal distress syndrome and miscarriages by pregnant women who consumed energy drinks.

Banning energy drinks or increasing regulation might seem to be in the public interest. However, companies are quick to point out that there is not always evidence that health events such as seizures are the direct result of caffeine toxicity.

Energy drink enthusiasts point out that the drinks often contain beneficial ingredients such as gingko biloba, which may improve memory, and açai berries, which contain antioxidants. Some who are opposed to bans and regulation describe the targeting of energy drink companies as reminiscent of political anti-tobacco campaigns that used children's health as an excuse to punish successful companies. They state that the health risks of tobacco are widespread and costly, while energy drinks provide a benefit in addition to the risks. Opponents of regulation also argue that in a free market system consumers should be able to make their own individual health and food choices.

1. The article presents arguments by those who propose barring energy drinks from the market and those who are opposed to a ban. In your response, analyze both positions to determine which one is best supported. Use specific evidence from the passage to support your claim.

   Write your answer below or type your response on a computer. Take up to 45 minutes to respond.

The Writing Process

✏ **Draft**

To provide details, paraphrase information from the passages. Explain the author's meaning and the connection to your ideas.

Use the questions on page 329 to evaluate your response.

2. A medical report says that, while 100 milligrams of caffeine might have some health consequences, it is generally safe for teenagers to consume 100 milligrams of caffeine in one day. Your city proposes two potential laws: a ban on drinks that contain more than 100 milligrams of caffeine per serving and a ban on selling energy drinks to anyone 18 or younger. Write a response in support of one of these laws over the other. Use specific evidence from the passage to support your claim.

Write your answer below or type your response on a computer. Take up to 45 minutes to respond.

> ### Remember the Concept
>
> Use a **Statement and Support** organizational structure for extended responses.
>
> Identify a central idea, supporting ideas, and conclusion. Find support for each of your ideas.

Use the questions on page 329 to evaluate your response.

Organizing Workplace Documents

Connections

Have you ever...

- Composed a memo to your supervisor or department?

- Added to workplace documentation, such as a manual or an online help database?

- Written a letter to a client?

Writing tasks are common in the workplace, from a simple email to a corporate business plan. Because these documents are for the workplace, they are formal. They should be well-organized and should use clear, professional language.

Workplace documents vary widely. They may include:

- Memos and emails.

- Proposals and reports.

- Documentation of processes, procedures, and technical information.

- Employee evaluations.

- Meeting agendas and minutes.

- Press releases.

How you organize a workplace document will depend on the writing task. What is the purpose of the document? Who is the audience? What procedures or templates exist for the task? However, all workplace documents need to be accurate and clear. A workplace document should always communicate clearly, and good organization helps with clear communication.

Workplace Documents: Type, Purpose, and Audience

To organize a workplace document, examine the document type, purpose, and audience. Based on that examination, choose a structure for the task.

Imagine you work for a non-profit organization. You must write a departmental email setting up a meeting to plan a spring fundraiser. At the meeting, participants will plan for the fundraiser, identify tasks that need to be done, and assign tasks. The theme, budget, sponsors, and marketing will need to be determined. Last year, the fundraiser was called Plant-a-Tree and raised $126,000. This year, the goal is to raise $160,000.

Plan: Examine the Document Type

Many workplace documents have set templates or traditional formats. What type of document are you creating? What are the rules or procedures for the type of document? If you are unsure about the requirements for a specific type of document, research to find more information.

?   **1.** What are the organizational elements of an email?

An email has recipients, a subject line, and a body. It can include attached files. The body of an email is typically treated similarly to a letter, with a greeting, a few paragraphs of text, and a signature.

Plan: Examine the Purpose and Audience

Think about the purpose and audience for the writing task. How will your goal affect the structure and organization of the document? What organization will communicate clearly with the audience?

?   **2.** What is the purpose and audience of this document? How will the purpose and audience affect the organization?

The purpose is to set up a meeting for the department to plan a fundraiser. The audience is the department members. The organization should highlight the meeting time and place and explain what participants need to do to prepare for the meeting.

Plan: Outline a Structure

Based on your understanding of the document type, purpose, and audience, outline a structure for your document. What sections and formatting will the document have? What information will you cover in each section? What organizational structures will you use?

3. Use the table below to outline what information you will include in each section of the email.

To
Subject

 Send

Your outline might be:

To Department Members
Subject Spring Fundraiser Planning Meeting
Greeting Beginning: Time, date, and purpose of meeting Middle: Goals of the meeting, preparation needed for the meeting Ending: Remind of last year's fundraiser and the purpose of the meeting Signature

Send

 ## *Draft*

Based on your outline, draft the document. Where they are appropriate, use subheads, bulleted lists, numbered lists, or other formatting elements to highlight important information.

4. On a computer or on a separate sheet of paper, draft an email for this scenario. Use the email address fundraisingteam@education-plus.org for the department.

You might write the following email:

To fundraisingteam@education-plus.org
Subject Spring Fundraiser Planning Meeting
Hello everyone, Our spring fundraiser is swiftly approaching and will require a good deal of preparation. I have scheduled a fundraiser planning meeting on January 10 at 2:30 P.M. in Conference Room #2. In this meeting, we will discuss strategies and tasks for this important event. We will assign tasks to participants and work out a rough schedule. This year, we hope to raise $160,000 with our spring fundraiser. In the planning meeting, we will determine the theme, location, budget, sponsors, and marketing to reach this goal. Be prepared to share your creative ideas and strategies. Also consider what role you would like to fill in the fundraiser preparation. Last year's Plant-a-Tree event was a smashing success, raising $126,000. I'm sure we can make this year's event as good if not better! Thank you for all your dedicated work. I look forward to seeing you all on January 10 at 2:30. Sincerely, Abigail Einhorn Fundraising Coordinator

 ## *Evaluate: Check for Clarity*

Evaluate the document. Is it clear? Does the organization suit the purpose and audience? Are important elements highlighted?

5. Evaluate the email. What revisions could you make for clarity? How could you highlight important information for the recipients?

The email is clear, but important information could be highlighted. You could put the meeting date and time in the subject line, for example. The phrase "theme, location, budget, sponsors, and marketing" could be formatted as a bulleted list to highlight the important points on the meeting's agenda.

Practice It!

Imagine that you are an advertising project manager. You have been assigned to create a new marketing campaign for Klean Floss, a dental product. The bulk of the campaign will use television ads, direct mail, and email to reach new customers. Advertisements will focus on the benefit of a clean feeling from using Klean Floss, combined with a mail-in offer for a free sample. The total budget for the campaign is $285,000. Write a client memo to Myra Sommers, Marketing Manager, at Klean Floss, Inc. that briefly explains the new marketing campaign and invites Ms. Sommers to a presentation on July 5th at 2:00 P.M. at the JTM Marketing office.

1. How would you format a memo to a client? What sections or elements should it have?

2. What is the purpose and audience of this document? How will the purpose and audience affect the organization?

3. Create an outline for this memo.

4. Write a draft of the memo.

 5. Evaluate your draft. What revisions could you make for clarity? How could you highlight important information for the recipients?

Use the following scenario for exercises 6 through 10.

Imagine that you need to write documentation for your office about how to use the office's email program. Choose an email program that you can access and complete any necessary research. Document how to use the program's main features, including any common mistakes or problems that users may have.

 6. How would you format software documentation for your coworkers? What sections or elements should it have?

 7. What is the purpose and audience of this document? How will the purpose and audience affect the organization?

 8. Create an outline for this document.

9. Write a draft of the document.

 10. Evaluate your draft. What revisions could you make for clarity? How could you highlight important information for the recipients?

Use the following scenario for exercises 11 through 15.

Imagine that you are manager of a Topping Sporting Goods store. You need to write a cover letter for the quarterly report that details the quarterly earnings for your store. Compose a cover letter addressed to the Chief Financial Officer, Margot Foster, which includes the following information. This quarter, your store made 16% more profit than last year at the same time. The marketing expenses rose by 3%, and you credit the increased marketing for increased sales. Based on the success, you recommend expanding the marketing budget by another 2%. You also plan to hire an additional cashier because of the increase in business.

11. How would you format a business letter? What sections or elements should it have?

12. What is the purpose and audience of this document? How will the purpose and audience affect the organization?

13. Create an outline for this document.

14. Write a draft of the document.

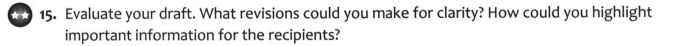 **15.** Evaluate your draft. What revisions could you make for clarity? How could you highlight important information for the recipients?

Check Your Skills

Write well-organized workplace documents for the following scenarios.

1. Imagine that you are a human resources assistant at XYZ Corporation. XYZ has decided to pay for 75% of any full-time employee's membership at City Fitness gym to encourage employee health and fitness. Write an email to your colleagues that explains the new gym membership program.

   Write your answer below or type your response on a computer. Take up to 45 minutes to respond.

Use the questions on page 329 to evaluate your response.

2. Imagine that you work as an office manager at a busy dental practice, Sierra Dental Health. Write a memo to all the employees, including the dentists, dental assistants, and receptionists, outlining a new policy for cancellations. According to the new policy, clients who cancel their dental appointments less than 24 hours before the scheduled appointment will be charged a $25 cancellation fee.

Write your answer below or type your response on a computer. Take up to 45 minutes to respond.

> ### Remember the Concept
>
> To organize workplace documents:
>
> - Evaluate document type, purpose, and audience.
> - Outline the document.
> - Draft.
> - Evaluate for clarity.

Use the questions on page 329 to evaluate your response.

Developing Ideas, Arguments, and Evidence

Good writing depends on good content. A developed idea or argument is one that you have thought about and looked at from various perspectives. You can describe your ideas in detail and make connections with other ideas.

The writing process helps you develop your ideas, arguments, and evidence so that you will have something compelling to say.

 ### Plan

When you begin to plan, you will identify ideas for your writing. What is your central idea? What are supporting ideas? During planning, find specific evidence and details to help develop your ideas.

 ### Draft

As you draft, you flesh out your ideas. Explain the connections between supporting ideas and your central idea, and explain the connections between details and your ideas. Defining connections is an important part of developing ideas.

 ### Evaluate

Evaluate whether your ideas are well developed. Do you give details and specifics?

This section will help you develop strong support for your ideas through the following lessons.

- **Developing Ideas**

  A developed idea is backed by details and explanations. Your idea is clearly communicated to the reader. This lesson will give you a strategy to develop your ideas.

- **Developing Strong Support**

  One of the most important types of writing is persuasive writing. In persuasive writing, you will state your position and present evidence to support that position. In this lesson, you will learn to evaluate the evidence that you use to support your ideas. The best support is specific, timely, accurate, and relevant.

- **Evaluating Arguments**

  Throughout life, you will read or listen to other people's arguments. Perhaps you will need to evaluate a scientific paper's conclusions. Perhaps you will need to make a decision about a ballot initiative or a candidate for governor. Perhaps you will need to write a report comparing applicants for a position at your company. In all of these circumstances, you will need to evaluate arguments. In this lesson, you will learn to evaluate and write about others' arguments.

- **Citing Evidence and Connecting with Claims**

  When you develop an argument, it is essential to make a connection between your evidence and your claim. This lesson gives you a strategy to build a "chain of evidence" connecting to your claim.

- **Drawing Conclusions**

  Drawing conclusions based on evidence is a critical skill. In this lesson, you will learn a strategy to draw conclusions.

Developing Ideas

Have you ever...

- Given someone directions for a project?

- Run out of things to say when writing a paper?

- Read an email that didn't give you enough details?

The details are important. If you're explaining how to complete a project, readers need enough information to follow the instructions. If someone sends you an email, you don't want that person to leave out important information. If you're writing a paper, you need enough details to fully explain your ideas. That's what **developing** your ideas means—giving enough information and explanation so that others can completely understand your meaning.

A developed idea is one that you have thought out fully. You have looked at it from different perspectives and described it in detail. A developed idea should have:

- Supporting ideas that give further information about your central meaning.

- Specific details that explain and support your idea.

- Explanations that connect supporting ideas, details, and the central idea.

The writing process helps you develop your ideas. When you plan, you think through your ideas. How are your ideas related? What details support your ideas? How do those details support your ideas? When you draft, you should continue to develop your ideas. Add explanations that make your ideas clear and show how your ideas and details are connected. As you work, you will evaluate your writing. Have you included all the details and explained all your thoughts?

Expand Your Ideas

Your ideas have more depth than you realize at first. Thinking through related ideas and supporting details helps you develop and communicate your ideas.

Imagine that you need to recommend one of your company's insurance policies to a coworker who anticipates having about $1,000 in medical expenses in the next year. The Bronze policy costs $55 per paycheck ($1,430 per year). It includes 20% coinsurance for most types of expenses, meaning that the insured person pays 20% of the expenses. Before any expenses are covered, you must pay a $1,500 deductible. The Silver policy costs $98 per paycheck ($2,548 per year). It includes 10% coinsurance for most types of medical expenses and has a $400 deductible. Your coworker wants to understand what her expenses will probably be like and what would happen if she had an unexpected large medical expense. Write an email explaining your recommendation.

Plan Ideas and Details

When you plan, expand your central idea, like blowing up a balloon. Add supporting ideas and details. What ideas are related to your central idea? What details help explain your ideas?

1. Add your central idea, supporting ideas, and details to the graphic organizer.

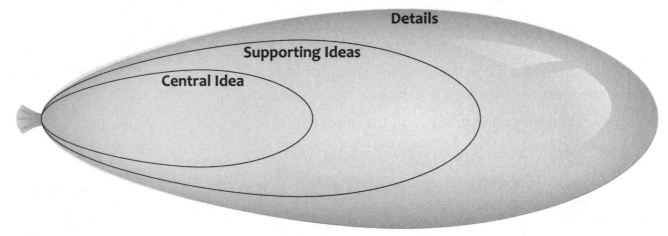

Your central idea might be to recommend the Bronze policy. One supporting idea is that the total expected expenses will be less. Another supporting idea is that unexpected expenses will not be too large a burden. Your details might include:

- The Bronze policy costs about $1,000 less per year.

- With the Silver policy, expected additional expenses are about $500. With the Bronze policy, expected additional expenses are about $1,000.

- The total savings with the Bronze policy is about $500.

- For an unexpected expense, the Bronze policy coinsurance would be 10% more of the expenses. The difference in the cost per paycheck approximately covers the difference in deductibles.

Draft Ideas and Details

When you draft, expand your idea further by adding connections, explanations, and organization. Organize your thoughts in a logical order, and connect your ideas and details. Explain each idea and detail to develop your central idea.

?   **2.** Draft a response based on the graphic organizer.

You might write:

> I recommend the Bronze policy for your situation. Your total expected expenses for the year would be lower. The Bronze policy costs about $1,000 less per year out of your paycheck, and you would likely pay around $1,000 per year in medical expenses. The total costs would be about $2,500. With the Silver policy, your total costs would be about $500 more, because you would be paying $2,500 out of your paychecks plus a $400 deductible and 10% coinsurance on additional expenses. Large unexpected expenses would cost more, but the additional expenses wouldn't be too large a burden. The difference in the cost per paycheck approximately covers the difference in deductibles, so your main additional expense would be the coinsurance, which is 10% higher. If you are concerned about a potential large medical expense, you should consider the Silver policy. However, because of your low expected expenses, the Bronze policy is probably the better option.

Evaluate Ideas and Details

Evaluate your work. Are there clear connections between your ideas? Do you fully explain your ideas and details?

?   **3.** Evaluate, revise, and edit your response.

Submit

When you are satisfied with your response, check it one last time and then submit it. In this scenario, you would send the email.

Build Your Writing Skills

Write a response that recommends the other plan. Why might your coworker choose each plan?

Practice It!

Use the following passage for exercises 1 through 3.

Funding for NASA has come under fire as unnecessary government spending. Critics point to poverty, crime, unemployment, education, and other immediate issues that could benefit from the money spent on NASA, which had a budget of almost $18 billion in 2012. Those opposed to the space agency point to private space exploration projects such as SpaceX and Virgin Galactic as a better way to explore space in the future. The risks and costs of space exploration are great, critics say, while the benefits are intangible.

On the other hand, NASA supporters point out that the agency's budget is only 0.6% of the $3 trillion budget. The benefits may not be immediately tangible, but supporters say that those benefits are far-reaching. They point to the moon landing as an iconic moment in U.S. history that promotes science and technology. The money spent on space exploration has resulted in a long list of sometimes unexpected innovations "from solar panels to implantable heart monitors, from cancer therapy to light-weight materials, and from water-purification systems to improved computing systems" according to NASA[1].

[1]Source: "Benefits Stemming from Space Exploration" by the International Space Exploration Coordination Group, Sept. 2013, available at http://www.nasa.gov/sites/default/files/files/Benefits-Stemming-from-Space-Exploration-2013-TAGGED.pdf

1. Plan a response explaining which argument in the passage is stronger. Use the following graphic organizer.

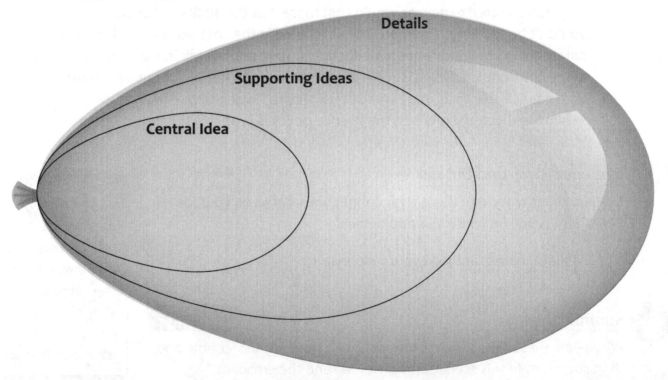

Details

Supporting Ideas

Central Idea

2. Draft your response. Organize your thoughts in a logical order, and connect your ideas and details. Explain each idea and detail to develop your central idea.

3. Evaluate your response. Revise and edit your work until you are satisfied with your response.

Use the following passage for exercises 4 and 5.

Humans become infected with roundworms by drinking unfiltered water containing copepods (small crustaceans) which are infected with larvae of D. medinensis. Following ingestion, the copepods die and release the larvae, which penetrate the host stomach and intestinal wall. After maturation into adults and copulation, the male worms die and the females (length: 70 to 120 cm) migrate in the subcutaneous tissues towards the skin surface. Approximately one year after infection, the female worm induces a blister on the skin, generally on the distal lower extremity (foot). The blister ruptures, and when this lesion comes into contact with water, the female worm emerges and releases larvae. The larvae can then be ingested by a copepod. After two weeks, ingested larvae have developed into infective larvae. Ingestion of the copepods closes the cycle.

Source: Adapted from "Parasites—Dracunculiasis (also known as Guinea Worm Disease)—Biology" by the CDC. http://www.cdc.gov/parasites/guineaworm/biology.html

 4. Parasites depend on hosts and live in or on the host's body. Explain how the parasite D. medinensis (roundworm) depends on hosts throughout its life cycle. Include multiple pieces of evidence from the passage to support your answer.

Plan your response by adding your central idea, supporting ideas, and details to the graphic organizer.

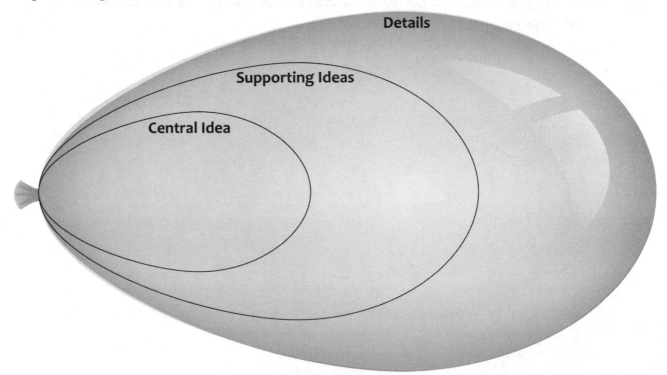

 5. Draft and evaluate your response. Type your response on a computer if possible. If a computer is unavailable, use a separate sheet of paper.

Check Your Skills

Use the following passage for exercises 1 and 2.

The question of whether or not to raise the minimum wage periodically arises for states and for the federal government. Some workers are asking for a national minimum wage increase to $15 per hour, while many object that a higher minimum wage will stifle business and ultimately hurt the economy.

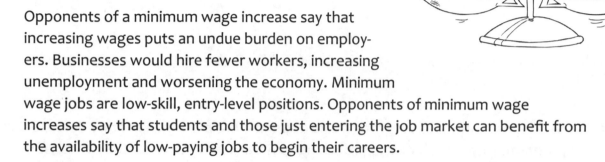

Opponents of a minimum wage increase say that increasing wages puts an undue burden on employers. Businesses would hire fewer workers, increasing unemployment and worsening the economy. Minimum wage jobs are low-skill, entry-level positions. Opponents of minimum wage increases say that students and those just entering the job market can benefit from the availability of low-paying jobs to begin their careers.

According to opponents, a minimum wage increase would also cause increased prices. They claim it would hurt the poor, since low-income households will suffer most from the loss of minimum wage jobs combined with increased prices for goods and services. In addition, opponents say that small businesses would be hurt, since they would suffer most from increased employment costs.

An increased minimum wage puts money directly in the pockets of spenders, supporters state. Those working a minimum wage job spend money on food, transportation, and other necessities. An increase of minimum wage income would mean more money in the economy, spurring growth. A study by the Federal Reserve Bank of Chicago found that after the minimum wage was increased, households with at least one minimum-wage worker spent $700 more every three months. At the same time, an increased minimum wage would get many workers off of government assistance such as food stamps and welfare, supporters claim.

Supporters of increasing the minimum wage note that the minimum wage has not kept up with inflation. In 2014, a full-time worker earning the federal minimum wage would make $15,080 a year. A family of four supported by two full-time minimum wage workers would be below the poverty level. Supporters of an increase state that a full-time job should pay a living wage, one that can cover basic living expenses.

1. The passage presents arguments supporting and opposing increasing the minimum wage. In your response, analyze both positions to determine which is best supported. Use relevant and specific evidence from the passages to support your response.

Take approximately 45 minutes for this task. Use the space below for planning, and type your answer on a computer to prepare for computer responses. If a computer is unavailable, write your answer on a separate sheet of paper.

 2. "A nation that continues year after year to spend more money on military defense than on programs of social uplift is approaching spiritual death. America, the richest and most powerful nation in the world, can well lead the way in this revolution of values.... There is nothing but a lack of social vision to prevent us from paying an adequate wage to every American citizen." —*Martin Luther King, Jr.*

From *Where Do We Go from Here: Chaos or Community?* by Martin Luther King, Jr., 1967

Develop an argument about how the passage reflects the issue expressed in the quotation. Incorporate relevant, specific evidence from the quotation, the passage, and your own knowledge to support your analysis.

Take approximately 25 minutes for this task. Use the space below for planning, and type your answer on a computer to prepare for computer responses. If a computer is unavailable, write your answer on a separate sheet of paper.

> *Remember the Concept*
>
> **Expand your central idea by adding:**
>
> - Supporting ideas
> - Details
> - Connections
> - Explanations

Use the questions on page 329 to evaluate your response.

Developing
Strong Support

Connections

Have you ever...

- Changed a friend's mind?

- Almost agreed with someone's argument, until you learned the source of his or her information?

- Heard a rumor that you knew wasn't true?

Before people will agree with a claim, they will usually look for a reason to do so. "Because I said so," rarely works to persuade. To convince others to agree with a position, you must include strong support to back up your claim. Developing good support is crucial to creating a successful argument.

An argument includes a claim (the central idea that you want to prove), evidence, and reasoning. Evidence and reasoning is the support for your claim. With strong evidence and clear, logical reasoning, a claim can be convincing and persuasive.

Good evidence has four attributes. It is **Specific**, **Timely**, **Accurate**, and **Relevant**.

Each of these attributes helps create convincing support. Without all four of these attributes, a claim loses credibility, and the argument is not persuasive.

When evaluating your own support or analyzing others' arguments, test evidence by asking, "Is it **STAR Support**?"

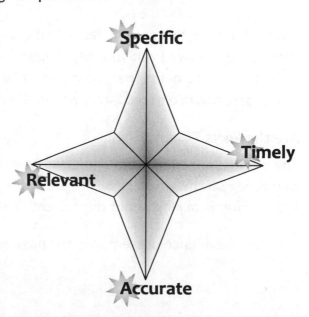

STAR Support

Specific, timely, accurate, and relevant evidence makes a claim more convincing.

- Look for STAR Support when you read and evaluate arguments.

- Use STAR Support in your own writing.

Ecotourism brings visitors to natural destinations to raise money and awareness to preserve natural environments. However, ecotourism is fundamentally flawed. It grows by 10 to 15 percent worldwide each year. That means more construction, trash, and use of local resources. An article in *USA Today* states, "one study in a Costa Rican national park found that wild monkeys turned into garbage feeders, becoming familiar with the presence of ecotourists and eating the food and rubbish left behind."[1] Ecotourism causes more harm than good. It is probably often developed in unsustainable ways, despite its stated goals.

---

[1]Source: From "Positive & Negative Effects of Ecotourism" by Rita Kennedy, Demand Media. *USA Today,* http://traveltips.usatoday.com/positive-negative-effects-ecotourism-63682.html

Evaluate What You Read for STAR Support

Are There Specific Facts?

To analyze an argument, find specific facts that the writer uses. If the writer uses no specific facts to support the argument, then the argument is mostly opinion.

?   **1.** What specific facts does the writer use to support the argument?

The writer gives two specific facts: that ecotourism grows 10 to 15 percent each year and that a study showed wild monkeys began feeding on ecotourists' trash. The writer also makes two statements that are vague and unspecific: that ecotourism means more construction, trash, and use of resources and that ecotourism is developed in unsustainable ways.

Are the Facts Timely?

The world is constantly changing, and new information is learned every day. Is the information timely? If the writer is talking about the Great Depression, expect facts from the 1930s. If the writer is talking about the current drop-out rates, the facts should be recent.

?   **2.** Is the evidence presented in the passage timely?

The passage doesn't give enough information to determine if the facts are timely without additional research. The facts may or may not be current.

Are the Facts Accurate?

Accurate

If an argument contains inaccurate facts, then the support is invalid. Misreadings, information used out of context, and second-hand knowledge can all lead to support that sounds great but is inaccurate. To spot inaccuracies, ask:

- Is the source credible?

- Does the information make sense?

?   **3.** Is the support for the argument accurate?

You can't always tell if information is accurate without checking other sources. However, you can tell that the author gives no sources for most of the facts. The only source is an article in *USA Today* that quotes an unnamed study. This source is a newspaper, which lends it credence, but the study itself would be a better source. The information in the passage makes sense, but the sources are vague.

Are the Facts Relevant?

Relevant

Do the facts actually support the claim? Examine the logical connection that the author makes between the fact and the central idea. Does it make sense?

?   **4.** Is the support for the argument relevant?

The statement that ecotourism involves construction, trash, and use of resources gives a reason that growth of 10 to 15 percent is relevant. Causing wildlife to eat garbage is a negative impact of ecotourism, though the author doesn't specifically state why it is a problem. The quotation is specific. However, facts about overall ecological impact of ecotourism (use of resources, impact of construction, and creation of trash) would be more relevant. The author's statement that ecotourism is developed in unsustainable ways is relevant, but it lacks any specific factual support.

The Writing Process

Plan

Do not be mislead when you plan your writing. Irrelevant or inaccurate support is sometimes used to distract a reader from an argument.

Use STAR Support in Your Writing

When you write:

- Use **Specific** facts, including details, to support your argument.

- Use **Timely** facts when you are researching. Look at when an article or book was written.

- Use **Accurate** facts and check quotations. Do not misrepresent the author.

- Use **Relevant** facts. Explain how your facts support your claim.

?   5. Write a paragraph evaluating the strength of the author's argument. Use specific facts from the passage and include logical connections that show how the facts are relevant to your central idea.

You might write:

> The author's argument is not well supported, since it relies on vague statements. The author states that ecotourism grows 10 to 15 percent annually, but the passage lacks clear reasons why this growth is negative. It is logical that ecotourism results in construction, trash, and resource use, but what is the impact of construction? How much trash is generated? How many resources are used? How does this compare to the benefits of ecotourism? The author quotes one study that found wild monkeys in Costa Rica began eating trash from ecotourism. This is not a beneficial result. However, there are unanswered questions. How prevalent is this result in areas where there is ecotourism? Are there other studies with similar findings? The author states that ecotourism is "probably often developed in unsustainable ways," but gives no evidence for this statement. The use of the words "probably often" shows that the author is merely speculating. Ecotourism may be harmful, but the author does not provide specific evidence for a convincing case.

Specific evidence includes an indirect quote ("ecotourism grows 10 to 15 percent annually") and a direct quote ("'probably often developed in unsustainable ways'"). The indirect and direct quotes are accurate, and the response includes explanations of why the quotations show that the argument is not well supported. You can use direct quotes in your writing, but do not use too many. Restate ideas to show that you understand them.

The Writing Process

Plan

Verify facts before you use them in an argument.

Imagine your city council is hearing arguments for and against reopening an abandoned drive-in movie theater. The developer is requesting taxpayer money to contribute to the renovation and in return pledges to have a free family movie night every other month for the first two years.

 1. Which of the following is irrelevant to the developer's argument?

   a. The movie theater would increase business in an otherwise unsightly area.

   b. The theater would draw visitors from out of town and support other businesses.

   c. The movie theater used to show a double feature every Saturday night.

   d. People who remember the theater support its renovation.

 2. Which specific information would help the developer make his case stronger?

   a. How renovating drive-in theaters has spurred economic growth in similar towns

   b. Why the theater closed down

   c. What movies would show there over the next three years

   d. Information about the current movie theater that shows movies indoors

3. A local citizen argues, "It is unfair for taxpayers to pay for business development. A drive-in theater would just encourage young people to drink in their cars. When the theater was open in the 1980s, it caused a lot of traffic. This theater is a bad idea."

   a. Does the argument provide specific facts? How does this affect the argument?

   b. Does the argument provide timely facts? How does this affect the argument?

   c. Does the argument provide accurate facts? How does this affect the argument?

   d. Does the argument provide relevant facts? How does this affect the argument?

Use the following passage for exercises 4 and 5.

Our city should install sidewalks along all our paved streets. Currently, only 50% of our streets have sidewalks beside them. This puts our children and all pedestrians in danger as they walk to school, stores, and neighbors' homes. Our citizens should not be afraid to walk to the park or the grocery store. Last year, two people were injured because they were hit by cars as they walked along the shoulder of a street. One is paralyzed and confined to a wheelchair. The benefits of installing sidewalks surely outweigh the cost. We require bicyclists to wear helmets; we should have roads with sidewalks. It is a matter of our safety.

 4. Examine the passage for STAR Support.

    a. What is the best example of specific evidence in the passage? Why?

    b. What one sentence is an example of irrelevant support? Why?

    c. What statement in the passage has questionable accuracy? Why?

5. Using STAR Support, write a paragraph evaluating the argument in the passage.

Build Your Writing Skills

When you see vague support, always ask how it could be made more specific.

Check **Your Skills**

Use the following passages for exercise 1.

National Parks Are Best Preserved by Government

Despite the claim that privatizing the National Park Service would create a stronger and more accessible collection of travel destinations, the best protector of national parks is the national government. As a non-profit institution, the function of government is to preserve democracy—and therefore the symbols of democracy—for citizens. Once public lands leave public control, they may be lost forever. Preservation is far from certain once a private corporation controls the land.

In the past, private industry has attempted to purchase state parks. In most cases, this has resulted in less public access at a greater cost to each visitor. The government created the parks; the government should keep control of them. The government may not be a perfect steward. However, for the people's land, the people's government is still the most appropriate regulator.

Privatizing Can Better Preserve and Maintain

National parks should be turned over to private corporations to run. As seen in other resources once regulated as monopolies, such as telephone services and some utilities, private corporations can manage large projects more efficiently, sometimes so efficiently that profit is possible. The 20th century has seen truly hideous mismanagement of national forests and parks, with amenities and roads in disrepair, parks understaffed, and the safety of campers and hikers left to suffer. The 21st would only see the continuation of shutdowns and poorly staffed parks. Our treasured wilderness areas and monuments deserve better.

The United States has long stood as an example of how private industry can revolutionize industries. National parks should be seen as tourist destinations as well as national legacies. Private industry has outperformed government in creating destinations of choice and should be permitted to apply its models of efficiency to national parks to ensure that our treasures remain standing and accessible through the 21st century.

1. Analyze the two arguments to determine which position is best supported. Use relevant and specific evidence from both passages to support your response.

Write your answer below or type your response on a computer. Take approximately 45 minutes to respond.

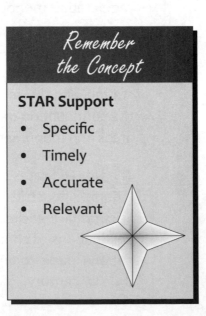

Remember the Concept

STAR Support

- Specific
- Timely
- Accurate
- Relevant

Use the questions on page 329 to evaluate your response.

Evaluating Arguments

Connections

Have you ever...

- Watched an infomercial for a new product?

- Listened to a talk radio show about a political topic?

- Read an editorial in a newspaper or online?

Commercials, talk radio, TV shows, and editorials all present arguments. A commercial tries to convince you to buy a product. A talk show or editorial presents an opinion. How do you know who to believe or what evidence you can trust? How do you explain why one argument is more believable than another?

Arguments can be crafted to make you respond emotionally or to seem logical, even if they are not. Many arguments sound perfectly reasonable the first time you read or hear them. On further examination, you may begin to see weaknesses.

A successful argument proves its claim using relevant evidence and sound reasoning. To evaluate whether an argument is credible and sound, describe the elements of the argument:

- Is its claim clear?

- Is the evidence credible?

- Is the speaker reliable?

After you describe the claim, evidence, and speaker, use this information to write an evaluation of the argument.

Describe the Claim, Evidence, and Speaker

When you evaluate an argument, you aren't giving your own opinion of the topic. Your goal is to objectively analyze the author's argument. This skill will help you write about arguments and make decisions about controversial topics.

When you describe the claim, evidence, and speaker, you assign value. For example, if you describe a claim as unreasonable and unclear, then it is not a strong claim. If you describe evidence as specific, credible, and from a trusted source, it is strong evidence.

Examine the following argument.

Two years of college education should be available free to all qualified U.S. students. By 2018, over 60 percent of jobs will require workers with at least some college education, but public support of education is down in 48 states. At the same time, employers are cutting back (or at least not expanding) their training programs. They are, in essence, expecting candidates to show up fully qualified, according to an article in the *Las Vegas Review-Journal*.[1]

Two years of free postsecondary education would address the problem of filling jobs with qualified workers. Government investment in free higher education would stimulate the economy by allowing college graduates more spending capacity. More people would attend college if finances weren't a barrier. Other countries who make this investment see a payoff in the quality of their work forces and lifestyles.

The benefits of this policy are obvious. Students would be more motivated to graduate high school, knowing that they have options after they graduate. Under this policy, students would decide immediately on a major or training program best suited to them and would be more likely to finish quickly and begin working.

Currently, a college degree is out of reach to many students, limiting their potential. A lack of college education prevents young adults from being financially stable enough to support a family, buy a home, or start a business. Even those who graduate college aren't assured of financial security. Those who leave college owing thousands in student loans and still can't find work are in grave financial situations. A free two-year degree would help many young people get started in careers. This would benefit individuals and also the society to which they contribute.

---

[1] "By 2018, 60 percent of job openings will require college education," Eli Amdur, *Las Vegas Review-Journal,* available at http://www.reviewjournal.com/news/education/2018-60-percent-job-openings-will-require-college-education

Describe the Claim

First, identify the claim, which is the idea that the writer is attempting to prove. Summarize the claim in one sentence. Then, describe the claim. You can use the following words to describe the claim. Identify reasons for your description.

Claim

Negative ➡	Claim	⬅ Positive
Unreasonable	Somewhat reasonable	Reasonable
Unclear	Somewhat clear	Clear

? 1. Identify and describe the claim of the argument, giving reasons for your description.

The claim is clear: that two years of college education should be free to U.S. students. It is stated at the beginning of the argument. The claim is somewhat reasonable. The government provides many services and could expand public education by two years. However, this would incur significant costs and changes in the educational system.

Describe the Evidence

Use **STAR Support** criteria to examine the evidence. Is it **Specific, Timely, Accurate,** and **Relevant**? Be sure to evaluate the source. Is the source untrustworthy or unknown? Is the source an expert?

Evidence

Evidence must also be **sufficient**. There must be enough evidence to prove the claim. Use the following words to describe evidence.

Negative ➡	Evidence	⬅ Positive
Insufficient/vague	Some evidence	Specific
Out-of-date	Unknown date	Timely
Inaccurate	Unknown source	Accurate
Irrelevant	Somewhat relevant	Relevant

? 2. Describe the evidence in the argument, giving reasons for your description.

One piece of evidence that is specific, timely, accurate, and relevant is that over 60% of jobs will require degrees by 2018. This fact comes from a newspaper article. Other statements are vague, such as the idea that students would quickly decide on majors. This idea isn't supported by specifics and seems mainly to be speculation. It has no source. Overall, the evidence seems insufficient, especially since it does not address the costs of the proposal.

Speaker

Describe the Speaker

The speaker is the author of an argument. Some speakers are biased, such as a company trying to sell a product. Others are reliable experts.

Many speakers are unknown, except through their arguments. A speaker who makes contradictory statements or uses emotional pleas to distract from the argument is not trustworthy. Also examine how the speaker addresses arguments from the opposition. Does the author ignore opponents?

Negative ➡	Speaker	⬅ Positive
Untrustworthy/biased	Unknown	Expert
Ignores or misrepresents opponents	Acknowledges opponents	Addresses legitimate counterarguments

?   **3.** Describe the speaker, giving reasons for your description.

The speaker's expertise or bias is unknown. He or she acknowledges that the opposition exists but does not address any counterarguments. The speaker is also somewhat contradictory. The statement that college graduates often cannot find jobs undermines the idea that two years of free college is a solution.

Write an Evaluation

Combine your descriptions of the claim, speaker, and evidence to write an evaluation. Start with a central idea that states the overall strength or weakness of the argument and use specific details to explain your descriptions of the claim, speaker, and evidence. Your evaluation should have a beginning, middle, and ending.

?   **4.** Write a paragraph evaluating the argument.

See the Answers and Explanations section on page 384 for a sample response.

Evaluating Arguments

Practice It!

Use the following passage for exercises 1 through 4.

Holiday parades are a waste of public resources. They are admittedly festive and happy occasions, but they serve no civic purpose that couldn't be otherwise served by a concert, fireworks show, or fair. Marching bands can be heard at football games, and balloons and floats are simply unnecessary diversions.

At famous parades, such as the Macy's Thanksgiving Day Parade or Mardi Gras, viewers, who are often inebriated, gather in the streets only to watch other people walk at various speeds. These parades block traffic and create trash. They require police and emergency responder overtime. This cost would be better spent funding environmental programs, shelters, education, and other public services.

1. Describe the claim in the passage, giving reasons for your description.

2. Describe the evidence in the passage, giving reasons for your description.

3. Describe the speaker in the passage, giving reasons for your description.

4. Write a well-organized paragraph evaluating the argument. Include suggestions to improve the argument.

The Writing Process

Evaluate

When you evaluate your writing, describe your claim, evidence, and yourself as a speaker. Look for ways to develop your reliability as a speaker. One way is by acknowledging the opposition and respectfully responding to counterarguments.

Use the following passage for exercises 5 through 8.

Driverless cars are our future, and we should encourage their development by passing laws allowing driverless cars on roads throughout the country. Nevada, Florida, and California already have laws allowing driverless cars. These software-controlled cars have successfully navigated San Francisco's steep and twisting Lombard Street and driven over 300,000 miles of tests. Only one accident has happened during testing: a human driver rear-ended a driverless car. With their incredible record of safety, driverless cars will reduce drunk driving, make commutes more productive, and reduce insurance costs. In a March 2012 video posted by Google, a legally blind man goes through a drive-through in a self-driving Toyota Prius. This video highlights the benefits of driverless car technology to disabled people. Why not allow this safe and beneficial technology to flourish?

5. Describe the claim in the passage, giving reasons for your description.

6. Describe the evidence in the passage, giving reasons for your description.

7. Describe the speaker in the passage, giving reasons for your description.

8. Write a well-organized paragraph evaluating the argument. Include suggestions to improve the argument.

> *Build Your Writing Skills*
>
> To compare two arguments, compare your evaluations of the claim, evidence, and speaker. It will help you determine which argument is stronger and why.

Check Your Skills

Use the following passages for exercise 1.

The presence of royalty gives a nation a sense of pride and history that should be cherished and honored. Great Britain is an excellent example of what a royal family can add to the culture. The constitutional monarchy allows Britain to experience the best of both worlds: the continuity of tradition and the progressive possibilities of a democracy.

Around the world, people celebrate royal weddings and births. When Prince Charles and Lady Diana married, it was an international sensation. An estimated 750 million people watched. The birth of Prince George of Cambridge in 2013 spurred composer Paul Mealor to write a new lullaby, "Sleep On." Shared events like this bring a nation together, forming cultural milestones.

The family of the Prince of Wales: Engraving by Shyubler. Published in the magazine *Niva*, published by A.F. Marx, St. Petersburg, Russia, 1888

In Great Britain and other nations with historic monarchies, the royal family is a link to the past. Although royal roles may be ceremonial, a royal family allows the average citizen to celebrate a shared history and national pride.

Royalty devalues the average citizen. A monarchy flies in the face of the idea that "all men are created equal." If royalty were eliminated, any loss of tradition would be more than replaced by a thirst for innovation, improvement, and individuality.

Through its monarchy, Great Britain makes a silent statement that some people are inherently better than others. Members of the royal family have special treatment because of an accident of birth. In an article on CNN, Graham Smith details the problems with British monarchy. He states, "It is secretive, having recently lobbied successfully to have itself removed entirely from the reaches of our Freedom of Information laws; it lobbies government ministers for improvements to its financial benefits and for its own private agenda; it is hugely costly—an estimated £202 million a year."[1] The British monarchy is outdated, undemocratic, and costly. On the other hand, the U.S. system of democracy, where anyone might earn the presidency, encourages self-improvement because birth is not destiny.

---

[1]Source: "Why UK should abolish its 'failed' monarchy" by Graham Smith on CNN.com
http://www.cnn.com/2012/05/30/world/europe/uk-jubilee-republicans/index.html

1. Analyze the two arguments to determine which position is best supported. Use relevant and specific evidence from both passages to support your response.

Write your answer below or type your response on a computer. Take approximately 45 minutes to respond.

> ### Remember the Concept
>
> Describe the **claim, evidence,** and **speaker** to evaluate an argument.

Use the questions on page 329 to evaluate your response.

Citing Evidence and Connecting with Claims

Connections

Have you ever...

- Realized halfway through a movie how it would end and told your reasons to a friend?

- Explained how you found the solution to a problem?

- Given evidence for your opinion in an argument?

Evidence is important. When you make a decision, you use evidence to come to a conclusion. When you speculate about what will happen, you use evidence to form an opinion. When you solve a problem, you use evidence to find a solution.

When you make a claim—an idea you want to prove—you will need to back up that claim with evidence. Imagine that you want to show that a character in a story is selfish. Your evidence is that the character takes a prize away from his best friend. You need to show why taking the prize was selfish. It is important that you make a clear connection between your claim and the evidence that you present. The reader needs to understand *why* the evidence supports the claim. When you connect evidence with your claim, you show the reader your reasoning and make your argument more convincing.

Your writing needs a strong chain of reasoning:

- You need strong evidence that supports your writing.

- You need a strong connection between the evidence and your claim.

- You need a strong claim that is supported by the evidence.

If all the links of the chain are in place, your writing will present a convincing argument.

Building a Chain of Evidence

Build a chain of evidence by defining the claim and evidence, making connections, and organizing your argument in a logical way.

Imagine that you need to recommend a candidate to interview for a sales position. The following are summaries of two candidates' résumés. Examine the summaries and write a paragraph recommending one of the two candidates.

Miguel Velasquez has a BS in English and went to school on a scholarship. He has two years of sales experience. He says that he is looking for a position where he can grow with the company and that he enjoys helping customers find the products they need.

Angela Goren has a BA in communications and a year and a half of sales experience. She says that she has used your products and enjoys them. She also says she can clearly communicate the benefits of your products to customers. In her last sales job, she received a promotion after six months.

Identify the Claim

The claim is your point of view. Your chain of evidence proves your claim, so the claim is the foundation of the argument. The claim should be clear and specific.

?   **1.** Identify the claim for your recommendation.

Your claim might be that Angela Goren is the better candidate for the job because of her familiarity with the company and her success in sales. To decide on a candidate, ask: Which claim can I support with the evidence?

Define the Evidence

Strong evidence makes a strong chain. Because you have identified your claim, you should already have ideas about your evidence. Find specific details that support your claim.

?   **2.** Define two to four specific pieces of evidence from the passage to support your claim.

You might identify the following evidence for choosing Angela:

- She has a BA in communications.

- She is familiar with the company and its products.

- She received a promotion in her former job.

Explain the Connection

For each piece of evidence, write a sentence explaining the connection with the claim. Why does it support the claim?

?   3. Write sentences explaining why each piece of evidence supports your claim.

You might write:

- Because of her BA in communications, Angela may have good communication skills.

- Because she knows the company's products, Angela may need less training.

- Because she received a promotion after six months, Angela has shown skill in sales.

Organize the Evidence and Connections

Organize your chain of evidence. Begin with your claim, and then put your evidence in a logical order. Include your connections for each piece of evidence.

?   4. Organize your claim, evidence, and connections.

You might decide to put the most convincing evidence first and start by talking about her promotion, then her familiarity with the company, and finally her BA in communications.

Draft, Evaluate, and Submit

Use your organized claim, evidence, and connections to finish drafting your work.

?   5. Draft and evaluate your recommendation on a computer or a separate sheet of paper.

See the Answers and Explanations section on page 387 for a sample recommendation.

Practice It!

Today, Mars is cold and dry, and liquid water is not stable on the surface. However, more than 3.5 billion years ago, climatic conditions appear to have been favorable for the presence of liquid water. How did its climate produce conditions favorable for rainfall and runoff? Most effort has been focused on proposing that the early Martian atmosphere was different because of a different mass and composition.

Carbon dioxide, methane, and SO_2 get the most attention, but each has its own unique issues and problems. Clouds form in CO_2 atmospheres that may limit the greenhouse potential, and vast beds of carbonates have not yet been detected as would be expected when CO_2 and liquid water coexist for extended periods of time. Methane requires a large continuous source to counter its removal by photolysis. And SO_2 may not build up to high enough levels to be effective since it readily oxidizes to sulfate aerosols which can cool the surface.

Another possibility is that wet conditions on early Mars were created by large impact events, which induced significant climate change. It is obvious that impactors have pummeled the Martian surface in the distant past. These could have temporarily altered the climate and produced episodes of intense rainfall.

Source: Adapted from NASA AMES Mars Climate Modeling Group, "Early Mars."
http://spacescience.arc.nasa.gov/mars-climate-modeling-group/past.html

  1. Compare the possible reasons that the passage gives for warm, wet conditions on early Mars. Explain which reason seems most logical.

   a. Identify your claim.

   b. Define two to four pieces of evidence.

    c. For each piece of evidence, write one sentence connecting it to the claim.

    d. Organize your claim, evidence, and connections in a logical sequence.

 2. Draft your response based on your claim, evidence, and connections.

 3. Evaluate your response. Revise and edit your work until you are satisfied with your response.

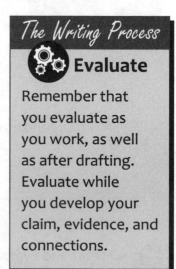

The Writing Process

Evaluate

Remember that you evaluate as you work, as well as after drafting. Evaluate while you develop your claim, evidence, and connections.

Use the following passage for exercises 4 and 5.

Many school districts are removing drink machines from schools or replacing them with machines dispensing bottled water. Supporters of removing the machines state that sugary drinks, including soda, sugared teas, and sports drinks, contribute to childhood obesity and add little nutritional value. Teenagers get about 15% of their calories from beverages, and a recent study found that where only sodas are banned from campuses, students still bought as many sugary drinks.

Some opponents, however, point to the study as evidence that drink bans are ineffective. The study found that in schools that banned all sugary drinks, students still consumed the same quantity of those drinks. The policies only lowered access to sugared drinks at school. Opponents recommend that schools focus on health education instead of eliminating free choice. They also point out that drink sales provide needed revenue for schools and protest that eliminating a source of school funding is unwise.

 4. Evaluate the arguments for and against drink machines in schools. Write a response supporting a claim that one position is best supported.

    a. Identify your claim and two to four pieces of evidence.

    b. For each piece of evidence, write one sentence connecting it to the claim.

    c. Organize your claim, evidence, and connections in a logical sequence.

 5. Draft and evaluate your response. Type your response on a computer if possible. If a computer is unavailable, use a separate sheet of paper.

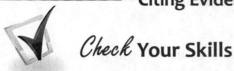

Check **Your Skills**

Use the following passage for exercises 1 and 2.

Net neutrality is an important and often misunderstood political issue. The term "net neutrality" means ensuring that all websites have equal access to Internet bandwidth, so that individual websites such as Netflix or YouTube can't be slowed or blocked by Internet providers (ISPs) such as cable and phone companies. According to a recent court ruling, the FCC does not have the right to enforce net neutrality without declaring ISPs as common carriers, which are necessary utilities such as electricity or water.

Supporters of net neutrality are concerned that ISPs could charge websites for bandwidth, limiting online competition, development and innovation of new websites, and the availability of free web services. The prices of web-based services could rise if ISPs began charging websites for bandwidth.

Those in favor of net neutrality are also concerned that ISPs could ban or charge competitors, while starting their own competing web services. Some suggest that ISPs could ban any website or service for any reason, including political reasons. Companies could theoretically block news services, organizations, or blogs that they oppose, or they could stop consumers from posting content on Twitter or Facebook, perhaps even banning any posts that criticize the ISPs.

Opponents of net neutrality want an open market for ISPs. An unregulated Internet, they state, means the ability to experiment with new business practices and innovate ways to improve the Internet. Those who want deregulation are concerned that net neutrality means increasing government power over business. They are in favor of businesses competing in a free market, without regulation. They argue that classifying Internet providers as utilities is stifling to business.

Without net neutrality, opponents say that ISPs will be able to manage Internet bandwidth better. Large-scale Internet services, such as websites that stream high-resolution videos, use a large portion of bandwidth. With net neutrality, the costs for this high usage by large companies are pushed onto consumers, opponents say.

1. The passage presents arguments supporting and opposing net neutrality. In your response, analyze both positions to determine which is best supported. Use relevant and specific evidence from the passages to support your response.

Take approximately 45 minutes for this task. Use the space below for planning, and type your answer on a computer to prepare for computer responses. If a computer is unavailable, write your answer on a separate sheet of paper.

 2. "A wise and frugal government, which shall restrain men from injuring one another, shall leave them otherwise free to regulate their own pursuits of industry and improvement, and shall not take from the mouth of labor the bread it has earned—this is the sum of good government." —*Thomas Jefferson*

From the First Inaugural Address by Thomas Jefferson, 1801

Develop an argument about how the passage about net neutrality reflects the issue expressed in the quotation. Incorporate relevant, specific evidence from the quotation, the passage, and your own knowledge to support your analysis.

Take approximately 25 minutes for this task. Use the space below for planning, and type your answer on a computer to prepare for computer responses. If a computer is unavailable, write your answer on a separate sheet of paper.

> **Remember the Concept**
>
> **Build a Chain of Evidence**
>
> - Identify the claim.
> - Define the evidence.
> - Explain the connections.
> - Organize the evidence.

Use the questions on page 329 to evaluate your response.

Drawing Conclusions

Connections

Have you ever...

- Decided to buy one product instead of another based on online reviews?

- Settled a disagreement based on arguments from two friends?

- Made a deduction about a person based on their actions?

When you draw a conclusion, you evaluate evidence and make an inference or decision based on that evidence. Scientists draw conclusions based on the results of experiments. Historians draw conclusions based on historical documents. Voters draw conclusions based on debates and information about the candidates. Businesspeople draw conclusions based on reports.

Drawing conclusions involves examining evidence and using logic to make decisions based on the evidence. When you draw conclusions, get a **KICK** from the evidence. Ask yourself:

- What do I **K**now?

- What can I **I**nfer?

- What can I **C**ompare?

- What are the **K**ey ideas?

Based on your examination of the evidence, you can draw a logical conclusion.

Learn It!

Getting a KICK from the Evidence

To draw a conclusion, examine the evidence. A conclusion is a logical deduction, decision, or judgement that you make after considering evidence.

A study at University College London looked at the Health Survey for England to analyze health and eating habits for 65,226 people. They found that people who ate seven or more portions of fruits and vegetables per day were 25% less likely to die of cancer, 31% less likely to die of heart disease, and 42% less likely to die of any cause compared to those who ate less than one portion of fruits and vegetables. Researchers also found that eating fresh vegetables caused the greatest reduction in death rate. They found the following figures:

Portions of Fruits and Vegetables	1–3	3–5	5–7	7+
Reduced Death Rate	14%	29%	36%	42%

The researchers adjusted their results for factors that affect the death rate: sex, age, cigarette smoking, social class, Body Mass Index, education, physical activity, and alcohol intake. Deaths within a year of the food survey were not included. The United Kingdom government health guidelines recommends five portions of fruits and vegetables per day.

Source: Adapted from "Seven a day keeps the reaper at bay" by UCL News, available at http://www.ucl.ac.uk/news/news-articles/0414/010413-fruit-veg-consumption-death-risk

What Do You Know?

First, ask what you know. What evidence do you have to consider?

? **1.** What do you know based on the article?

The article gives results from one study at the University College London. It gives figures for reduced rates of death based on the amount of fruits and vegetables eaten per day. Both the information in the table and the figures in the article give specific information.

What Can You Infer?

Examine the evidence and make inferences. What can you logically say is true, based on what you know?

? **2.** What inferences can you make based on the evidence?

From the evidence, you can infer that eating more fruits and vegetables increases a person's health. The more fruits and vegetables those in the study ate, the lower the chance of death.

What Can You Compare?

Often, drawing conclusions involves comparisons. You can compare data, arguments, or other information. Making comparisons helps you make decisions.

? **3.** What comparisons can you make based on the evidence?

In this article, you can compare reduced death rates between groups. You can also compare the UK health guideline of five portions of fruits and vegetables a day to the study results.

What Are the Key Ideas?

Identify the most important ideas based on your examination of the evidence. What values are most important? What evidence is most relevant?

? **4.** Identify the key ideas based on the evidence.

The key idea in the article is that as fruit and vegetable consumption increases likelihood of death decreases. Another key idea, although it's not emphasized in the article, is that vegetables have more of an effect than fruit.

Draw a Conclusion

Based on your examination of the evidence, draw a conclusion. Make a positive statement of your logical conclusion.

? **5.** Based on the evidence, draw a conclusion about the UK health guidelines.

Based on the results of this study, the UK health guidelines recommend too few portions of fruits and vegetables. Eating seven portions would have more benefits.

Practice It!

Use the following passage for exercises 1 through 5.

Computer-graded essays are becoming the norm on standardized tests, and often students are unaware that their essays may be graded by a computer. Grading programs begin with hand-scored essays. The programs then evaluate computer-readable features, such as the total number of words, grammatical features, and spelling features. The program compares these objective features to human scores and creates a mathematical model that predicts the score based on analysis of computer-readable features. This model is used to score essays. Some educators and test-takers are concerned about computer-graded essay exams. Proponents state that computer scoring is quick, inexpensive, and accurate. Human scores are often used alongside computer scoring to ensure accuracy. Opponents are concerned that computer scoring could encourage students to target computer-readable skills and ignore content and creativity.

1. What do you know based on the passage?

2. What inferences can you make based on the evidence and arguments?

3. What comparisons can you make based on the evidence and arguments?

4. Identify the key ideas based on the evidence and arguments.

5. Based on the evidence and arguments, draw a conclusion about how computer grading should be used in standardized essay tests.

Use the following passage for exercises 6 through 10.

Texting has become a social phenomenon. Some young people send and receive hundreds of texts a month. What are the consequences of massive texting? Proponents of texting state that it increases the use of written language, which increases literacy. A University of Toronto study concluded that texting is a rich linguistic environment, similar to spoken language.[1] Opponents point to the use of spelling shortcuts and acronyms in texting. They state that young people will learn bad language habits from extensive texting. An article in *The Telegraph* in 2004 reported that students used text message language in school exams.[2] Text messaging, for better or worse, is likely to have long-term consequences.

[1] Source: "Linguistic Ruin? LOL! Instant Messaging and Teen Language" by Sali A. Tagliamonte and Derek Denis, University of Toronto, 2008. Available at http://web.uvic.ca/ling/coursework/ling395/395_LOL.pdf

[2] Source: "Pupils resort to text language in GCSE exams" by Julie Henry, *The Telegraph*, 2004. Available at: http://www.telegraph.co.uk/education/educationnews/3346533/Pupils-resort-to-text-language-in-GCSE-exams.html

6. What do you know based on the passage?

7. What inferences can you make based on the evidence and arguments?

8. What comparisons can you make based on the evidence and arguments?

9. Identify the key ideas based on the evidence and arguments.

10. Based on the evidence, draw a conclusion about which argument is stronger.

Use the following passage for exercises 11 through 15.

A study by Australian and U.S. researchers showed that a compound can reverse muscle aging in mice, countering aging-related ailments.[1] Human trials may begin shortly. The benefits of reducing diabetes, arthritis, and other diseases are clear. High costs of health care and elderly care could be reduced, and quality of life could be improved. However, some are concerned about potential negative consequences. Could counteracting aging lead to overpopulation, stagnation, and unemployment? A larger population demands more food, space, and other resources. If experienced employees maintain their health, they may stay in the workforce and edge out younger college graduates. Longer-lived, healthier retirees could use up their retirement funds and need living assistance. Will the problems outweigh the rewards? Will society adapt to a longer and healthier life?

[1]Source: "Australian and US scientists reverse ageing in mice, humans could be next" by Ashley Hall, ABC News. Available at http://www.abc.net.au/news/2013-12-20/scientists-develop-anti-ageing-process-in-mice/5168580

11. What do you know based on the passage?

12. What inferences can you make based on the evidence and arguments?

13. What comparisons can you make based on the evidence and arguments?

14. Identify the key ideas based on the evidence and arguments.

15. Based on the evidence, draw a conclusion about whether the negative consequences of counteracting aging would outweigh the benefits.

Check **Your Skills**

Use the following passage and your understanding of drawing conclusions for exercises 1 and 2.

In December 2012, the *Journal News* in Westchester County, New York posted an interactive map on its website that showed the names and addresses of registered pistol owners in the area. Many people protested this use of information.

Since owning a gun is not a crime, critics complained that the map was unfair, implying that gun owners are a danger for neighbors. Gun advocates complained that the map invaded the privacy of gun-owners by distributing their names and addresses, making them potential targets of criminals looking to steal weapons. Others complained that, although the information came from government records, there was no way to ensure its accuracy.

The newspaper defended its actions, stating that readers were interested in knowing whether any gun-owners lived in their neighborhood. Supporters often cite the freedom of information as a benefit to society, arguing that all information of interest should be made freely available. The information was released by the government under the Freedom of Information Act.

 1. The passage presents arguments supporting and opposing the *Journal News* releasing a map of the location of gun permit holders. In your response, analyze both positions to determine which is best supported. Use relevant and specific evidence from the passage to support your response.

Take approximately 45 minutes for this task. Use the space below for planning, and type your answer on a computer to prepare for computer responses. If a computer is unavailable, write your answer on a separate sheet of paper.

Use the questions on page 329 to evaluate your response.

2. "Every increase of knowledge may possibly render depravity more depraved, as well as it may increase the strength of virtue. It is in itself only power; and its value depends on its application. " —*Sydney Smith*

From *Dictionary of Burning Words of Brilliant Writers* by Josiah Hotchkiss Gilbert, 1895

Develop an argument about how the passage about releasing gun permit information reflects the enduring issue expressed in the quotation. Incorporate relevant, specific evidence from the quotation, the passage, and your own knowledge to support your analysis.

Write your answer below or type your answer on a computer. Take approximately 25 minutes for this task.

> *Remember the Concept*
>
> To draw conclusions, ask yourself:
>
> - What do I **Know**?
> - What can I **Infer**?
> - What can I **Compare**?
> - What are the **Key** ideas?

Use the questions on page 329 to evaluate your response.

Issues in Revising and Editing

Everyone has special problems in writing. Some people can never remember how to spell certain words. Other people tend to use too many words. Still others misuse specific words. Identifying the special problems in your writing that interfere with communication is important. Keeping a record of recurring errors in your writing, from illogical organization to misused commas, will help you improve your revising and editing.

When you revise your writing, you look at larger problems. Revising involves reviewing your central ideas, supporting ideas, details and evidence, organization, and logic. It also involves reviewing your sentence construction and grammar. If your sentences are difficult to understand, you may need to make changes to the structure of your paragraph or the content of your sentences. This section will focus on identifying and fixing confusing language.

When you find language that's confusing, ask what the underlying problem is. Do you understand clearly the idea you are trying to express? Do you need to make changes to the structure and content of your writing to clarify your ideas?

When you edit your writing, you look closely at the language of each sentence. The goal of editing is to find and correct errors and to improve the way you express ideas. When you revise, you are looking at the big picture; when you edit, you are looking at the details.

In this section, you will use the **FREE** process to identify and fix language errors. To make your writing error-FREE:

- **Focus** on one sentence.

- **Read** the sentence aloud.

- Check for common **Errors**.

- **Evaluate** the changes.

The following sections will help you fix specific types of errors.

- **Obstructions to Communication**
  This lesson will help you identify and fix common obstructions to communication, including wordiness, awkward sentence structure, illogical word order, and misplaced modifiers.

- **Word Usage**
  Using the correct word is key to communication. This lesson will give you a strategy to check for correct use of pronouns, transitional words, conjunctions, and formal language.

- **Spelling, Capitalization, and Punctuation**
  Spelling, capitalization, and punctuation interfere with communication when there are many errors, errors involving commonly confused words, or confusing punctuation errors. In this lesson, you will learn to find and correct spelling, capitalization, and punctuation errors.

- **Sentence Structure**
  Incorrect sentence structure can cause confusion and miscommunication. This lesson will help you identify problems with fragments, run-ons, subordination or coordination, subject-verb agreement, and parallel structure.

Obstructions to Communication

Connections

Have you ever...

- Had difficulty using badly written instructions?
- Received an incomprehensible email from a client?
- Misunderstood a text from a friend?

Errors in grammar and language can seem to make sense to the writer, but completely confuse the reader. The reason why we have language rules is so that we can communicate clearly. Some of the most common obstructions to communication involve confusing word order or too many words.

Imagine two children talking through two tin cans connected by a string. The sound waves travel across the string from one tin can to the other. If the string is straight and taut, the sound travels easily. If the string is twisted, tied, or blocked, the sound is obstructed.

Confusing sentences, awkward structure, extra words, dangling modifiers, or illogical word order can all cause twists and turns in your language. They prevent clear communication from traveling to your reader.

To clarify sentences, think about your purpose and audience. What are you trying to communicate? How will your reader understand it? Then, think about the parts of your sentence. Who is the actor? What is the action? What are the important details that need to be included? Identify the best way to clearly communicate your idea to the reader.

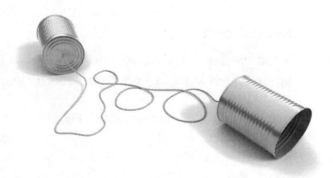

FREE to Fix Obstructions to Communication

You can identify obstructive language by thinking like a reader. What will your reader understand from your writing?

Imagine you are writing a speech for a PTA meeting about the overuse of rewards for children. You have written the following paragraph.

Children benefit from an authentic feeling of accomplishment, and a participation award or trophy doesn't provide that feeling. When receiving trophies for no reason, the trophies don't have any meaning that they should have for them. Soon, no trophy or award will have any meaning for our children. Children need to learn that they can achieve a reward through work and practice. They shouldn't think that rewards are meaningless and arbitrary.

Focus on a Sentence

When you are looking for obstructions to communication, you need to keep in mind the context and organization of your writing. However, it's still important to look at each sentence separately. You can identify problematic sentences as you read your writing and then examine them more closely.

1. Read through the passage to understand the context and organization of the writing. Then, choose a problematic sentence to examine for obstructions to communication.

The second sentence has problems that obstruct communication. Focus on this sentence:

> When receiving trophies for no reason, the trophies don't have any meaning that they should have for them.

Read Aloud

Read the sentence aloud, and think about what you hear. Is the language confusing? Do you know which words to emphasize? Is it clear what words and phrases reference?

2. Read the sentence aloud. Fix any obstructions to communication that you notice.

You might notice that the last part of the sentence doesn't make a lot of sense. It's not clear who the word "them" references, and "that they should have" seems unnecessary. You might revise the sentence to eliminate the last phrase:

> When receiving trophies for no reason, the trophies don't have any meaning.

Look for Common Errors

Watch for the following errors:

- **Dangling modifiers:** Clauses and phrases that describe a word not clearly stated

- **Wordiness:** Redundant or unnecessary words

- **Awkwardness** or **Illogical Word Order:** Unnatural-sounding phrasing that makes the sentence difficult to understand

? 3. Check the sentence for common errors. Fix any problems that you find.

This sentence contains a dangling modifier. The clause "When receiving trophies for no reason" is a dangling modifier. Who is receiving the trophies? The sentence doesn't say. You might revise this sentence by making it clear who receives the trophies:

> When children receive trophies for no reason, the trophies don't have any meaning.

Evaluate the Corrected Sentence

Read over the corrected sentence. Can you do anything to improve communication?

? 4. Read the corrected sentence and make any improvements.

You might decide that you could revise "don't have any meaning" to "have no meaning" to make the sentence simpler:

> When children receive trophies for no reason, the trophies have no meaning.

> **Build Your Writing Skills**
>
> Dangling modifiers are common at the beginning of the sentence. When a sentence begins with a modifier, look for the word it references.

Practice It!

Use the following passage for exercises 1 through 4.

A trigger is anything that causes or worsens asthma symptoms. Asthma attacks can be triggered by many indoor allergens and irritants, such as molds, dust mites, pet dander, secondhand smoke, and cleaning chemicals. Having asthma, any individual should look for which triggers are the ones which trigger that one's asthma attacks or worsen them, also. Asthma sufferers may respond to one or several triggers. Working with a doctor to identify and avoid triggers can help reduce asthma episodes.

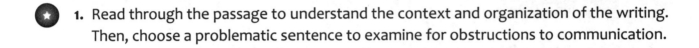

1. Read through the passage to understand the context and organization of the writing. Then, choose a problematic sentence to examine for obstructions to communication.

2. Read the sentence aloud. Fix any obstructions to communication that you notice.

3. Check the sentence for common errors. Fix any problems that you find.

4. Evaluate the corrected sentence and make any improvements.

Use the following passage for exercises 5 through 8.

Starting a car share program in our neighborhood is an excellent project for our community council. A car share program will save our community members money and provide transportation for residents who don't have a car during the day. Additionally, a car share program will allow our community to invest in fuel-efficient vehicles. In a recent poll, 86% of neighborhood residents expressed interest in joining a car share program. These results of the poll show that there is enough interest in a car share program in our community and among our community members to make one a financially viable choice for our community.

5. Read through the passage to understand the context and organization of the writing. Then, choose a problematic sentence to examine for obstructions to communication.

6. Read the sentence aloud. Fix any obstructions to communication that you notice.

7. Check the sentence for common errors. Fix any problems that you find.

8. Evaluate the corrected sentence and make any improvements.

Use the following passage for exercises 9 through 12.

Plato said, "When there is an income tax, the just man will pay more and the unjust less on the same amount of income."[1] Many complain that a complex tax system makes it easier for the unjust to avoid paying fair taxes. Remaining controversial, how to fix the current complex tax system and make it simpler continues to be elusive. Some favor a flat tax, which would tax income at the same rate for everyone. Proponents say that a flat tax would be both simple and fair. However, others favor a simplified progressive tax. Under a progressive tax, those who earn less pay a lower tax rate. Those who earn more pay a higher tax rate. Supporters of a progressive tax say that it removes an undue burden on the poor and middle class, shifting a greater tax burden to those who can afford it.

Source: Plato, *The Republic*, Book 1, approximately 380 BC

⭐ **9.** Read through the passage to understand the context and organization of the writing. Then, choose a problematic sentence to examine for obstructions to communication.

⭐⭐ **10.** Read the sentence aloud. Fix any obstructions to communication that you notice.

⭐⭐ **11.** Check the sentence for common errors. Fix any problems that you find.

⭐⭐ **12.** Evaluate the corrected sentence and make any improvements.

> ## Writing Tip
>
> To use FREE for multiple choice or drop-down exercises:
>
> - **Focus** on the whole sentence.
> - **Read** the sentence with each answer choice.
> - Check each answer for common **Errors**.
> - **Evaluate** the sentence with your chosen answer.

Check Your Skills

Use the FREE process to choose the best answer for exercises 1 through 4.

I am writing to express my appreciation for the excellent service I received at Bluebell Car Service in Cordova, Vermont. On January 3, I visited the station (1) _____ Jack Montoya serviced my car (2) _____ He completed the oil change quickly and efficiently, and he also noticed that my car tires needed to be replaced. (3) _____ I am very appreciative of the (4) _____

1. Which is the best option to correctly complete blank 1?
   a. to get for my 2005 Toyota Corolla an oil change.
   b. to get an oil change for my 2005 Toyota Corolla.
   c. for my 2005 Toyota Corolla, to be getting an oil change.
   d. for my 2005 Toyota Corolla to get an oil change.

2. Which is the best option to correctly complete blank 2?
   a. while there.
   b. while being there.
   c. while I was there.
   d. being while I was there.

3. Which is the best option to correctly complete blank 3?
   a. Because of his help, I avoided the inconvenience and expense of a blown tire.
   b. Helping me, I avoided the inconvenience and expense of a blown tire.
   c. Because of his help, avoiding the inconvenience and expense of a blown tire.
   d. Helping me avoided the inconvenience and expense of a blown tire.

4. Which is the best option to correctly complete blank 4?
   a. excellent customer service receiving.
   b. excellent customer service of which I received.
   c. excellent customer service that I received.
   d. excellent customer service I was receiving of.

Use the FREE process to choose the best answer for exercises 5 through 8.

Vaccines prevent dangerous, even deadly, diseases. Vaccines greatly reduce the possibility of infection **(5)** _____ Vaccines imitate infections without causing illness. **(6)** _____ do cause the immune system to produce T-lymphocytes and antibodies. **(7)** _____ the false infection may cause minor symptoms. These symptoms, such as a low-grade fever or headache, are normal **(8)** _____

★ 5. Which is the best option to correctly complete blank 5?

    a. by the body's natural defenses causing development of immunity.

    b. by the development of the body's natural defenses into immunity.

    c. by causing development of immunity by the body's natural defenses.

    d. by causing the body's natural defenses to develop immunity.

★ 6. Which is the best option to correctly complete blank 6?

    a. These imitation infections

    b. Imitating infections,

    c. When imitating infections,

    d. When the infections imitated,

★ 7. Which is the best option to correctly complete blank 7?

    a. After having received a vaccine,

    b. After receiving a vaccine,

    c. After a patient receives a vaccine,

    d. After a vaccine receiving,

★ 8. Which is the best option to correctly complete blank 8?

    a. and should not cause concern.

    b. and should be not something to cause concerning.

    c. and should not cause concern, worry, or upset.

    d. and should not be a concerning aspect or cause.

> ### Remember the Concept
>
> Use FREE to find and fix obstructions to communication.
>
> - Identify potential problem areas and **Focus** on a sentence.
>
> - **Read** aloud to find confusing wording.
>
> - Check for common **Errors**, including dangling modifiers, wordiness, awkward structure, and illogical word order.
>
> - **Evaluate** the corrected sentence.

Word Usage

Have you ever...

- Been surprised when a teacher used slang?

- Become confused about whether something you were reading was in the past or present?

- Had a spellchecker replace your typo with the wrong word?

Choosing the correct word is essential for communication. Each word conveys a specific meaning in a sentence. Using an incorrect word can easily cause either misunderstanding or confusion. Understanding how to correct common errors in word usage will improve your writing.

Common errors in word usage include:

- Wrong or confusing pronouns.

- Mismatched subjects and verbs.

- Logical connecting or transition words with the wrong meaning.

- Casual or informal language in formal writing.

- Double negatives.

When you speak to a friend, you have a lot of help communicating. You use tone of voice, hand gestures, and common knowledge to communicate. When you write, you don't have these helpers. This makes choosing the correct word especially important.

Using FREE to Fix Word Usage

The following table explains common word usage errors.

Pronoun Usage	What does the pronoun reference? It should be clear who you mean by "he," "she," or "they."
Subject-Verb Agreement	Does the subject match the verb? "John sit in the front" should be "John sits in the front."
Verb Tense	Are all the verbs the same tense? "Barry went to the store and then drives to work" should be "Barry went to the store and then drove to work."
Transition Words	Are transition words appropriate? Use the transition with the right meaning. "However" shows contrast, while "likewise" shows similarity.
Connecting Words	Are connecting words appropriate? Use the connecting word with the right meaning. "Because" or "so" shows cause. "Yet" or "but" shows contrast.
Informal Language	Is your language appropriate for your purpose and audience? Avoid slang and informal language in formal writing.
Double Negatives	Do you use two negative words? Two negatives change the meaning to positive. "I never owed no one money" should be "I never owed anyone money."

Focus on a Sentence

Word usage errors are easy to miss. Focus on one sentence at a time to thoroughly check your work for usage errors. If you tend to make verb tense errors, be sure to check verb tense in the whole text, not just each sentence. Your verb tense should be consistent and logical throughout your writing.

Use the following sentence for the exercises in word usage.

When Abigail met with her accountant, she point out that Abigail's filing system is screwy.

Read Aloud

Read the sentence aloud. Often you can identify subject-verb agreement errors, double negatives, informal language, and inappropriate connecting words or transitions by reading aloud.

? **1.** Read the sentence aloud. Fix any errors that you find.

You might notice that "she point out" sounds wrong. The singular subject "she" needs a singular verb "points out." You might also notice the word "screwy." This slang term should be replaced with more formal language. You might correct the sentence like this:

> When Abigail met with her accountant, she points out that Abigail's filing system is flawed.

Look for Common Errors

Next, check for common errors that might be missed when you read aloud. Consistent verb tense is sometimes hard to identify by reading aloud. Subtle subject-verb agreement and pronoun usage errors can also be easy to miss.

? **2.** Check the sentence for common errors. Fix any errors that you find.

When you look for errors, you might notice that the verb tense is inconsistent in the sentence. The verb "met" is past tense, while "points out" and "is" are present tense. You might correct the sentence like this:

> When Abigail met with her accountant, she pointed out that Abigail's filing system was flawed.

Evaluate the Corrected Sentence

Read the sentence again. Are there remaining errors? Can you improve the wording?

? **3.** Evaluate the corrected sentence and improve the language, if possible.

When you review the sentence, you might notice that the pronoun "she" is ambiguous. Is it referring to Abigail or the accountant? You might correct the sentence like this:

> When Abigail met with her accountant, the accountant pointed out that Abigail's filing system was flawed.

Build Your Writing Skills

The pronouns "each," "either," "neither," "no one," "nobody," "everyone," "someone," "anyone," "everybody," "somebody," and "anybody" are singular. "Neither Jacob nor Paulo is ready" is correct. "Neither Jacob nor Paulo are ready" is incorrect.

Practice It!

Edit the following passage in exercises 1 through 20.

Gravitational attraction from the sun and the moon are responsible for tides. The moon's gravity has their strongest effect on the side of the Earth that is closest, but water nearest the moon is pulled toward the moon. The moon's gravitational force was ginormous enough to form a bulge of water near the moon. On the other hand, the sun causes a second bulge of water near the sun. As the Earth, sun, and moon rotate, the tides don't never cease to rise and fall.

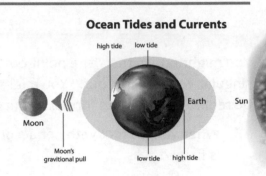

Ocean Tides and Currents

1. Focus on a sentence to check for word usage. Write the sentence here.

2. Read the sentence aloud. Fix any errors that you find.

3. Check the sentence for common errors. Fix any errors that you find.

4. Evaluate the corrected sentence and improve the language, if possible.

5. Focus on another sentence to check for word usage. Write the sentence here.

6. Read the sentence aloud. Fix any errors that you find.

7. Check the sentence for common errors. Fix any errors that you find.

8. Evaluate the corrected sentence and improve the language, if possible.

---

9. Focus on another sentence to check for word usage. Write the sentence here.

10. Read the sentence aloud. Fix any errors that you find.

11. Check the sentence for common errors. Fix any errors that you find.

12. Evaluate the corrected sentence and improve the language, if possible.

---

13. Focus on another sentence to check for word usage. Write the sentence here.

14. Read the sentence aloud. Fix any errors that you find.

15. Check the sentence for common errors. Fix any errors that you find.

> *Build Your Writing Skills*
>
> When you join two or more singular subjects with the word "or," the verb should be singular: "A raven or a crow is out in the field."

16. Evaluate the corrected sentence and improve the language, if possible.

_____

17. Focus on another sentence to check for word usage. Write the sentence here.

18. Read the sentence aloud. Fix any errors that you find.

19. Check the sentence for common errors. Fix any errors that you find.

20. Evaluate the corrected sentence and improve the language, if possible.

_____

21. What common word usage errors do you make? How can you improve your word usage?

22. What types of word usage errors are most difficult for you to find? Why? How can you improve your ability to find these errors?

> ### Build Your Writing Skills
>
> A title is singular, even if it sounds plural: "_The Simpsons_ is still a popular TV show after many years on the air."

Check Your Skills

Use the FREE process to choose the best answer for exercises 1 through 4.

I am writing in regards to the accident that took place on my property on April 18. **(1)** _____ a blue Chevrolet crashed through a fence and into a tree. **(2)** _____ was severely damaged, and the estimated damages to my property **(3)** _____ $1,600 to repair. I am enclosing the landscaping company's estimate, **(4)** _____ states that the work will take three to six weeks.

---

1. Which is the best option to correctly complete blank 1?

    a. However,

    b. By that date,

    c. Therefore,

    d. On that date,

2. Which is the best option to correctly complete blank 2?

    a. It

    b. They

    c. The tree

    d. The fence and tree

3. Which is the best option to correctly complete blank 3?

    a. will cost

    b. were costing

    c. will

    d. was

4. Which is the best option to correctly complete blank 4?

    a. it

    b. they

    c. who

    d. which

Use the FREE process to choose the best answer for exercises 5 through 8.

Many states have lotteries and (5) _____ the proceeds to fund education. This policy may seem like an easy and effective way to fund education, but it is (6) _____ The (7) _____ is that it unfairly taxes the poor, (8) _____ they are the demographic who purchase lottery tickets.

---

5. Which is the best option to correctly complete blank 5?

    a. use

    b. uses

    c. using

    d. used

6. Which is the best option to correctly complete blank 6?

    a. not never a good idea.

    b. not never a bad idea.

    c. not a never good idea.

    d. not a good idea.

7. Which is the best option to correctly complete blank 7?

    a. major no-no about a lottery

    b. hidden problem with a lottery

    c. stuff you don't realize about a lottery

    d. actual thing going on in a lottery

8. Which is the best option to correctly complete blank 8?

    a. after

    b. whereas

    c. while

    d. since

Remember the Concept

Use FREE to find and fix word usage errors.

- **Focus** on a sentence.

- **Read** aloud to find verb errors, double negatives, informal language, and incorrect words.

- Check for common **Errors**, including verb tense, subject-verb agreement, and pronoun errors.

- **Evaluate** the corrected sentence.

Spelling, Capitalization, and Punctuation

Connections

Have you ever…

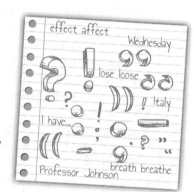

- Confused two words that sound alike but are spelled differently?

- Seen a funny post about comma usage, such as "Let's eat Grandma," versus "Let's eat, Grandma"?

- Received an email written in all capital letters?

Correct spelling, capitalization, and punctuation help with understanding. There are many rules for these elements of language mechanics. Focusing on specific problems in your own writing and common errors can help you improve your writing.

Be aware of the following issues. In capitalization:

- Capitalize titles or descriptors when they are part of a name: "Uncle Joaquin" versus "my uncle;" "Chevron Corporation" versus "the corporation."

- Don't capitalize words for emphasis. **Incorrect:** "The movie is based on a True Story." **Correct:** "The movie is based on a true story."

In punctuation:

- Don't use unneeded commas, exclamation points, or semicolons. Never use emoticons such as :) in formal writing.

- Connect sentences properly with a comma and a conjunction or with a semicolon.

- Use apostrophes correctly for possessive nouns and pronouns.

In spelling:

- Don't use informal acronyms or shorthand, such as "B4" instead of "before."

- Watch for words that sound alike but are spelled differently, such as "its" and "it's."

Learn It!

Using FREE to Fix Language Mechanics

Keep a diary of errors that you discover in your own writing, and identify your most common errors. Focusing on common errors will help you the most. Also keep in mind the errors that are most common among writers.

	Incorrect	Correct
Capitalization in Context	Professor Freeman introduced us to another Professor.	Professor Freeman introduced us to another professor.
Unnecessary Capitalization	The theme of the story was True Love Conquers All.	The theme of the story was true love conquers all.
Unnecessary Commas	Before shopping, I checked online, to find the sales.	Before shopping, I checked online to find the sales.
Overused Punctuation	The proposition is a bad idea! I'm voting against it; you should, too!	The proposition is a bad idea. I'm voting against it. You should, too.
Sentence Connections	We bought three dozen but we might need more.	We bought three dozen, but we might need more.
Emoticons	The devastating ending was a surprise to us all :(	The devastating ending was a surprise to us all.
Apostrophes	The book is not her's. Its either Maurices' or the Smith's book.	The book is not hers. It's either Maurice's or the Smiths' book.
Acronyms or Shorthand	I would like 2b a dentist someday. IMHO, it is the best occupation.	I would like to be a dentist someday. In my humble opinion, it is the best occupation.
Homonyms	I can't bare to leave home today. You're party can wait.	I can't bear to leave home today. Your party can wait.
Commonly Confused Words	I can't eat desert. It has a bad affect on my weight.	I can't eat dessert. It has a bad effect on my weight.

Focus on a Sentence

Spelling, capitalization, and punctuation errors can happen anywhere, and they can be difficult to find. Focus separately on each sentence in your writing to check for errors.

Use the following sentence for the exercises in language mechanics.

When you decide too purchase a new Computer, the first step is to identify you're needs, for software, storage, and processing.

Read Aloud

Read the sentence aloud. Focus on pausing for punctuation and sounding out words you commonly misspell or confuse.

?   **1.** Read the sentence aloud. Fix any errors that you find.

You might notice that the comma between "needs" and "for" sounds unnecessary. You might correct the sentence like this:

> When you decide too purchase a new Computer, the first step is to identify you're needs for software, storage, and processing.

Look for Common Errors

Checking for common errors is essential in spelling, capitalization, and punctuation. Many of these errors are difficult to find by reading aloud.

?   **2.** Check the sentence for common errors. Fix any errors that you find.

You might identify that the word "you're" is used instead of "your." Also, the word "computer" should not be capitalized. You might correct the sentence like this:

> When you decide too purchase a new computer, the first step is to identify your needs for software, storage, and processing.

Evaluate the Corrected Sentence

Read the sentence again to check for errors you may have missed. Errors often clump together. If you found errors in a sentence, look for other errors near it.

?   **3.** Evaluate the corrected sentence and fix any remaining errors.

The word "too" is used instead of the word "to." Correct the sentence like this:

> When you decide to purchase a new computer, the first step is to identify your needs for software, storage, and processing.

Practice It!

Edit the following passage in exercises 1 through 20.

Their are four basic laws of Supply and Demand, each describing the affects of a different relationship of supply and demand. First, if demand increases and supply, does not change, a shortage occurs, leading too higher prices. Second, if demand decreases and supply does not change; a surplus occurs and this leads to lower prices. Third, if demand does not change and supply increase's, a surplus occurs, which causes lower prices. Finally, if demand does not change and supply decreases, a shortage occurs, than this situation causes higher prices.

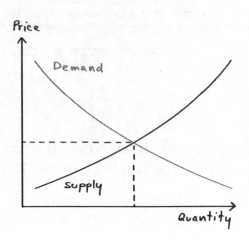

1. Focus on a sentence to check for spelling, capitalization, and punctuation errors. Write the sentence here.

2. Read the sentence aloud. Fix any errors that you find.

3. Check the sentence for common errors. Fix any errors that you find.

4. Evaluate the corrected sentence and fix any additional errors.

5. Focus on another sentence to check for spelling, capitalization, and punctuation errors. Write the sentence here.

6. Read the sentence aloud. Fix any errors that you find.

7. Check the sentence for common errors. Fix any errors that you find.

8. Evaluate the corrected sentence and fix any additional errors.

9. Focus on another sentence to check for spelling, capitalization, and punctuation errors. Write the sentence here.

10. Read the sentence aloud. Fix any errors that you find.

11. Check the sentence for common errors. Fix any errors that you find.

12. Evaluate the corrected sentence and fix any additional errors.

13. Focus on another sentence to check for spelling, capitalization, and punctuation errors. Write the sentence here.

14. Read the sentence aloud. Fix any errors that you find.

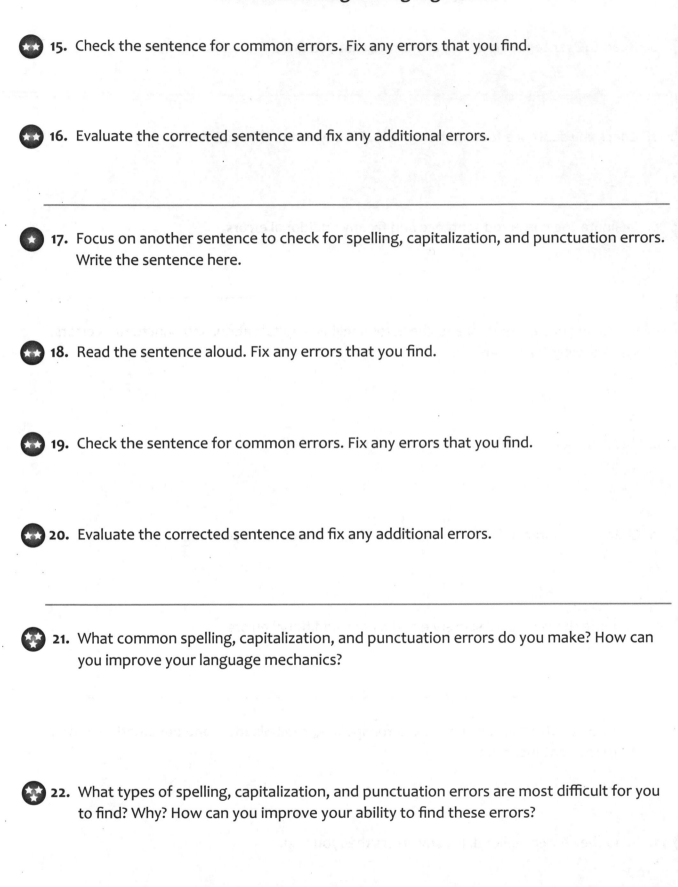

15. Check the sentence for common errors. Fix any errors that you find.

16. Evaluate the corrected sentence and fix any additional errors.

17. Focus on another sentence to check for spelling, capitalization, and punctuation errors. Write the sentence here.

18. Read the sentence aloud. Fix any errors that you find.

19. Check the sentence for common errors. Fix any errors that you find.

20. Evaluate the corrected sentence and fix any additional errors.

21. What common spelling, capitalization, and punctuation errors do you make? How can you improve your language mechanics?

22. What types of spelling, capitalization, and punctuation errors are most difficult for you to find? Why? How can you improve your ability to find these errors?

Check Your Skills

Use the FREE process to choose the best answer for exercises 1 through 4.

How old should a child be to have a smartphone? Some parents give
(1) _____ smartphones at six or seven years old. However, many people worry what smartphones **(2)** _____ How does a smartphone affect
a young child's brain? We don't know the **(3)** _____ of smartphones
for children would rather be safe than sorry. Others discount these concerns, stating that smartphones are just as likely to have positive effects. Smartphones may
train children's brains to have superior **(4)** _____

---

1. Which is the best option to correctly complete blank 1?

   a. there children

   b. their children

   c. they're children

   d. there children's

2. Which is the best option to correctly complete blank 2?

   a. might mean for a child's development.

   b. might mean for a childs' development.

   c. might mean for a childs development.

   d. might mean for a childs's development.

3. Which is the best option to correctly complete blank 3?

   a. answer but; opponents

   b. answer but opponents

   c. answer; but opponents

   d. answer, but opponents

4. Which is the best option to correctly complete blank 4?

   a. Spatial Awareness and Learning Skills.

   b. Spatial Awareness and learning skills.

   c. Spatial awareness and Learning skills.

   d. spatial awareness and learning skills.

Use the FREE process to choose the best answer for exercises 5 through 8.

Mankind has known about magnets for thousands of years. According to the
(5) _____, Thales of Miletus discussed the properties of magnets
sometime between 625 BC and 545 BC. Magnets are (6) _____ magnetic fields which attract or repel other objects. All materials have some magne-
tism. However, only permanent magnets, (7) _____ or other highly
magnetic material, are strong enough for people to feel. Magnets
(8) _____ physical forces.

⭐ **5.** Which is the best option to correctly complete blank 5?

    a. Philosopher Aristotle

    b. philosopher Aristotle

    c. Philosopher aristotle

    d. philosopher aristotle

⭐ **6.** Which is the best option to correctly complete blank 6?

    a. objects that produce

    b. objects, that produce

    c. objects that, produce

    d. objects that produce,

⭐ **7.** Which is the best option to correctly complete blank 7?

    a. maid from Iran

    b. made from Iran

    c. maid from iron

    d. made from iron

⭐ **8.** Which is the best option to correctly complete blank 8?

    a. are fascinating examples have

    b. are fascinating examples of

    c. our fascinating examples off

    d. our fascinating examples of

Remember the Concept

Use FREE to find and fix errors in mechanics.

- **Focus** on a sentence.
- **Read** aloud to find commonly confused words, misspellings, and incorrect punctuation.
- Check for common capitalization, punctuation, and spelling **Errors**.
- **Evaluate** the corrected sentence.

Sentence Structure

Have you ever...

- Read a sentence that was long and confusing?

- Felt confused by a short sentence that didn't seem to complete a whole thought?

- Been unsure how to join two sentences effectively?

Although there are an infinite number of possible sentences, sentences follow specific structures. Correct sentence structure makes your writing clear and easy to understand.

A sentence needs three elements: a subject, a verb, and a complete thought. If you can identify these elements of a sentence, you can find and fix many sentence structure errors. You should be familiar with the following common sentence errors:

- **Fragments:** A fragment is a partial sentence, lacking either a subject, a verb, or a complete thought.

- **Run-ons:** A run-on is a sentence where two or more main clauses are joined incorrectly. A **comma splice** is a type of run-on where two sentences are joined by a comma. Sometimes, the word "run-on" is used to describe a sentence that is overly long and confusing.

- **Lack of Parallel Structure:** Lists or groups of words or phrases should all have the same form, i.e. "I went *running, biking, and hiking* last week."

- **Lack of Subject-Verb Agreement:** The verb must match the subject, i.e. "Allison does" not "Alison do."

- **Subordination or Coordination Errors:** Two sentences can be joined with a comma and a coordinating conjunction (and, but, for, or, nor, so, yet). They can also be joined with a subordinating conjunction (such as after, although, because, before, if, since, that, unless, until, when, where, whether, which, while) without a comma.

Using FREE to Fix Sentence Structure

To find sentence structure errors, learn to identify:

- **Main clauses:** A subject, verb, and complete thought that could stand alone as a whole sentence.

- **Subordinate clauses:** A phrase with a subject and verb that begins with a subordinating conjunction. It cannot stand alone as a whole sentence.

	Incorrect	Correct
Fragment	When we went to the museum.	We went to the museum. When we went to the museum, we saw the dinosaur exhibit.
Run-on	We went to the museum, and we saw the dinosaur exhibit, and then we went to dinner.	We went to the museum and saw the dinosaur exhibit, and then we went to dinner.
Comma Splice	We went to the museum, we saw the dinosaur exhibit.	We went to the museum, and we saw the dinosaur exhibit.
Parallelism	We were visiting the museum and saw the dinosaur exhibit.	We visited the museum and saw the dinosaur exhibit.
Connecting Subordinate Clauses	We left early: because I had an appointment. Because I had an appointment; we left early.	We left early because I had an appointment. Because I had an appointment, we left early.
Connecting Main Clauses	We went to the museum and we saw the dinosaur exhibit.	We went to the museum, and we saw the dinosaur exhibit. We went to the museum; we saw the dinosaur exhibit.
Subject-Verb Agreement	Every month, we goes to the museum.	Every month, we go to the museum.

Focus on a Sentence

Focus on each sentence to find errors, but look at surrounding sentences to identify sentences that should be combined.

Use the following sentence for the exercises in sentence structure.

> After Jen left for work; Terrance was doing the dishes, picked up the living room, and washing the car, then he took Ella to preschool.

Read Aloud

Read the sentence aloud. Try to identify main clauses and subordinate clauses. Does the sentence sound complete? Does it sound long or complex? Do lists of words and phrases go together and sound correct? Do subjects and verbs sound right together?

?   **1.** Read the sentence aloud. Fix any errors that you find.

You might notice that the multiple verbs in the sentence don't use parallel structure. You might correct the sentence like this:

> After Jen left for work; Terrance did the dishes, picked up the living room, and washed the car, then he took Ella to preschool.

Look for Common Errors

Check for errors that might be difficult to notice, such as errors in punctuation. Are main clauses and subordinate clauses joined properly? Are there comma splices?

?   **2.** Check the sentence for common errors. Fix any errors that you find.

You might notice that a semicolon is used incorrectly to join a subordinate clause to a main clause. You might correct the sentence like this:

> After Jen left for work, Terrance did the dishes, picked up the living room, and washed the car, then he took Ella to preschool.

Evaluate the Corrected Sentence

Read the sentence again to check for any additional errors.

?   **3.** Evaluate the corrected sentence and fix any remaining errors.

This sentence contains a comma splice. It's common to have a comma splice before the word "then," which cannot join two sentences. You could add the word "and," but a better choice might be to separate the two sentences:

> After Jen left for work, Terrance did the dishes, picked up the living room, and washed the car. Then, he took Ella to preschool.

Practice It!

Edit the following passage in exercises 1 through 20.

In 2014, the United Nations' International Court of Justice ruled that Japan's Antarctic whaling was a commercial program, it was not a scientific endeavor. After the United Nations ruled that the whaling program was not scientific; Japan cancelled its 2014 Antarctic whaling hunt. Since many types of whales are endangered species. Japanese whaling, a historic, part of culture, and commercial tradition, has been a controversial issue. While whaling are still controversial, international bans on whaling are proceeding.

1. Focus on a sentence to check for sentence structure errors. Write the sentence here.

2. Read the sentence aloud. Fix any errors that you find.

3. Check the sentence for common errors. Fix any errors that you find.

4. Evaluate the corrected sentence and fix any additional errors.

5. Focus on another sentence to check for sentence structure errors. Write the sentence here.

6. Read the sentence aloud. Fix any errors that you find.

7. Check the sentence for common errors. Fix any errors that you find.

8. Evaluate the corrected sentence and fix any additional errors.

---

9. Focus on another sentence to check for sentence structure errors. Write the sentence here.

10. Read the sentence aloud. Fix any errors that you find.

11. Check the sentence for common errors. Fix any errors that you find.

12. Evaluate the corrected sentence and fix any additional errors.

---

13. Focus on another sentence to check for sentence structure errors. Write the sentence here.

14. Read the sentence aloud. Fix any errors that you find.

15. Check the sentence for common errors. Fix any errors that you find.

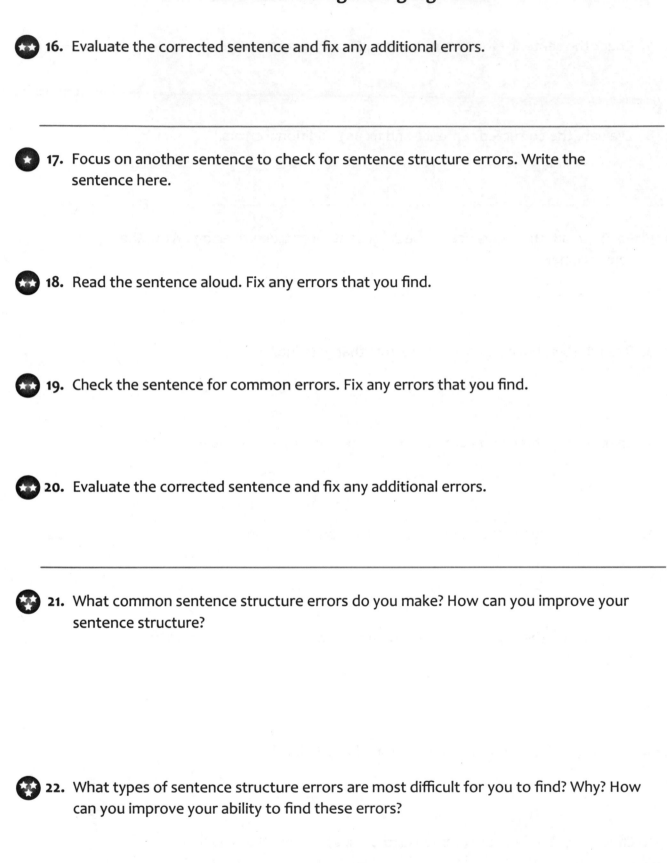

16. Evaluate the corrected sentence and fix any additional errors.

_____

17. Focus on another sentence to check for sentence structure errors. Write the sentence here.

18. Read the sentence aloud. Fix any errors that you find.

19. Check the sentence for common errors. Fix any errors that you find.

20. Evaluate the corrected sentence and fix any additional errors.

_____

21. What common sentence structure errors do you make? How can you improve your sentence structure?

22. What types of sentence structure errors are most difficult for you to find? Why? How can you improve your ability to find these errors?

Check Your Skills

Use the FREE process to choose the best answer for exercises 1 through 4.

The El Niño weather phenomenon occurs when temperatures in the equatorial Pacific Ocean **(1)** _____ When El Niño **(2)** _____ has effects on weather throughout the globe. El Niño can cause floods in the U.S. and Peru, tropical cyclones in the East Pacific, and **(3)** _____ Observations of the tropical Pacific are **(4)** _____ scientists to predict short term climate variations.

1. Which is the best option to correctly complete blank 1?

   a. being unusually high.

   b. be unusually high.

   c. is unusually high.

   d. are unusually high.

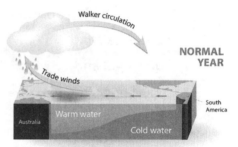

2. Which is the best option to correctly complete blank 2?

   a. occurs, it

   b. occurs and it

   c. occurs, and it

   d. occurs; it

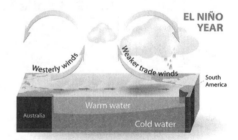

3. Which is the best option to correctly complete blank 3?

   a. droughts in the West Pacific.

   b. drying in the West Pacific.

   c. droughtiness in the West Pacific.

   d. dryness in the West Pacific.

4. Which is the best option to correctly complete blank 4?

   a. invaluable. Because they allow

   b. invaluable; because they allow

   c. invaluable, and because they allow

   d. invaluable because they allow

Use the FREE process to choose the best answer for exercises 5 through 8.

In 1963, the United States enacted sanctions against Cuba, making trade
(5) _____ these sanctions are the longest-standing in the U.S. Those
who support continuing the trade embargo against Cuba **(6)** _____
that the sanctions still show U.S. disapproval of the communist regime. Others
oppose the **(7)** _____ they have been ineffective in removing that
regime. Opponents claim that the only effect of the sanctions is to limit economic
(8) _____ the controversy, it is doubtful that the U.S. will lift sanctions
soon, and Cuban trade will likely remain illegal.

★ **5.** Which is the best option to correctly complete blank 5?

    a. illegal, and

    b. illegal and

    c. illegal,

    d. illegal; and

★ **6.** Which is the best option to correctly complete blank 6?

    a. argues

    b. argue

    c. arguing

    d. is arguing

★ **7.** Which is the best option to correctly complete blank 7?

    a. sanctions. Because

    b. sanctions, and because

    c. sanctions; because

    d. sanctions because

★ **8.** Which is the best option to correctly complete blank 8?

    a. opportunity, and despite

    b. opportunity. Despite

    c. opportunity and despite

    d. opportunity; and despite

> ### Remember the Concept
>
> Use FREE to find and fix sentence structure errors.
>
> - **Focus** on a sentence.
> - **Read** aloud to identify run-ons, fragments, subject-verb agreement errors, or a lack of parallel structure.
> - Check for common **Errors,** including comma splices and coordination or subordination errors.
> - **Evaluate** the corrected sentence.

Writing Practice

The best way to improve your writing is by practicing. When you write, you are communicating your ideas to your readers. If you can clearly and effectively communicate, you will be more successful in the workplace, in school, and in every-day tasks.

To improve, focus on using the writing process as you practice.

Plan: Don't start writing until you have planned. Read, think, and define what you want to write.

Draft: Drafting will be easier if you have planned well. Organize what you want to say, and add connections, explanations, and transitions.

Evaluate: Think critically about your writing. Check that you have a clear, logical organization, specific details, and effective language. Revise and edit your writing to improve it and eliminate errors.

Submit When you are satisfied with your writing, do one last check for errors. Complete any final formatting and submit your work. That might mean hitting "send" on a email or turning in a paper to your instructor.

As you work, be sure to self-evaluate your performance. To self-evaluate your practice, use the questions on page 329.

This section includes lessons to practice four important types of writing.

- **Practice in Everyday Writing**
  Writing is an important part of everyday life, in the workplace and at home. This lesson will give you practice in everyday writing tasks.

- **Practice for Reasoning through Language Arts**
  Learn a process to evaluate and compare opposing arguments about a variety of topics. This type of writing will improve your analytical skills and will allow you to communicate your critiques of written materials.

- **Practice in Social Studies Writing**
  Social studies writing involves analyzing works from many time periods. The same issues affect people in different eras and cultures. Learn to make connections between past and present ideas.

- **Practice in Science Writing**
  In science, written communication is essential. Scientists must communicate clearly and exactly. They explain experiments, studies, results, and conclusions. Writing about science shows that you understand scientific concepts. This lesson introduces a strategy for science writing.

Practice in Everyday Writing

Have you ever ...

- Written a personal statement for a college application?

- Written a response in an online forum?

- Written an email to a client?

Writing is a growing part of everyday life. In the workplace, employees write emails, letters, reports, and memos. Online, individuals write posts, responses, and comments. At home, consumers write letters and emails to companies. Citizens write letters and emails to the government, newspapers, and organizations. The better you can express yourself, the better you can accomplish your goals.

Practicing your everyday writing is important. The more you practice, the more your writing will improve. Tasks that are important to you provide the best writing practice. Consider:

- Do you have family or friends who are far away? Write letters to your parents, children, or friends.

- Do you have an important topic that you want to communicate to others? Try starting a blog or commenting in an online forum.

- Are you interested in a particular career? Try writing to companies or individuals to find out more about the career, make contacts, or offer your services as a volunteer.

- Are you planning on going to college? Practice writing college applications or emails to admissions officers.

The Writing Process for Everyday Writing

Think about your writing task. What is your purpose? Who is your audience? The requirements of your task will inform the choices that you make.

Imagine you have received the following letter at work. Write a response that thanks the sender for buying the product and suggesting the improvement. Let her know that your engineering department is evaluating the suggested improvement and that she can contact human resources if she is interested in an internship or potential employment.

Dear Perez-Madison Company:

My name is Lei Thompson, and I am an engineering student. I recently ordered the PM870 Adjustable Monitor Wall Mount and attempted to install it. The wall mount seemed flimsy when it was installed because of the shape of the bracket that attaches the mount to the wall.

I designed a support to attach to the bracket and printed the support with a 3D printer at my school. I am enclosing the design specs of this bracket and how it fits with the wall mount. I hope you will evaluate this bracket. Feel free to include this piece in your design in the future to improve your product.

Now that the additional support is in place, I am very pleased with the wall mount. The adjustable arm is very well designed and provides the versatility that I need for my computer's second monitor.

Thank you for your time and attention.

Sincerely,

Lei Thompson

Plan

Depending on your task, planning can take a few minutes or a few weeks. The amount of time you take to plan depends on the schedule and scope for your project. When you plan, focus on purpose, audience, and organization:

- Purpose: Why are you writing? What do you need to achieve?
- Audience: Who will read your writing?
- Organization: What is the beginning, middle, and ending of your writing?

? **1.** Plan your response.

Purpose:	Audience:
Beginning:	
Middle:	
Ending:	

You might write:

Purpose:	Audience:
To acknowledge the letter, show appreciation, and let the sender know the status	Lei Thompson, engineering student and customer

Beginning:

Thank the sender and let her know that the idea is appreciated and being evaluated.

Middle:

Explain the process of evaluation of new ideas: from customer service staff, to engineering department, to management.

Encourage the customer to continue with engineering studies. Encourage the customer to contact human resources for possible future employment or internships.

Ending:

Encourage the customer to continue to buy products and contact us with any suggestions.

Draft

Based on your planning, draft your response. Be sure to format your response appropriately. Letters, emails, reports, and memos each have required formats.

?   **2.** Draft your response.

You might write:

Dear Ms. Thompson:

Thank you for taking the time to develop a suggested improvement to our product and for sending us your detailed plans. We appreciate your business and your well-thought-out idea.

Our office was very impressed with your design, and we have passed it on to our engineering department for evaluation. All ideas that come to our office are first evaluated by the customer service staff. Ideas of merit, such as yours, are then evaluated by the engineering department. The engineering department then creates a proposal for management. If your idea is recommended and the proposal is approved, it will be implemented in future production. We will be sure to let you know the results of our evaluation.

We would like to encourage you in your engineering study. Your idea was innovative and well presented. If you would like to contact our human resources department, we would certainly be interested in learning more about you and your plans for the future. We have some summer internships available, and we actively recruit new engineering graduates.

We hope that you continue to buy our products and encourage you to contact us with any further suggestions.

Sincerely,

Javier Robles

Evaluate and Submit

Evaluate your writing:

- Is it appropriate for your purpose? Does it accomplish your goal?

- Is it appropriate for your audience? Is the writing clear? Is the language appropriate?

- Is the central idea clear and well-supported?

- Are there sufficient specific details?

- Is the format appropriate and correct?

3. Evaluate your response. What are its strengths and weaknesses? What can you do to improve your everyday writing in the future?

> **Build Your Writing Skills**
>
> In the workplace and at home, you will need to write for many different purposes and audiences. Practice writing for a variety of real-world writing tasks, including letters, memos, emails, reports, and applications. You will become a better all-around writer.

Use the following scenario and passage for exercises 1 through 3.

Imagine you are applying to college. You need to write a personal statement to go with your application. The college provided the following writing prompt.

What major do you intend to study? Discuss how you became interested in this major and describe any experience you have had relevant to the field. Include any activities, employment, volunteer work, or internships. What have you learned from your experiences?

1. Complete the graphic organizer to plan your response.

Purpose:	Audience:
Beginning:	
Middle:	
Ending:	

2. Draft a response to the prompt based on the graphic organizer. Type your answer on a computer. If a computer is unavailable, write your answer on a separate sheet of paper.

 3. Evaluate, revise, and edit your response. Make sure your ideas are organized and connected logically. Check your response for errors.

Use the following prompt and passage for exercises 4 through 6.

Write a cover letter to apply for the following position.

Parken-Todd Media Group, Inc. seeks a creative, enthusiastic communication manager. You will work closely with our web team to write, edit, and proofread web content. Working with the project manager and social media team, you will manage our web communications plan and documentation.

---

4. Complete the graphic organizer to plan your response.

Purpose:	Audience:
Beginning:	
Middle:	
Ending:	

5. Draft a response to the prompt based on the graphic organizer. Type your answer on a computer. If a computer is unavailable, write your answer on a separate sheet of paper.

6. Evaluate, revise, and edit your response. Make sure your ideas are organized and connected logically. Check your response for errors.

Use the following prompt and passage for exercises 7 through 9.

Write a letter to the editor in response to the following newspaper opinion article. Critique the article's position and express either your agreement or disagreement.

Take Money out of Politics

What's wrong with politics? The answer is simple— money. As elections become more and more expensive, large donors have more and more power. The U.S. presidential election in 2012 cost seven billion dollars. Much of that money came from corporations, unions, and wealthy individuals. These wealthy donors have influence because candidates depend on their donations.

The solution to this problem is publicly funded elections. Taking the money out of politics levels the playing field, allowing more candidates to run for office, and removes some of the advantages for incumbents, who generally receive more donations than their opponents. Public office shouldn't be reserved exclusively for the wealthy and those supported by wealthy donors.

Once all candidates have equal budgets, the focus of campaigns can be removed from fundraising. Candidates should be focusing on outlining their policies and positions for the electorate, not on raising money for misleading television commercials. An election with a limited budget that focuses on ideas and reasonable debate would improve our country.

It is a shame that we spend billions of dollars on elections when we don't have enough money to fund public education and other social programs. The money wasted on extravagant campaigns could be put to good use improving our society and our economy.

Money needs to be forced out of politics. It will never leave on its own; political influence is too valuable for corporations and high-powered individuals. We need to reform our laws to enforce publicly funded elections at every level.

7. Complete the graphic organizer to plan your response.

Purpose:	Audience:

Beginning:

Middle:

Ending:

8. Draft a response to the prompt based on the graphic organizer. Type your answer on a computer. If a computer is unavailable, write your answer on a separate sheet of paper.

9. Evaluate, revise, and edit your response. Make sure your ideas are organized and connected logically. Check your response for errors.

Check **Your Skills**

Use the writing process to practice everyday writing with the following tasks.

 1. Imagine your landscaping company's 25th anniversary is approaching. Write a letter to your customers in honor of the anniversary. In your letter, thank your customers for their business and loyalty. In addition, present an offer for 25% off in honor of your 25th anniversary.

Write your answer below or type your response on a computer.

Use the questions on page 329 to evaluate your response.

Use the following passage for exercise 2.

Dear Homeowner:

A city home inspector inspected your property on April 10 and found the following code violations:

- Weeds in excess of four inches in width or breadth.

- Excessive weeds adjacent to sidewalks.

Please work with us by correcting these violations by April 24. A second property inspection will occur on that date. If you need to contact us regarding this notice, please reference notice number A34991.

Sincerely,

Joshua Linman
Home Inspector

2. Write a letter in response to this notice to inform the inspector that you will be on vacation from April 12 through April 21 and request an extension to complete the weeding on your property.

Write your answer below or type your response on a computer.

Use the questions on page 329 to evaluate your response.

3. Find an article about a current event in a newspaper, magazine, or online. Write a blog post about the article.

Take approximately 45 minutes for this task. Type your response on a computer to prepare for computer responses. If a computer is unavailable, write your answer on a separate sheet of paper.

Remember the Concept

For everyday writing:

- **Plan:** Think about your purpose and audience. Organize your writing with a beginning, middle, and ending.

- **Draft:** Draft your writing in the proper format.

- **Evaluate:** How well does your writing accomplish your goals?

Use the questions on page 329 to evaluate your response.

Practice for Reasoning through Language Arts

Have you ever...

- Made a choice between two products?

- Explained to someone why you made a decision?

- Tried to convince a friend how to vote in an election?

If you have, then you have compared two arguments, evaluated them, and drawn conclusions. Evaluating conflicting points of view is a valuable skill. You might need to evaluate candidates for a job, companies who provide a service, or competing products. In college courses, you might evaluate competing hypotheses or interpretations of topics in sociology, economics, or literature.

Reasoning through language arts means using reading and writing to think and reason. When you reason using language arts, you evaluate what you read and express your evaluation in writing. Often, this involves evaluating and comparing logical arguments.

To evaluate and compare arguments, identify the opposing claims and the support for each claim. Which argument has the stronger support? What are the strengths and weaknesses of each argument?

Evaluating and comparing arguments is not about your personal opinion. It is about the strength of the arguments. You might disagree with strong arguments or agree with weak ones. Your goal is to objectively evaluate the strength of arguments, whether or not you agree with them.

Comparing Arguments

The following prompt asks you to compare two arguments. You need to evaluate the arguments and then build your own argument about the information in the passage.

The passage presents arguments both supporting and opposing a 10 cent tax on grocery bags. In your response, analyze both positions to determine which one is best supported. Use relevant and specific evidence from the passage to support your response. Take approximately 45 minutes for this task.

On Thursday, the city council heard speakers on the proposal to require grocery stores to charge a 10 cent tax per bag for disposable grocery bags. The following is a summary of arguments from supporters and opponents.

Speakers supporting the proposal stated that a tax on bags would reduce waste by encouraging shoppers to bring their own bags. They cited the wide availability of inexpensive reusable bags and noted that grocery stores use a high volume of both paper and plastic bags, producing significant waste.

Plastic grocery bags cannot be recycled in the city's curbside recycling program and have a low rate of recycling, according to information provided by the city's recycling contractor and local supermarkets. The tax revenue would be used to improve the city's recycling and green energy programs. Those improvements could include distributing free reusable bags to some consumers.

Speakers opposing the proposal stated that a 10 cent tax would be a burden on consumers. They stated that stores should have a choice whether or not to provide bags to consumers and that consumers should have a choice whether to invest in reusable bags. The proposal effectively forces consumers to either pay a tax or buy reusable bags.

Speakers stated that since groceries are not taxed to avoid undue burdens on the impoverished, grocery bags should not be taxed either. One speaker called the proposal a "forgetful consumer tax," noting that shoppers who forgot their bags at home would be charged. Opponents also stated that grocery bags are likely to be reused by consumers, who will have to buy more garbage bags and other products to use at home.

Plan: Build the Framework (15 minutes)

Start by planning your response. Compare writing your response to constructing a building. You need a framework before you can complete the walls and roof. Write your:

- **Central Idea:** Which argument in the passage is stronger? Explain your reasoning.

- **Details:** Identify details that support your idea and explain the connection.

- **Conclusion:** Summarize and expand on your central idea. Explain your conclusion.

1. Plan your response to the prompt.

Central Idea:	Explanation:
Restate a Detail:	Explanation:
Restate a Detail:	Explanation:
Restate a Detail:	Explanation:
Restate a Detail:	Explanation:
Conclusion:	Explanation:

You might write:

Central Idea: Proponents have a stronger argument.	Explanation: Their argument includes more specific data than the opposition.
Restate a Detail: Supporters say plastic grocery bags are inconvenient to recycle and are recycled less often than other items.	Explanation: This data is from a reliable source and shows the waste produced by the current system.

Restate a Detail: Opponents say a 10 cent tax is a burden.	**Explanation:** This statement doesn't include any data to support it, but could be a strong argument with supporting data.
Restate a Detail: Opponents point out groceries have no tax because food is a necessity. They compare the grocery bag tax to this.	**Explanation:** The statement sounds logical, but the impact on poorer consumers is still not established.
Restate a Detail: Opponents say consumers reuse grocery bags and will buy other types of bags if grocery bags are taxed.	**Explanation:** This is speculation.
Conclusion: The opposition's argument lacks data.	**Explanation:** The opposing argument could be stronger, but it needs data to show the burden on the consumer.

Draft: Construct the Structure (20 minutes)

Use your central idea, details, and conclusion to construct your response. Your introduction should include your central idea and explanation. Use the details you identified to write the body, and end with the your conclusion.

? **2.** Draft your response.

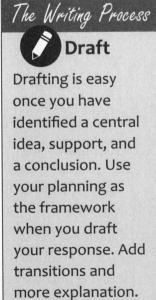

The Writing Process

Draft

Drafting is easy once you have identified a central idea, support, and a conclusion. Use your planning as the framework when you draft your response. Add transitions and more explanation.

You might write:

> Based on the specific data provided by speakers, the proponents of charging the tax on grocery bags have a stronger argument. Their position includes better supported arguments than the opposition, which lacks good support for its ideas.
>
> The supporting argument is based on the idea that reducing waste should be a societal goal. The argument identifies grocery bags as a problem. Supporters say plastic grocery bags are inconvenient to recycle and are recycled less often than other items. This data is from a reliable source. Given this information, reducing the use of disposable grocery bags seems a reasonable goal.
>
> The opposition fails to clearly support its claims. Opponents say a 10 cent tax is a burden, but the passage does not include any data to support this statement. How much of a burden would the tax create? Supporters suggest that tax revenues might finance a free reusable bag program, but the opposition doesn't respond to this. However, the potential burden on consumers could be a strong argument if it included data about the impact on consumers.
>
> Opponents point out groceries have no tax because food is a necessity. They compare the grocery bag tax to this policy. This is a logical argument based on existing tax laws, but the impact on poorer consumers is still not established. Other items sold at grocery stores are taxed, including toilet paper and soap, and grocery bags are not food items.
>
> One of the more problematic claims of the opposition is that consumers reuse grocery bags and will buy more trash bags and other bags if grocery bags are taxed. This is speculation. The author cites no source and gives no specific data. The use of the word "likely" shows that the argument is speculative instead of based on facts.
>
> The opposition's central idea is that taxes are a burden and that consumers should be left to choose the best path. The supporters' argument is based on the value of eliminating waste and the wastefulness of grocery bags. The opposition's points are arguably more weighty; this tax might unfairly affect the poor. However, those arguing against the tax need data to show the burden on the consumer.

 ### *Evaluate and Submit: Add Finishing Touches (10 minutes)*

In a timed response, be sure that you evaluate your work as you write. Organize your response around a strong central idea and include specific details. Explain the significance of quotations from the passage. Take a few minutes after you draft to review, revise, and edit your work. Improve your writing and eliminate errors. When you are satisfied with your response, submit your work.

Use the following passages for exercises 1 through 3.

The passages present arguments both supporting and opposing increased oil drilling in the Gulf of Mexico. In your response, analyze both positions to determine which one is best supported. Use relevant and specific evidence from the passages to support your response. Take approximately 45 minutes for this task.

The U.S. has natural reserves of oil in the Gulf of Mexico that are not being utilized, although they could improve our economy, lower consumer costs, and increase government revenues.

Domestic oil production means more jobs to boost local economies. Oil is a massive industry that should be encouraged to promote our economy. While creating jobs, an increased oil supply will also mean lower gas prices. Local oil reserves also eliminate the need to transport oil across the ocean and reduce our dependence on foreign oil.

In addition to these benefits, state and federal governments will see increased revenue from leases to oil companies for drilling. Some are concerned about safety and the environment. However, with modern technology, oil can be drilled safely, without harming wildlife and natural environments. There is no reason to let oil reserves sit at the bottom of the Gulf of Mexico, unused.

Further drilling in the Gulf of Mexico is unnecessary and dangerous. Our money would be better spent elsewhere. Deep-water oil drilling is an extreme risk to the environment and likely to produce more harm than benefits. Oil spills are common occurrences. They disrupt local industries, including fishing and tourism, while oil companies do little to correct the damages. Saying that it won't happen again is naive. The Deepwater Horizon spill in 2010 spilled almost five million barrels of oil. Oil cleanup continued for a year, and damage to human health, fishing and tourism, and marine habitats continue today. The damage to the environment and wildlife is also costly.

In addition to the hazards, oil drilling only increases the damage fossil fuels cause to our environment. There are only 18 billion gallons of off-shore oil reserves in the entire U.S. coastline, extending our oil reserves perhaps two and a half years. Spending money investing in clean, renewable energy such as wind and solar would be more productive than investing in costly, damaging oil production.

1. Complete the graphic organizer to plan your response. Take approximately 15 minutes to plan your response.

Central Idea:	Explanation:
Restate a Detail:	Explanation:
Restate a Detail:	Explanation:
Restate a Detail:	Explanation:
Restate a Detail:	Explanation:
Conclusion:	Explanation:

2. Draft a response to the prompt based on the graphic organizer. Take approximately 20 minutes to draft your response based on your planning. Type your answer on a computer to prepare for computer responses. If a computer is unavailable, write your answer on a separate sheet of paper.

 3. Evaluate, revise, and edit your response. Make sure your ideas are organized and connected logically. Check your response for errors. Take approximately 10 minutes for this task.

Use the following passage for exercises 4 through 6.

The passage presents arguments both supporting and opposing buying pets from breeders. In your response, analyze both positions to determine which one is best supported. Use relevant and specific evidence from the passage to support your response. Take approximately 45 minutes for this task.

Pet breeders are a popular way to buy a particular pet suited to a particular taste. However, pet breeders come under fire because shelters are filled with unwanted dogs and cats. The controversy over pet breeders is not likely to end soon.

Pet breeders and buyers of purebred pets often accuse opponents of unfairly lumping respectable breeders in with breeders who mistreat dogs. They say that, while abuses should be punished, breeders fill an important function.

A prospective pet owner, supporters state, has a right to choose a pet that is appropriate to his or her lifestyle. According to the U.S. Humane Society, almost 40% of dogs are returned to a breeder, given to a shelter, euthanized, or abandoned within a year. A lack of compatibility is a primary reason that pets are abandoned, according to supporters of breeding. Dogs and cats that are adopted from shelters often have physical or emotional problems that will cause problems for pet owners, proponents of breeders state. Breeders help match prospective pet owners with suitable pets.

On the other hand, those opposed to breeders cite health problems found in many purebred dogs. Inbreeding causes a high risk of cancer, heart disease, arthritis, skin diseases, and neurological disorders. Bulldogs have breathing difficulties because of their purebred features; basset hounds suffer from spinal, skin, and joint issues. Golden retrievers are particularly susceptible to cancer.

Opponents also state that dog breeding encourages and legitimizes puppy mills and backyard breeders that mistreat dogs and keep them in unhealthy conditions to make an easy dollar off the high demand for purebred dogs. With thousands of rescued dogs and cats in shelters, opponents of breeders maintain that prospective pet owners can be matched with appropriate pets without breeding.

4. Complete the graphic organizer to plan your response. Take approximately 15 minutes to plan your response.

Central Idea:	Explanation:
Restate a Detail:	**Explanation:**
Restate a Detail:	**Explanation:**
Restate a Detail:	**Explanation:**
Restate a Detail:	**Explanation:**
Conclusion:	**Explanation:**

5. Draft a response to the prompt based on the graphic organizer. Take approximately 20 minutes to draft your response based on your planning. Type your answer on a computer to prepare for computer responses. If a computer is unavailable, write your answer on a separate sheet of paper.

6. Evaluate, revise, and edit your response. Make sure your ideas are organized and connected logically. Check your response for errors. Take approximately 10 minutes for this task.

Check **Your Skills**

Use the following passages for exercise 1.

Nuclear power is a necessary part of a clean energy plan to help reduce our dependence on fossil fuels and limit the effects of global climate change. Nuclear power plants do not release carbon dioxide or other pollutants into our atmosphere; they only emit steam. Nuclear energy is the most important source of clean energy available today, producing cheaper energy than wind power, solar power, or coal.

Accidents have happened at nuclear power plants, including the recent disaster at Fukushima, but these incidents are preventable with good oversight, planning, and regulation. The Fukushima power plant began operation in 1971, and newer plants are safer and more reliable. We should not let fear keep us from clean, inexpensive energy that we can produce with today's technology.

Nuclear power is unsafe and a poor investment for our future. In 2011, the Fukushima nuclear plant was hit by a tsunami, and hundreds of thousands of residents were put in danger of radiation exposure and increased cancer risks. This incident shows the dangers of nuclear power to humans and the environment. Massive amounts of radiation were released, and it will take years to clean up the affected water.

Accidents aren't the only danger from nuclear power. Hazardous waste remains radioactive for thousands of years, stored in concrete basins. There is no solution for eliminating this waste except storing it indefinitely. While solar power is fast becoming cheaper and more efficient, nuclear power remains expensive. Cost estimates that suggest nuclear is cheaper leave out expenses such as construction and waste storage. With advancing technology, we have better options than nuclear.

---

 1. The passages present arguments both supporting and opposing nuclear power. In your response, analyze both positions to determine which one is best supported. Use relevant and specific evidence from the passages to support your response.

Take approximately 45 minutes for this task. Type your answer on a computer to prepare for computer responses. If a computer is unavailable, write your answer on a separate sheet of paper.

Use the questions on page 329 to evaluate your response.

Use the following passage for exercise 2.

In the United States, only nine states do not have laws banning text messaging for all drivers. Text message bans are meant to keep drivers from distractions and prevent accidents. However, some people object to the laws as ineffective and unnecessary.

Opponents to cell phone bans note that there are already laws against driver distractions. They recall laws that lowered speed limits to 55 miles per hour to pre-vent accidents. Drivers still sped; in fact, speeding was the norm on many highways. Anti-texting laws will be the same, opponents say. In fact, texting will be more dangerous, because drivers will try to hide their mobile devices, creating more distractions. As evidence, oppo-nents cite a study of insurance claims in four states covering several months before and after a texting-while-driving ban. The study shows that accidents increased by nine percent.

Others dismiss this study, calling for more long-term studies that do not only focus on the first few months of a new regulation. Proponents of laws against texting while driving cite statistical evidence that texting is hazardous while driving. The FCC states that 11% of 18- to 20-year-old drivers who survived car accidents reported that they were sending or receiving texts at the time of the crash. In a survey by the Pew Research Group, 40% of American teens reported being in a car when the driver put people in danger by using a cell phone. A single text message takes the driver's eyes off the road for approximately 4.6 seconds, according to the U.S. Department of Transportation. During that time, a car driving 55 miles per hour will travel the length of a football field.

2. The passage presents arguments both supporting and opposing bans on texting while driving. In your response, analyze both positions to determine which one is best supported. Use relevant and specific evidence from the passages to support your response.

Take approximately 45 minutes for this task. Type your answer on a computer to prepare for computer responses. If a computer is unavailable, write your answer on a separate sheet of paper.

Use the questions on page 329 to evaluate your response.

Use the following passage for exercise 3.

Since New York City's 2013 attempt to limit soda sizes in restaurants to 16 ounces or less, the availability of large soda sizes has become a topic of controversy. Many people objected to the limit as excessive government regulation. Others supported it as an initiative to improve public health.

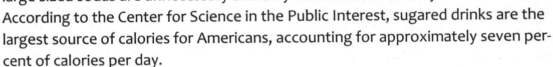

The goal of the ban on large soda sizes was to limit consumption of sugared drinks with little or no nutritional value. Those supporting the ban cite the public health costs of obesity. In 2010, the U.S. Centers for Disease Control (CDC) reported 35.7% obesity among American adults. The estimated health costs related to obesity, including indirect costs, are over $100 billion. Supporters state that large sized sodas are unnecessary and only contribute to obesity. According to the Center for Science in the Public Interest, sugared drinks are the largest source of calories for Americans, accounting for approximately seven percent of calories per day.

Those who oppose a ban on large drinks claim that it is an unnecessary regulation that limits business, interferes with consumers' free choice, and does not attack the root problems of obesity. Some argue that targeting one type of food is unjustified, when no one food causes obesity. Others note that there are no studies on the effectiveness of banning large sugared sodas. Sugared sodas are known to cause weight gain, but the results of regulations and limits on soda sizes are unknown. Since nearly 80% of sugared sodas are sold in stores that wouldn't be affected by a restaurant ban, the regulation would probably not affect the regular soda drinkers who would most benefit from a reduction in sugar intake.

 3. The passage presents arguments both supporting and opposing limits on soda sizes in restaurants. In your response, analyze both positions to determine which one is best supported. Use relevant and specific evidence from the passages to support your response.

Take approximately 45 minutes for this task. Type your answer on a computer to prepare for computer responses. If a computer is unavailable, write your answer on a separate sheet of paper.

Remember the Concept

Plan: Build the Framework

Draft: Construct the Structure

Evaluate: Add the Finishing Touches

Submit

Use the questions on page 329 to evaluate your response.

Practice in Social Studies Writing

Have you ever...

- Used the phrase "all men are created equal"?

- Argued with a friend about whether a new law was constitutional?

- Voted for a presidential candidate?

The U.S. government is built on fundamental principles outlined in the Constitution and other founding documents. The country's founders considered principles such as freedom, equality, representative government, privacy, and justice. Throughout U.S. history, we have debated and changed our ideas about these fundamental and lasting concepts.

Events throughout U.S. history—the Civil War, the American Civil Rights Movement, prohibition, the Great Depression, the internment of Japanese-Americans during World War II—have affected our views of governance. The discussion is not over. Is freedom more important than security? What do we mean by an equal society? What are just punishments? Concepts such as liberty and self-determination have spurred dialogue, change, and even war. The U.S. Constitution addresses these concepts, yet there is still active and passionate discussion about many of these issues today.

Enduring social issues are important to us all. They shape our culture and our laws. This lesson will give you practice thinking and writing about fundamental issues in society and the links between the past and the present.

The Relationship Bridge

The following prompt asks you to do an important task: identify and explain the relationship between two expressions of an enduring issue at different times or places. In your response, you will build a bridge between the two passages.

Develop an argument about how President Bush's speech reflects the enduring issue expressed in the quotation from Nelson Mandela. Incorporate relevant and specific evidence from the quotation, the passage, and your own knowledge to support your analysis. Take approximately 25 minutes for this task.

For to be free is not merely to cast off one's chains, but to live in a way that respects and enhances the freedom of others.

—*Nelson Mandela*

Source: From *Long Walk to Freedom* by Nelson Mandela, 1995

Three weeks ago we celebrated our nation's Independence Day. Today we're here to rejoice in and celebrate another "independence day," one that is long overdue. With today's signing of the landmark Americans with Disabilities Act, every man, woman, and child with a disability can now pass through once-closed doors into a bright new era of equality, independence, and freedom....

This historic act is the world's first comprehensive declaration of equality for people with disabilities—the first. Its passage has made the United States the international leader on this human rights issue.... Our success with this act proves that we are keeping faith with the spirit of our courageous forefathers who wrote in the Declaration of Independence: "We hold these truths to be self-evident, that all men are created equal, that they are endowed by their Creator with certain unalienable rights." These words have been our guide for more than two centuries as we've labored to form our more perfect union. But tragically, for too many Americans, the blessings of liberty have been limited or even denied. The Civil Rights Act of '64 took a bold step towards righting that wrong. But the stark fact remained that people with disabilities were still victims of segregation and discrimination, and this was intolerable. Today's legislation brings us closer to that day when no Americans will ever again be deprived of their basic guarantee of life, liberty, and the pursuit of happiness.

—*President George H.W. Bush, July 26, 1990*

Source: From "Remarks of President George Bush at the Signing of the Americans with Disabilities Act," July 26, 1990, available at http://www.eeoc.gov/eeoc/history/35th/videos/ada_signing_text.html

Plan: Describe the First Passage (2 minutes)

To build a bridge, first build bridge ends. Examine one passage to help you quickly organize your thoughts, especially in a timed exercise. To build the bridge end:

- Read the prompt and the first passage.

- Identify the societal issue in the passage and what you know about the context.

- Summarize the opinion.

1. Identify the issue in the quotation from Nelson Mandela and summarize the opinion.

Bridge End	Connection	Bridge End
Issue:		Issue:
Summary:		Summary:
Context:		Context:

The issue in this quotation is freedom. The opinion is that we should not only be concerned with our own freedom, but with others' freedoms. The clue to the context is its author, Nelson Mandela, who fought against the racial segregation of Apartheid in South Africa.

Plan: Describe the Second Passage (4 minutes)

Repeat the process with the second passage. In this case, the second passage is longer. As you read, write down the quotations from the passage that describe the speaker's perspective well. This will help you build evidence to use in your writing.

2. Identify the issue in the second passage and summarize the opinion.

Bridge End	Connection	Bridge End
Issue: Freedom		Issue:
Summary: We should be concerned with others' freedoms, not just our own.		Summary:
Context: Apartheid		Context:

The context of the passage is the Americans with Disabilities Act. Bush says the ADA enhances freedom by removing discrimination against people with disabilities. You might choose some key quotes: "a bright new era of equality, independence, and freedom;" "first comprehensive declaration of equality for people with disabilities;" "But the stark fact remained that people with disabilities were still victims of segregation and discrimination."

Plan: Your Thesis (4 minutes)

Fill in the connection between the two passages by defining the relationship between the two perspectives. State the relationship in a full sentence that you can use as a thesis.

3. Write your thesis, joining the ideas in the two passages.

Bridge End	Connection	Bridge End
Issue: Freedom Summary: We should be concerned with others' freedoms, not just our own. Context: Apartheid		Issue: Freedom Summary: The ADA enhances freedom by removing discrimination against disabled people. Context: ADA

Your thesis might be, "The Americans with Disabilities Act (ADA), which enhances freedom by removing discrimination against people with disabilities, fulfills Nelson Mandela's vision of finding freedom in ensuring others' freedom."

Draft (10 minutes)

Once you have written your thesis, you are ready to draft. Use your bridge as a reference as you write, incorporating your ideas about each passage to support your thesis. Start with your thesis to write your introduction. Use evidence from each piece of writing in the body. Then end your draft with a clear conclusion.

4. Draft your response.

You might write:

> The Americans with Disabilities Act (ADA), which enhances freedom by removing discrimination against people with disabilities, fulfills Nelson Mandela's vision of finding freedom in ensuring others' freedom. President Bush speaks about ending the "segregation and discrimination" affecting those with disabilities. Mandela's experience was with segregation and discrimination based on race. Both emphasize the need to protect freedom for all in a just society.
>
> President Bush calls the ADA an entrance into "a bright new era of equality for people with disabilities." The means to this equality is ensuring access to education, service, and jobs. The ADA mandates making public services accessible to those with disabilities. This is a mandate for the government to "respect and enhance" the freedom of Americans with disabilities. It levels the playing field so that individuals are not held back by their disabilities, but have the same opportunities as others.
>
> As the "first comprehensive declaration of equality for people with disabilities," the ADA was groundbreaking in providing new freedoms. Similarly, Nelson Mandela broke new ground in South Africa, where black citizens were once limited in where they could live and what they could do. While black South Africans were restricted by unfair laws, Americans with disabilities have historically been restricted by a lack of accessible services. Without a wheelchair ramp, a courthouse or school is inaccessible to someone without use of their legs. In South Africa, unfair laws were removed. In the U.S., the ADA removed barriers by building wheelchair ramps and other adaptations for those with disabilities. Both actions created more individual freedom and opportunity.
>
> Bush clearly connects those with disabilities to other groups who have experienced discrimination: "But the stark fact remained that people with disabilities were still victims of segregation and discrimination." He evokes the same idea of freedom in the quote by Nelson Mandela. Freedom hinges on expanding freedom for all by removing barriers and creating opportunity.

> **The Writing Process**
>
> 💡 **Plan**
>
> Present your thoughts in a logical order. Make connections between your ideas as you write, and never include a quotation without explaining its meaning.

Evaluate and Submit (5 minutes)

In a timed response, be sure that you evaluate your work as you write. Organize your response around a strong central idea, and include specific details. Explain the significance of quotations from the passage. Take a few minutes after you draft to review, revise, and edit your work. When you are satisfied with your response, submit your work.

Practice It!

Use the following passages for exercises 1 and 2.

Develop an argument about how the letter to the editor reflects the enduring issue expressed in the quotation from Benjamin Franklin. Incorporate relevant and specific evidence from the quotation, the passage, and your own knowledge to support your analysis. Take approximately 25 minutes for this task.

They who would give up essential Liberty, to purchase a little temporary Safety, deserve neither Liberty nor Safety.

—*Benjamin Franklin*

Source: From the Pennsylvania Assembly's Reply to the Governor, Nov. 11, 1755, by Benjamin Franklin

---

The U.S. government is taxed with assuring our security, but it is also taxed with securing our liberty. Without personal liberty, security is a burden instead of a boon. The actions of the National Security Agency (NSA) in collecting information about massive numbers of U.S. citizens with only the oversight of secret courts robs us of our liberty and disrupts the difficult balance of liberty and security.

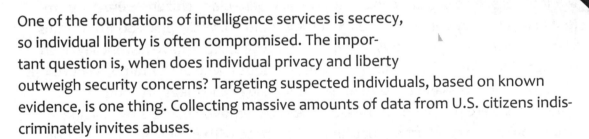

One of the foundations of intelligence services is secrecy, so individual liberty is often compromised. The important question is, when does individual privacy and liberty outweigh security concerns? Targeting suspected individuals, based on known evidence, is one thing. Collecting massive amounts of data from U.S. citizens indiscriminately invites abuses.

How are we to know that this data won't be abused for personal or political reasons? Should we not fear the potential corruption of our government? Data is a powerful tool. Massive, secret data collection is a frightening tool.

Many people fear terrorist attacks in the United States. Fear, though, has never been the basis of good governance. Good governance requires the rational weighing of important goals. It requires establishing a balance of values. We value security and protection. We also value liberty and freedom from unjust prosecution. The massive collection of phone and Internet data does not retain a balance between these values.

—*Lara Conroy, Letter to the Editor*

1. Complete the graphic organizer to summarize each passage and write a thesis.

Bridge End	**Connection**	**Bridge End**
Issue:		Issue:
Summary:		Summary:
Context:		Context:

2. Draft and evaluate a response to the prompt based on the bridge graphic organizer. Use a computer or draft your response in the workbook.

Use the following passages for exercises 3 and 4.

Develop an argument about how the blog post reflects the enduring issue expressed in the quotation from Carl Schurz. Incorporate relevant and specific evidence from the quotation, the passage, and your own knowledge to support your analysis. Take approximately 25 minutes for this task.

The Senator from Wisconsin cannot frighten me by exclaiming, "My country, right or wrong." In one sense I say so too. My country; and my country is the great American Republic. My country, right or wrong; if right, to be kept right; and if wrong, to be set right.

—*Carl Schurz*

Source: From remarks in the U.S. Senate, February 29, 1872, by Carl Schurz

---

I have heard many stories of citizens being harassed for taking cell phone videos of police officers. Recently, only blocks from my apartment, a police officer reportedly took a cell phone from a pedestrian who was filming an arrest. Events like this are worrying to me. Police officers have authority and power, so they should be scrutinized.

On the other hand, some communities are experimenting with filming all police officers on duty by making officers wear body cameras as part of their uniforms. The University of South Florida Department of Criminology and the Orlando Police Department are currently studying the effects of body cameras. Personally, I believe this study will show their value. In discussion groups, police officers I've talked to have applauded the use of body cameras. They believe that cameras integrated into police uniforms will stop many people from false complaints and help police officers avoid violent confrontations. That is one side of the story. If police officers are abusing their powers, cameras should also stop the harassment of undeserving citizens.

None of us wants to be filmed constantly or have our privacy compromised by surveillance. However, filming of on-duty police officers is a different matter. Police officers are public servants performing a public duty. They must be subject to oversight in their work.

—*Antonio Marquez, Blog Post*

3. Complete the graphic organizer to summarize each passage and write a thesis.

Bridge End	**Connection**	**Bridge End**
Issue:		Issue:
Summary:		Summary:
Context:		Context:

4. Draft and evaluate a response to the prompt based on the bridge graphic organizer. Use a computer or draft your response in the workbook.

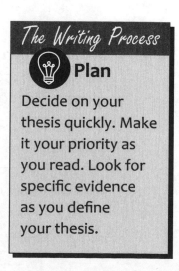

The Writing Process

Plan

Decide on your thesis quickly. Make it your priority as you read. Look for specific evidence as you define your thesis.

Check Your Skills

Use the following passages for exercise 1.

. . . nor shall any person be subject for the same offense to be twice put in jeopardy of life or limb; nor shall be compelled in any criminal case to be a witness against himself, nor be deprived of life, liberty, or property, without due process of law; nor shall private property be taken for public use, without just compensation.

—*Fifth Amendment to the U.S. Constitution*

Source: Bill of Rights, available at http://www.archives.gov/exhibits/charters/bill_of_rights_transcript.html

---

In June 2013, the U.S. Supreme Court ruled that silence could be used to prosecute suspects in a court of law. In the case of Salinas v. Texas, the suspect did not answer whether he thought his shotgun would match the shells from the murder scene. The prosecution used his silence as evidence against him. Suspects in criminal cases must be read their Miranda rights so that they understand their constitutional rights, including the right to remain silent. The Supreme Court ruled that because the defendant "did not expressly invoke" the Fifth Amendment right to remain silent, this right was then void.

In other words, the right to remain silent is only in effect if you state that you are taking advantage of that right (not merely if you remain silent). However, the idea of an inherent right is that you do not have to invoke the right. The right is inalienable—a right that cannot be removed. This Supreme Court ruling takes away the right to remain silent by requiring magic words to activate it. Isn't the right to remain silent simply the right not to speak? If you remain silent, you are invoking that right, whether or not you state it explicitly to the police.

—*Vera Morgan, Letter to the Editor*

---

1. Develop an argument about how the letter to the editor reflects the enduring issue expressed in the quotation from the U.S. Constitution. Incorporate relevant and specific evidence from the quotation, the passage, and your own knowledge to support your analysis.

   Take approximately 25 minutes for this task. Type your answer on a computer to prepare for computer responses. If a computer is unavailable, write your answer on a separate sheet of paper.

Use the questions on page 329 to evaluate your response.

Practice in Social Studies Writing

Use the following passages for exercise 2.

> The one pervading evil of democracy is the tyranny of the majority, or rather of that party, not always the majority, that succeeds, by force or fraud, in carrying elections.
>
> —*Baron John Emerich Edward Acton*

Source: Baron John Emerich Edward Acton, *The History of Freedom and Other Essays*, 1907

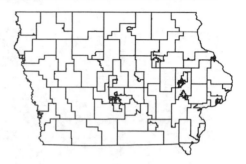

One of the most significant problems facing our society today is fair and representative districting. Democracy only works if our votes are represented. However, in too many states, those in power have drawn boundary lines of districts in order to stay in power.

Someone must draw and approve boundary lines for districts, but any politician doing so faces a conflict of interest. The shape of a politician's district, and the demographics of the people in that district, can dictate whether he or she can win the next election.

The only way to avoid unfair districts is to take districting decisions out of the hands of politicians. In 2010, the state of California created a non-partisan redistricting commission composed of five Democrats, five Republicans, and four members not affiliated with either major party. The commission was given criteria for equitable districts with reasonable geographic boundaries without regard for benefits or costs for incumbent politicians. Redistricting can be difficult, but this non-partisan independent commission is a step in the right direction. All of our states need to follow the path of independent redistricting to assure representation for every citizen. I have come to believe that this is a national problem and should be dealt with on the national level. Too many states will not implement fair redistricting on their own.

—*Elijah Banner, Letter to Senator*

 2. Develop an argument about how the letter reflects the enduring issue expressed in the quotation from Baron Acton. Incorporate relevant and specific evidence from the quotation, the passage, and your own knowledge to support your analysis.

Take approximately 25 minutes for this task. Type your answer on a computer to prepare for computer responses. If a computer is unavailable, write your answer on a separate sheet of paper.

Use the questions on page 329 to evaluate your response.

Use the following passages for exercise 3.

We are now forming a republican government. Real liberty is neither found in despotism or the extremes of democracy, but in moderate governments.

—*Alexander Hamilton*

Source: Alexander Hamilton, debates of the Federal Convention, June 26, 1787

The electoral college is an outdated feature of our democracy. No one goes into a voting booth to vote for an electoral college representative. We vote for the presidential candidates. Shouldn't our votes count, one for one across the nation, in the election of our president?

The debate over the electoral college often focuses on the 2000 presidential election. Democratic candidate Al Gore won the popular vote by over 500,000 votes. However, because of the electoral college system, the election went to Republican candidate George W. Bush. Each state sends representatives to the electoral college based on the election outcome in that state. This makes it possible for a candidate to win the popular vote and lose the election. While some consider this result to be a fluke, it happened. It could happen again, by a larger margin. Our democracy should count each voice, not each state.

Isn't it more democratic to vote directly for presidential candidates? Why should our federal government depend on a state-by-state count of electoral college representatives? It's time to do away with the electoral college.

—*George Olsen, Blog Post*

---

 3. Develop an argument about how the blog post reflects the enduring issue expressed in the quotation from Alexander Hamilton. Incorporate relevant and specific evidence from the quotation, the passage, and your own knowledge to support your analysis.

Take approximately 25 minutes for this task. Type your answer on a computer to prepare for computer responses. If a computer is unavailable, write your answer on a separate sheet of paper.

> *Remember the Concept*
>
> Create a Relationship Bridge to define the relationship between two passages.

Use the questions on page 329 to evaluate your response.

Practice in Science Writing

Connections

Have you ever...

- Voted on an issue involving science?

- Explained a new scientific study to a friend?

- Given a relative advice about how to deal with an illness or injury?

Developing the ability to comprehend and write about scientific subjects will benefit you in your life, your career, and your academic progress. From choosing a water filter to finding out information on health problems, you deal with science every day. Many careers and areas of study also deal with scientific topics. Health care deals with biology, physiology, and pharmaceutical research. Law enforcement deals with sociology, psychology, and public policy studies.

You will need to read and respond to scientific texts. You will also need to understand and design scientific experiments. When you write about scientific topics, you will show:

- Your ability to apply scientific knowledge to new situations.

- Your ability to comprehend new scientific information.

- Your existing knowledge of fundamental scientific concepts.

Responding to a Science Prompt

A science prompt will ask you to do a specific writing task, such as designing an experiment, evaluating an experiment, describing scientific knowledge, or applying a scientific principle.

Respond to the following scientific passage and prompt.

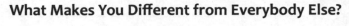

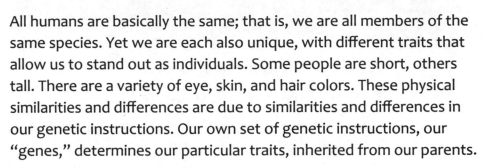

What Makes You Different from Everybody Else?

All humans are basically the same; that is, we are all members of the same species. Yet we are each also unique, with different traits that allow us to stand out as individuals. Some people are short, others tall. There are a variety of eye, skin, and hair colors. These physical similarities and differences are due to similarities and differences in our genetic instructions. Our own set of genetic instructions, our "genes," determines our particular traits, inherited from our parents.

Genes come in the form of DNA (deoxyribonucleic acid), a long, thread-like molecule that carries within its coil all of our genetic information. A genome is all of a living organism's DNA. It is the complete set of genetic instructions for building, running, and maintaining that organism. Virtually every single cell in the body carries a complete copy of all the DNA that makes up the genome.

All living things, from bacteria to plants to animals, have genomes, and every species has its own genome. Simple organisms, such as bacteria, have small genomes with several hundred to several thousand genes in them. By contrast, humans have a relatively large genome with about 30,000 genes. In any two humans, 99.9% of their DNA is identical. However, the entire set of genetic instructions is so large that the 0.1% variation allows for millions of possible differences. This tiny fraction of DNA where variations occur leads to the enormous diversity that makes each of us unique. Yet, the same variation that causes differences in our appearance also leads to differences in our likelihood of getting any particular disease. Knowledge about the effects of DNA variation between individuals can lead to better understanding of diseases and to advances in medicine.

Source: National Human Genome Research Institute, adapted from "From the Blueprint to You: A Brief Guide to Genetics," available at http://www.genome.gov/Pages/Education/Modules/BluePrintToYou/BlueprintCover02.pdf

The passage explains DNA variations in humans. When animals are bred, breeders choose to mate animals with particular traits so that their offspring inherit the desired traits. Explain the role of DNA variation in breeding. Take approximately 10 minutes for this task.

Plan: Identify the Task (1 minute)

Identify the task in the text and the prompt:

- Do you need to design an experiment?

- Do you need to apply information in the text to a new situation?

- Do you need to describe scientific knowledge?

? **1.** Identify the task from the prompt and passage.

The task is to apply information in the text to a new situation. The text gives you information about variations in DNA, specifically human DNA. The prompt asks you to apply that information to animal breeding.

Plan: Outline Central Idea and Details (2 minutes)

Identify a central idea immediately. Make a brief outline of details and a conclusion to support your central idea.

? **2.** Outline the central idea and details.

Central Idea:
Detail:
Detail:
Detail:
Detail:
Conclusion:

You might write the following outline:

Central Idea: DNA variation creates the variation in traits that allows breeders to choose animals to breed.
Detail: Most of the DNA of any species is the same and will be inherited from any parents of that species.
Detail: When breeders choose animals with specific traits, those traits are controlled by DNA.
Detail: The DNA variation in the parents is inherited by the children.
Detail: Because the children inherit the DNA variation, they also inherit the trait.
Conclusion: Without DNA variation within a species, breeding would not be possible.

Draft: Expand the Central Idea and Details (5 minutes)

Expand on the central idea, details, and conclusion in your outline. Add transitions and additional information to clarify your ideas and create fluid writing.

3. Draft your response.

You might write:

> DNA variation is the difference in DNA molecules from one individual to the next in a species. Because DNA controls inherited traits, DNA variation creates the varied traits that allow breeders to select animals to breed. Most of the DNA of any species is the same and will be inherited from any parents of that species. This portion of the DNA does not affect selective breeding. When breeders choose animals with specific traits, the DNA variation controlling those traits in the parents is inherited by the children, so the trait is also inherited. Without DNA variation within a species, breeding for specific traits would not be possible.

 ## Evaluate and Submit (2 minutes)

In a timed response, evaluate your work as you plan and write. Be sure that your response answers the prompt and has good content. Take a few minutes after you draft to review, revise, and edit your work. When you are satisfied with your response, submit your work.

Understanding Science Experiments

Understanding science experiments is crucial to developing science writing content.

Make a **hypothesis,** a proposed idea.	A black car's interior will heat quickly in the sun, because black absorbs the most light.
Identify an **independent variable** that you will change.	The color of the car is the independent variable.
Identify a **dependent variable** that you expect to change.	The heat inside the car is the dependent variable.
Identify a **control group** to verify how your variable is affecting results.	The control group can be blue cars and white cars.
Identify **constants** that remain the same so they don't affect results.	Constants would be the year and model of car, amount of sun, time in the sun, and type of pavement.
Include multiple trials.	You might plan to have 10 white cars, 10 black cars, and 10 blue cars.
Measure the dependent variable.	You might plan to put a thermometer in each car and record the temperature every 10 minutes.
Evaluate the data.	Did the black car heat more and faster than the other cars, as expected? Is there anything unexpected? What do you conclude about the hypothesis?
Plan next steps.	Based on the results, what new hypothesis can you make? What other experiments would you perform?

Practice It!

Use the following passage and prompt for exercises 1 and 2.

A large number of trees in a forest have died because of a beetle infestation. The owners of a nearby apple orchard are concerned that the beetles might infest their trees as well. A local scientist hypothesizes that the beetle infestations will not affect the orchard, since she believes the beetles will only infest specific types of trees.

Design a controlled experiment to test whether the beetles will attack the apple orchard. Include descriptions of data collection and how the scientist can determine whether her hypothesis is correct. Take approximately 10 minutes for this task.

 1. Complete the graphic organizer to outline your response.

Central Idea:
Detail:
Detail:
Detail:
Detail:
Conclusion:

 2. Draft and evaluate a response to the prompt based on the graphic organizer. Use a computer or write your response on a separate sheet of paper.

Use the following passage and prompt for exercises 3 and 4.

The box and whisker plot shows rainfall for the months of May through August in the town of East Harkinson. This year, East Harkinson received 4.26 inches of rain in May, 2.12 inches in June, 0.18 inches in July, and 3.14 inches in August.

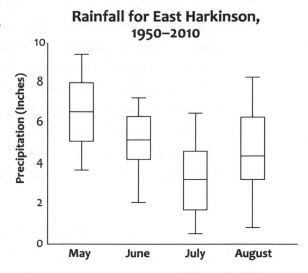

Rainfall for East Harkinson, 1950–2010

Based on the box and whisker plot, how would you characterize this year's rainfall for the town of East Harkinson? How does it compare to past years? Take approximately 10 minutes for this task.

3. Complete the graphic organizer to outline your response.

Box Plots

Central Idea:
Detail:
Detail:
Detail:
Detail:
Conclusion:

4. Draft and evaluate a response to the prompt based on the graphic organizer. Use a computer or write your response on a separate sheet of paper.

Use the following passage and prompt for exercises 5 and 6.

Clem bought a pack of generic batteries. He put one in his remote control and another in his hand-held mixer. A few weeks later, the remote and the mixer both died. Clem hypothesized that the generic batteries are a poor brand and don't last. He bought three more packs of batteries: one pack of the generic brand and one pack each of two major name brand batteries. How could Clem test his hypothesis?

Design a controlled experiment to test Clem's hypothesis about the generic brand's longevity. Include descriptions of data collection and how Clem can determine whether his hypothesis is correct. Take approximately 10 minutes for this task.

 5. Complete the graphic organizer to outline your response.

Central Idea:
Detail:
Detail:
Detail:
Detail:
Conclusion:

 6. Draft and evaluate a response to the prompt based on the graphic organizer. Use a computer or write your response on a separate sheet of paper.

Use the following passage and prompt for exercises 7 and 8.

A scientist hypothesized that increased runoff of Chemical A into Briar Lake had increased the presence of Bacteria B. The scientist performed a study to measure the amount of the chemical and the bacteria in Briar Lake and nearby Carson Lake, which lacks chemical runoff. The study had the following results.

Location	Chemical A	Bacteria B
Briar Lake—Site 1	1.02 mg per 100 mL	402 per 100 mL
Briar Lake—Site 2	2.59 mg per 100 mL	395 per 100 mL
Carson Lake—Site 1	0.12 mg per 100 mL	87 per 100 mL
Carson Lake—Site 2	0.01 mg per 100 mL	89 per 100 mL

The passage describes the results of a study. Describe your conclusions based on the results. Is the hypothesis correct or incorrect? What next steps would you take based on this study? Take approximately 10 minutes for this task.

7. Complete the graphic organizer to outline your response.

Central Idea:
Detail:
Detail:
Detail:
Detail:
Conclusion:

8. Draft and evaluate a response to the prompt based on the graphic organizer. Use a computer or write your response on a separate sheet of paper.

Check **Your Skills**

Use the following passage for exercise 1.

The biology department at a local university is evaluating their undergraduate general education coursework. The histogram shows the distributions of student grades in Biology 101. The department wants to raise grades without reducing the educational value or standards of the course. The department decides that identifying effective new teaching methods is the best course.

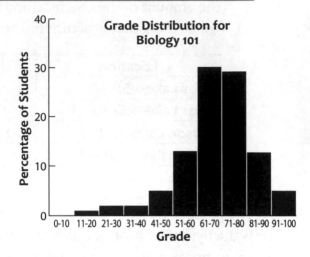

One teacher proposes that group work will improve grades. He proposes that students should spend 30% of class time working together in groups on specific biology projects aligned to the curriculum. Another teacher proposes that replacing lectures with Socratic questioning will be effective. She proposes that teachers should spend 30% of class time using Socratic questioning.

The department hypothesizes that either method will increase student performance compared to current teaching methods.

---

1. Design a controlled experiment that the department can use to test this hypothesis. Include descriptions of data collection and how the department can determine whether the hypothesis is correct.

Take approximately 10 minutes for this task. Write your response below or type your response on a computer.

Use the questions on page 329 to evaluate your response.

Use the following passage for exercise 2.

What causes surface tension on water? The answer is the force that binds water molecules together. Inside the water, a molecule binds to other molecules on every side. On the surface of the water, however, the water molecules are not completely surrounded. Because there are no water molecules above them, the water molecules at the surface bind more strongly to the molecules beside them. This creates a strong barrier of tightly bound molecules at the surface of the water. Sometimes people think of surface tension as a "film" at the surface of the water, but the surface of the water is not made of a different substance than any other part of the water. The molecules are simply more tightly bound together.

Water's Surface

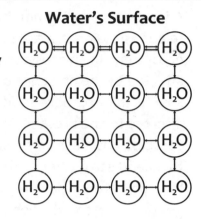

2. The passage explains surface tension on water. Based on the passage, explain how surface tension helps water striders and other small, light insects move and stand on the water's surface.

   Take approximately 10 minutes for this task. Write your response below or type your response on a computer.

Use the questions on page 329 to evaluate your response.

Use the following passage for exercise 3.

A food web is a diagram that shows the food relationships of animals and plants in an ecosystem. In an ecosystem, organisms are affected by the presence or absence of their food source. In turn, those food-source organisms are affected by the presence or absence of their food sources. This diagram shows a simplified food web for a land ecosystem. In this diagram, lions are top-level predators. They prey on wild cats, jackals, and goats. Therefore, the lions depend on wild cats, jackals, and goats. A lack of prey would impact the lion population. Similarly, the wild cats, jackals, and goats depend on their food sources: mice, rabbits, and plants.

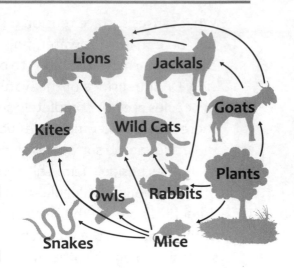

 3. Based on the passage and diagram, what would happen to this ecosystem if a deadly disease wiped out most of the mouse population?

Take approximately 10 minutes for this task. Write your response below or type your response on a computer.

> ### Remember the Concept
>
> To respond to science prompts:
>
> - **Plan:** Identify the task.
>
> - **Plan:** Outline central ideas and details.
>
> - **Draft:** Expand the central ideas and details.
>
> - **Evaluate:** Check for strong content and clear communication.

Use the questions on page 329 to evaluate your response.

Self-Evaluation of Your Writing

Evaluating your writing is an important skill. Use the following questions to rate your writing and identify problems. The more you practice the writing process and evaluate your results, the more your writing will improve. When you use the following questions, try to identify specific examples from your writing that show your writing's strengths and weaknesses.

You may make copies of this section to evaluate multiple writing assignments. Not every question will apply to every task, so you may skip evaluation questions that are not appropriate to the assignment. Average the scores for each question to rate your response as (3) excellent, (2) acceptable, or (1) not acceptable.

When you receive feedback from an instructor, compare the feedback to your self-evaluation. This will help you learn to evaluate your writing more effectively.

Creation of Arguments and Use of Evidence

1. How well do you create original logical arguments and set up a central idea or purpose that is connected to the prompt?

    (3) Exceptionally Well: The purpose is focused and clearly connected to the prompt.

    (2) Somewhat/Sometimes Well: The argument may stray from the purpose at times but typically shows some connection to the prompt.

    (1) Not Well: An argument may be present but lacks purpose or does not connect to the prompt.

2. How well does your writing use relevant and specific evidence?

    (3) Exceptionally Well: Evidence and explanations are specific and directly support the purpose. Evidence is from a reliable source.

    (2) Somewhat/Sometimes Well: Evidence may be loosely related or not relevant at times. More evidence may be needed.

    (1) Not Well: Evidence is lacking or does not come from a reliable source.

3. How well does your response evaluate the arguments in the passage?

    (3) Exceptionally Well: The response thoroughly analyzes the arguments in a passage. This includes evaluating claims, identifying assumptions or logical fallacies, and determining the credibility of sources.

    (2) Somewhat/Sometimes Well: The response partially analyzes the arguments and issues in the source text. Analysis may be too basic, limited, or include inaccuracies.

    (1) Not Well: The response minimally analyzes the issue or the argument presented in the source text. The response may completely lack analysis or show no understanding of the argument.

4. How could you improve in this category?

Development of Ideas and Organizational Structure

1. How well does your writing logically develop ideas and elaborate your central ideas with relevant details?

    (3) Exceptionally Well: Ideas are well developed and easy to follow. Most ideas are explained and supported.

    (2) Somewhat/Sometimes Well: Some ideas are not fully developed or are vague.

    (1) Not Well: Some ideas are not sufficiently developed or do not completely make sense. There is little elaboration of central or supporting ideas.

2. How well does your writing create a progression of ideas from one to the other that ties details to your central idea?

    (3) Exceptionally Well: The ideas progress in a way that makes sense. There is a clear connection between the main points and details that further develop them.

    (2) Somewhat/Sometimes Well: The ideas progress but details may be disorganized or fail to connect to supporting ideas or the central idea.

    (1) Not Well: The ideas are undeveloped or fail to make sense. There is little to no elaboration of ideas.

3. How well does your writing present a clear organizational structure that supports your purpose?

    (3) Exceptionally Well: The writing is organized in a way that shows the message and purpose. The writing uses effective transitions.

    (2) Somewhat/Sometimes Well: The organization of the writing is inconsistent or only partially effective. Transitions are used inconsistently.

    (1) Not Well: The writing has no clear organization and lacks effective transitions.

4. How well does your writing establish a style and tone that is appropriate to its intended audience and purpose?

    (3) Exceptionally Well: The writing uses a formal style and tone that shows awareness of the audience and purpose of the task.

    (2) Somewhat/Sometimes Well: The writing uses an inconsistent formal style and tone that shows awareness of audience or purpose.

    (1) Not Well: The writing uses an ineffective or inappropriate tone that demonstrates limited or no awareness of audience or purpose.

5. How well do you choose words and use a strong vocabulary?

    (3) Exceptionally Well: The writing includes specific, well-chosen words that help express ideas.

    (2) Somewhat/Sometimes Well: The writing may occasionally include misused words or words that vaguely express ideas.

    (1) Not Well: The writing includes frequent misused words, slang, or vague or repetitive language.

6. How could you improve in this category?

Clarity and Command of Standard English Conventions

1. How well does your writing apply the following: good spelling, correct subject-verb agreement, correct pronoun use, good use of modifiers and word order, correct capitalization, correct use of apostrophes, and correct use of punctuation?

    (3) Exceptionally Well: The writing correctly uses the above conventions.

    (2) Somewhat/Sometimes Well: There may be some misuse of the above conventions.

    (1) Not Well: There are many errors in the above conventions.

2. How well does your writing apply the following: correct clauses and parallel structure, good phrasing without awkwardness or wordiness, good transitions, correct sentence structures without run-ons and fragments, and good word usage?

    (3) Exceptionally Well: The writing shows correct use of sentence structure and flows together.

    (2) Somewhat/Sometimes Well: There may be some awkward sentences that make the meaning unclear. The writing flows well in places.

    (1) Not Well: Sentences are consistently awkward, choppy, repetitive, or rambling, and the meaning is unclear.

3. How well does your writing avoid errors in mechanics and conventions?

    (3) Exceptionally Well: There may be minor errors that do not interfere with understanding.

    (2) Somewhat/Sometimes Well: There may be many errors in mechanics and conventions that occasionally affect understanding.

    (1) Not Well: The writing does not demonstrate understanding of conventions and usage of language.

4. How could you improve in this category?

Answers and Explanations

This section provides answers and explanations for this workbook, including sample responses to prompts. There are many ways to approach writing tasks. The answers here provide examples of effective responses. Keep in mind that strong arguments can be made for either side of debated issues. Some explanations include examples of ineffective responses, which you can use to practice revision. Use these samples along with the self-evaluation questions in this workbook to help you evaluate and improve your writing.

The Writing Process — page 3

Plan, Draft, Evaluate — page 5

Plan, Draft, and Evaluate Your Writing

Practice It! — pages 8–10

1. Since the topic is likely unfamiliar, the best way for Sharon to begin planning is to read and research. While reading, she can brainstorm, take and organize notes, ask questions, and focus on a specific central idea. Once she has preliminary planning completed, she can brainstorm again and organize her ideas.

2. A topic that is too general often results in poor writing. Narrowing the focus to a specific central idea is an important part of planning, drafting, and evaluating. To decide on a central idea, Andrew can research the U.S. Congress, look at news articles, and read about historical topics. Andrew can make notes about interesting ideas and do some preliminary research to make sure he has access to enough information about the potential topics. Then, he needs to decide which idea is most interesting and best suited to writing a paper.

3a. Before Ralph begins writing, he should think about the information he has about his department's productivity. Does he need to do additional research? What is the best way to organize the report? What information does he need to cover? What kind of introduction and conclusion does he need?

3b. Ralph can draft an outline of his report and determine what sections he needs to write. He can organize his notes into sections and then use the outline and notes to write his draft.

3c. Ralph can evaluate his writing by reviewing his draft and making sure it is organized well and makes sense. He might ask, does it give enough information? Is the information easy to understand? Are the conclusions well supported? Does the report make reasonable suggestions?

4a. Mauricio is in the planning stage of the writing process. He has found some books and has brainstormed information he knows. He still needs to complete the planning stage before writing.

4b. A good way for Mauricio to proceed would be to read and research more information about submarines. He will need to take notes, ask questions, think about the information, and determine his central idea. Once he has a clear, focused central idea, he can organize his notes to prepare for drafting.

5a. The purpose is to show that you can clearly explain possible advantages of predicting solar flares based on the passage. No audience is specified, so the audience is an instructor or reader who will evaluate your writing. You can identify the effects of solar flares from the passage. Predicting solar flares will help with predicting these effects.

5b. You might write:

Predicting solar flares can provide benefits for government and business. Since long-distance radio signals are affected by solar flares, forewarning could allow radio broadcasters to prepare for interruptions. Satellite orbits are also vulnerable to solar flares. Predicting their occurrence could help NASA and other space agencies to correct satellite orbits and minimize damage. Solar flare prediction would help both business and government to be prepared. Innovators might even find ways to make solar flares beneficial by utilizing their effects.

5c. Evaluate your paragraph's organization, central idea, supporting details, and conclusion. Make sure your paragraph is clear and easy to understand.

6. Revising your work as you evaluate it might involve reorganizing, adding details, rewriting sentences or paragraphs for clarity, or adding explanations to connect ideas to the central idea. Depending on your task, you could completely rewrite your work. On the other hand, proofreading work when you are finalizing it is a smaller task. You might format your work, correct small spelling or grammar errors, or make minor changes to add clarity. The major revisions should be done when you draft and evaluate, before you are ready for final proofreading.

7a. The purpose is to critique an argument. Since no audience is specified, you will want to show your ability to evaluate and analyze the argument, showing both its good points and its problems. You might plan to identify the writer's specific arguments and evaluate their strengths and weaknesses.

7b. You might write:

The author's argument in favor of closing Bradley Branch Library is coherent but weak. The author argues that library services are being replaced by Internet services. While many resources are available over the Internet, libraries provide free access to books, magazines, and little-used research materials difficult to find elsewhere. Only limited books are available online without costs. Modern libraries also provide free access to the Internet, in order to assure that online resources are available across the community. The author "doubts" that the library is busy, showing that he or she is merely speculating. The author also says that patrons can travel to another branch, but the author does not acknowledge that residents with limited transportation who can benefit most from a local library might find traveling difficult. Overall, the author would benefit from additional research regarding the library's offerings and uses.

7c. Evaluate your paragraph's organization, central idea, supporting details, and conclusion. Make sure it is clear and easy to understand.

8. If you were writing a blog post about a recipe, you might plan your post by outlining the recipe, taking photos, making the recipe to test it, and brainstorming ideas for your introduction and conclusion. You could draft the post based on your planning and then evaluate it to make sure the recipe is clear and easy to follow. You also might want to evaluate whether your post is interesting for readers. Once your post is finalized, you can publish it to your blog.

Check Your Skills *pages 11–12*

1. The following is an example of an **effective** response. It includes specific details, follows a logical order, and has an introduction and conclusion.

Lee is experiencing a common problem among writers. Instead of fully utilizing the writing process, he focuses primarily on drafting. The result is writing that lacks content and is not thoughtfully crafted. Lee should begin by planning his writing, instead of jumping into the drafting stage. In the planning stage, Lee can research information about building a shed, as well as drawing from his own knowledge to brainstorm ideas. He should identify a focused central idea to help him organize his writing and create a strong introduction. He can organize his prewriting into an outline to help him write his first draft. As he plans and drafts, Lee should evaluate his work for clarity and good organization. He should also evaluate his work after he drafts. This evaluation may lead to a need for more planning and drafting as he revises and edits the blog post. When Lee reaches a point where his writing is finished, it is time for him to submit the post. He should complete one last review to correct any errors and improve the formatting, and then he can publish the post on his blog. A blog allows Lee to continue to revise his work, respond to others' comments, and write follow-up posts, so Lee might choose to continue the writing process even after his blog post is published.

The following is an example of an **ineffective** response. It contains some language errors, such as inconsistent verb tense, vague ideas, and repetition. Get some extra practice by revising the following response.

The writing process can help Lee write a better blog post. First, he can start with planning. When he skipped the planning stage, he ran out of ideas. During planning, he could brainstorm ideas for the body, introduction, and conclusion. Lee went straight to the drafting stage. Lee should not draft first. Drafting is a wrong way to start. If Lee started with planning, drafting will be easier. He can plan information, which he will use for drafting. As Lee writes and after he writes, he should evaluate his writing. This would give him ideas for revising. When he is satisfied with his blog post, he can submit the post.

2. The following is an example of an **effective** response. It clearly summarizes the argument in the passage and evaluates it using specific evidence.

The 1875 Supreme Court of Wisconsin had a misguided view of women. Its argument against allowing women to practice law in the court was that women must be protected and not exposed to real-world problems. However, women live in the real world. Duer Miller makes this point by noting that the court mentioned three crimes against women as too horrific for female lawyers to address. If a woman is abused or raped, should it fall to only men to decide on the consequences of that crime? If a woman is victimized, is it "reverence" and "faith" to stop women from talking about that crime? Women should be allowed to advocate for better treatment of women. Disallowing women from the courtroom by "protecting" them means that women receive no voice in crimes committed against them. Duer Miller's argument is compelling and convincing.

The following is an example of an **ineffective** response. The writer's reasoning is unclear and lacking specifics. Get some extra practice by revising the following response to better support its position.

Duer Miller's implied argument is that the Supreme Court demeaned women by trying to protect them. This is a poor argument in favor of women being able to argue in front of the court. The Supreme Court of Wisconsin ruled that women could not practice law in front of the court, so that is their ruling. Since this is a Supreme Court ruling, it was a good argument. Women don't have to argue in front of a court. That is a way that women don't always have to have the same jobs as men. It doesn't mean women aren't as good as men, the court respects them. Overall, Duer Miller's argument is not convincing.

Focus: Plan   *page 13*

Determining Purpose and Audience   *page 15*

KEYS to Purpose and Audience

Practice It!   *pages 18–20*

1. c. To persuade

2. d. All of the above

   All this information might affect voters' opinions about the proposition. The more relevant information the author knows about the audience, the better the author can persuade the audience.

3. You might want to know how your friends feel about painting or art. You might want to know your friends' schedules and possible objections to the project.

4. Knowing more about your audience can improve persuasive writing by allowing you to address your audience's concerns and appeal to your audience's values and beliefs.

5. The purpose is to persuade. You want to persuade your superiors that you have improved and therefore deserve a raise.

6. Your audience knows obvious aspects of your job performance, such as what projects you have been assigned. Your audience knows you personally and will be familiar with any aspects of your work that the company tracks. For example, your superiors might know how many clients you've signed or how many calls you've taken.

7. Your audience expects you to detail ways that your work performance has improved. Your audience also expects you to make a persuasive argument about why you deserve a raise.

8. You share knowledge of the workplace and company with your audience. You likely share common workplace experiences.

9. Your purpose is to persuade your superiors that you have shown improvement in your job performance over the last year and deserve a raise. Your audience is a boss or group of superiors who are judges of your work and who have knowledge of you as an employee, as well as knowledge of your workplace.

10. This is a formal, persuasive writing task. A good approach might be to brainstorm accomplishments over the last year. You can also compare your work performance from a year ago to your current performance. Your writing should include specific examples of how you have improved and helped the company.

11. You might write:

    Over the last three years, I have only had one 2% raise. The increase in salary was not enough to keep up with inflation. During my time here, I have become a valuable asset to the firm. Just last week, two clients went to the trouble of sending in emails praising my work and how much I have helped them. I am more knowledgeable about our products than anyone else in my department. As my yearly review approaches, I believe it is time that I receive a significant raise for my valuable work.

12. You might write:

    I was incredibly nervous to ask my supervisor for a raise. On the other hand, I knew that I deserved more money for everything that I do. I decided to write her an email, so that I could express myself thoughtfully. Believe me, I went over every word carefully. I couldn't believe how positive her response was! I will be meeting with her tomorrow to discuss the specifics, but I'm definitely getting that long-overdue raise.

13. Because the purpose differs, you will include different information in your writing. The persuasive paragraph will include a central idea about a raise and arguments that support that central idea. The narrative paragraph will tell about events and emotions. The audience also affects your writing. A paragraph to your supervisor will be more formal and businesslike. A paragraph to your friends will be more familiar. It can be informal and even humorous.

14a. Responses will vary. An example of an everyday audience might be a boss, client, or family member. That person will likely know about your personality and shared experiences.

14b. Responses will vary. The expectations of your everyday audience will depend on the context of your writing. A workplace audience will expect businesslike correspondence. A family member or friend will expect informal, friendly correspondence.

14c. Responses will vary. A workplace audience will share knowledge of your company and your work, as well as experiences that you have shared. A family member or friend will share common experiences and personal knowledge.

IMPACT for Writing Requirements

Practice It!   pages 23–24

1. Keywords include "explaining," "should or should not," "USPS," "reduce," "service," "take a stand," "three paragraphs," "advantages," "disadvantages," "recommendations," "impact," "rural," and "urban."

2a. For this prompt, you should:
- Explain why the USPS should or should not reduce delivery services to five days.
- Write at least three paragraphs.
- Include advantages and disadvantages of your recommendation.
- Explain the impact on rural and urban customers.

2b. Verbs are action words. When a prompt tells you what to do, it typically uses a verb to describe the action you should take. Verbs in the prompt that describe what you should do are "explain," "write," and "include."

3. You might argue in favor of five-day mail delivery, focusing on the effects of less mail delivery. You could argue that access to email, text messaging, and other forms of communication lessen the need for Saturday mail delivery.

   You might argue in favor of five-day mail delivery service focusing on the cost savings to the post office and organizing your writing in a problem-solution format.

4. You might choose the first idea because you could apply the argument to urban and rural customers. You might note that you would need to mention advantages and disadvantages. Cost savings is one advantage, and a disadvantage might be loss of service to people with less access to technology.

5. You might write:

   The USPS should reduce mail delivery to five days a week, eliminating Saturday delivery. No one truly relies on Saturday delivery anymore. Most non-retail businesses are closed, and individuals have many options for communication in our modern, technological society.

   Technology is supplanting the need for daily mail delivery. Email, text messaging, wireless phone service, and wireless Internet mean that important messages can be sent quickly and easily, without a stamp. Urban areas have significant access to new technology, and although some rural areas only have limited access to broadband Internet, the impact of reduced mail service should be minimal.

   The main advantage of eliminating Saturday mail delivery is reduced cost. The postal service can use this savings to improve other services. Some politicians have suggested that the USPS could offer basic local banking services to benefit the poor. This would help lower-class urban and rural residences more than an extra day of mail delivery. The disadvantages are minimal. Some personal and work deadlines may be more difficult to meet, such as getting an important package to a printer or delivering a birthday present on time. However, private delivery services do provide weekend deliveries for an extra fee. Occasional important deadlines could still be met.

   The idea of Saturday mail delivery is archaic. No one needs to receive bills and junk mail during the weekend, a time when most businesses are closed. Other, more efficient forms of communication are available, so it is natural that we no longer need the same mail services. A five-day delivery schedule will create a more efficient postal service.

Check Your Skills   *pages 25–26*

1a. The purpose of this persuasive writing task is to write an essay to persuade the scholarship board that you deserve a $1,500 scholarship. The audience is the scholarship board. This is a formal purpose and audience. The scholarship board does not know you, so part of the purpose is to introduce yourself, your accomplishments, and your goals. The board will expect an argument that shows how a $1,500 scholarship would be a good investment in your future.

1b. The prompt asks you to write an essay, describe your accomplishments and goals, and explain how a $1,500 scholarship would help you reach those goals. The response should be a persuasive essay that focuses on your positive accomplishments.

1c. The following is an example of an **effective** response. It clearly communicates the writer's accomplishments, goals, and reasons for deserving the scholarship.

I have been interested in studying the human brain since I was 16 years old. My grandmother was diagnosed with Alzheimer's disease at that time, and I helped care for her as she lost her grasp on the world around her. My grandmother was a significant influence on me as a child. Before she was affected by Alzheimer's disease, she often told stories of her work as a nurse and encouraged me to study medicine. In her honor, I hope to earn a degree in neurology and work to help others who suffer from dementia. A $1,500 scholarship would help me take my first step toward a premed degree and, eventually, a medical degree that would allow me to study degenerative brain disease.

My grandmother's illness threw our family into disarray. Soon, she needed 24-hour care, and some of that responsibility fell to me as a teenager. My high school studies floundered, and eventually I dropped out of school. However, the hours of caring for my grandmother gave me insight into the amount of suffering dementia can cause. After my grandmother passed away, I earned a high school diploma and started volunteering part-time in a local nursing home. My volunteer work has exposed me to many cases of dementia. I am able to talk to doctors and nurses about the effects of and treatments for brain diseases. The more I learn, the more interested I become in finding ways to prevent brain degeneration.

Recently, I have been accepted to Henley Community College. A $1,500 scholarship will allow me to complete my general education and transfer to a four-year college, where I can continue my premed degree. The journey to a medical degree is long, but I am committed to help those, like my grandmother, who suffer from degenerative diseases.

The following is an example of an **ineffective** response. It does not clearly address the purpose and is inappropriate for the audience.

I want to become a doctor, and I am already accepted into a community college. My grandmother was diagnosed with Alzheimer's disease when I was 16 years old, and I cared for her while she became ill. That was a terrible time. It's the reason I never finished high school. She was once a nurse, and I want to follow in her footsteps and become a doctor. I currently work in a nursing home as a volunteer, and I see many cases of dementia. I talk to the doctors and nurses about it all the time. It's very interesting, even though it is also sad. It's clear to me that Alzheimer's disease, which is linked to plaque forming in the brain, is a disease that should be both preventable and treatable. Advances are made in the field all the time. I need to do a lot more study, but when I have the necessary background, I know I can make a difference in studying dementia. In any case, that's what I want to do eventually. I will continue to work in the nursing home for now, while I attend community college.

2a. The purpose of this task is to show your understanding of an important historic event and its effects on today's world. The audience is a teacher or evaluator who will judge your ability to describe a historic event and its ramifications in today's world. The reader will be knowledgeable and able to evaluate your critical thinking about a historic event.

2b. You might decide to discuss the modern-day effects of the Wright brothers' first flight. This is a historic event with clear modern-day consequences. The task is informational and analytical, and a cause-and-effect structure with chronological description of the development of the aviation industry would likely be effective.

2c. The following is an example of an **effective** response. It draws connections between a historic event and modern-day consequences.

Just last week, a client flew to our Los Angeles office from New York to discuss a new project. Because we were able to meet in person, we made an effective start on a complex task. An important historic event made this moment possible. The Wright brothers' first flight in 1903 has led, in just over 100 years, to accessible worldwide travel that has changed the way we fight wars, do business, and think about the world.

At Kitty Hawk in 1903, the Wright brothers flew for 12 seconds over a distance of 120 feet. In less than five years, they had developed a practical fixed-wing plane. By 1911, military aircraft were being used for bombing and aerial photography. Aircraft technology quickly developed, and by World War I, the Red Baron was impressing pilots with his flying expertise. By the time World War II began, airplanes were an essential part of war. After World War II, commercial aviation had its start. For the first time, people and cargo could be transported quickly and easily across vast distances.

Air travel is something modern people tend to take for granted. It takes only about eight hours to fly across the United States or from London to New York. International corporations use modern flight for cargo and communications. Delivery services fly their own aircraft to get packages across the country. In the news, the use of military drones is debated, while large companies consider the possibilities of drones for delivering products to customers' doorsteps.

Even the moon landing can be traced back to the first flight, less than seventy years previously. The advancements of the Wright brothers changed the world. Flight is now how human beings move.

The following is an example of an **ineffective** response. It does not clearly address the prompt and lacks focus on the modern-day ramifications of the first powered flight.

The Wright brothers first flew from Kitty Hawk in 1903. On December 17, 1903, Orville Wright flew a spruce-and-muslin plane for 12 seconds. It was the first successful powered flight. The plane had a gasoline engine that the brothers made in their bicycle shop. The Wright Flyer is on display in the Smithsonian Institution today. One of the results of this first powered flight is that today you can pay hundreds of dollars, wait in a long line, and get x-rayed by an invasive machine just to sit on a flying bus for eight hours and fly from New York to Los Angeles. The development of flight was very important. We have implemented the Wright brothers' technology in a lot of ways, both good and bad.

Reading and Thinking for Writing
page 27

Reading for Writing

Practice It! *pages 30–31*

1. Your goal is to formulate an opinion on whether you agree or disagree with the author and reasons for that opinion.

2. The central idea is that high schools should be separated by gender, with only male or only female students.

3. Responses will vary. You might note specific arguments that the author makes.
   - All-male and all-female high schools keep students focused on studies.
   - Coed schools are distracting because of a growing interest in the opposite sex.
   - Success in high school is crucial to success in the future.

   Noting your thoughts or criticisms of these arguments will be helpful in writing your response.

4. You might write:

> Coed schools are a better choice for high school students than separate schools for males and females. The author's position against coed schools rests on one point only: that removing the opposite sex from schools will increase concentration. The author concludes that this increased concentration will cause increased success in high school and in life. However, the author does not include any evidence that students in non-coed schools perform better. The author certainly does not address any potential problems with schools for only one gender. While high school is a difficult time full of distractions, non-coed high schools are likely to cause more problems than they solve. Keeping male and female students separated because of potential distractions ignores students' needs. Young men and women need to learn to deal with others of different genders in life and in the workforce. Keeping students separate hinders the development of important social skills. Learning to work together is an important part of learning. Overall, the author's argument is weak, and without evidence, the argument for coed schools is stronger.

5. The goal is to apply the concept of freedom of speech to the argument in the passage.

6. The central idea of the passage is that the president should only be criticized thoughtfully and respectfully.

7. You might note aspects of the author's argument that relate to freedom of speech.
   - Criticizing the president is free speech.
   - The mode of speech is part of freedom of speech, and the author tries to dictate mode of speech (respectful and thoughtful).
   - Freedom of speech has limits. For example, you can't yell "fire!" in a crowded theater.
   - The author's argument is more about discourse, i.e. the usefulness of the criticisms, not about causing harm.

8. You might write:

> The author argues that criticisms of the president should be thoughtful and respectful. However useful the author's argument might be for positive discourse, it is contrary to our country's valued freedom of speech. Criticisms of the president are free speech. Arguably, criticisms of the government are the most important free speech. Part of freedom of speech is the way speech is phrased. The tone of speech (angry, loud, or mocking) is part of the meaning. Freedom of speech does have limits. You can't yell "fire!" in a crowded theater, and you can't goad a loyal follower to attempt assassinating the president. However, the author's argument is more about discourse and the usefulness of criticisms of the president than about dangerous or inciting speech. Disrespectful or thoughtless speech about the president might have negative consequences, but it would depend on the speech and circumstances. Calling for only thoughtful and respectful speech is limited. Sometimes anger, mockery, or disrespect are important aspects of speech.

Idea Clustering

Practice It! *pages 34–36*

1. Responses will vary. The following is an example of a completed idea cluster.

2. Responses will vary. You might identify potential issues with allowing younger drivers on the road.

3. You might write:

Raising the driving age to 18 is good policy because it will prevent accidents. Driving is a responsibility. Older drivers are more mature and better able to make good decisions for safe driving. While younger teenagers still need transportation, they typically have more options. Schools provide busses. Cities provide public transportation. Often, work or school is close enough to walk or ride a bike. Even if preventing younger teens from driving causes slight inconveniences, it is a small trade-off for safety. Mixing teens and cars is a recipe for accidents. Raising the driving age can alleviate the dangers of irresponsible teen driving.

4. Responses will vary. The following is an example of a completed idea cluster.

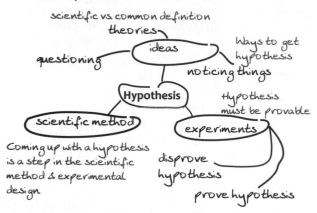

5. Responses will vary. Idea clustering can be helpful for generating new ideas for your writing and grouping ideas in a logical order.

6. You might write:

A hypothesis is a provable scientific idea that has predictable results. To form a hypothesis, observe the world around you. Notice patterns in the world and question cause and effect. Form an idea about what causes specific behavior or consequences. Once you have formed a hypothesis, such as "The wildflowers in my yard will grow fastest in full sun," you can design a test to prove or disprove the hypothesis. The design of the experiment depends on the hypothesis, and the hypothesis provides the criteria to evaluate the experimental results. The hypothesis is an essential part of the scientific method and experimental design.

7. Responses will vary. The following is an example of a completed idea cluster.

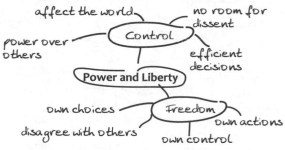

8. Responses will vary. The idea cluster may help you make connections between the consequences of individual power and individual liberty.

9. You might write:

The quotation states that a free government must not give power to an individual that would endanger public liberty. Liberty involves some conflict. Each individual makes his or her own choices and governs his or her own actions. People won't always agree or make the same choices. If a single person has complete power, that person can interfere with liberty by limiting individual choices and actions. The more power is concentrated in one person or group, the more danger this person or group represents to freedom.

Check Your Skills

pages 37–38

1. Example notes might be:
   - Independent field biologists work as observers on fishing boats and at-sea processing facilities.
   - The goal of observers is economic and ecological sustainability for fisheries.
   - The West Coast Groundfish Trawl Catch Share Program includes a certified observer on all trips of participating ships.
   - Observers record data about caught and discarded fish, endangered or threatened species, diversity and condition of fish, seabird sightings, and marine mammals.
   - Observers record biological data, including sex, length, and weight of fish.

2. Responses will vary. The following is an example of a completed idea cluster.

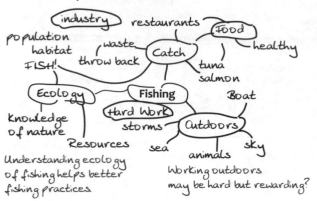

3. You might write:

> Imagine sitting at a sea-side restaurant enjoying a grilled tuna steak. The fishing industry brought that tuna from the deep sea to the plate. Fisheries depend on the health of fish populations and the health of the ocean itself. To maintain this health, field biologists work as observers on fishing boats or at-sea fish processing facilities. Observers collect data about fishing and wildlife to help improve fishing practices and further economic and ecological sustainability for fisheries. If you are interested in marine ecology and would enjoy working outdoors, it is worth investigating becoming a fishing industry observer.

Choosing an Organizational Structure   *page 39*

RE-PAC Your Ideas

Practice It!   pages 43–44

1. The purpose is to write a persuasive argument to convince readers of the local paper of your position on children owning mobile phones. The readers of the local paper are the audience. They live in your area and may share some of your experiences.

2. Responses will vary. The following is an example of a completed idea cluster.

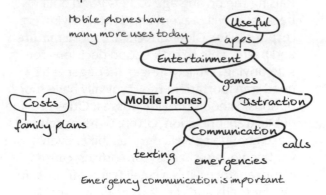

3. Purpose: Persuade
   Audience: Local newspaper readers

Structure	Statement and Support	Problem and Solution
Beginning	Statement: mobile phones are bad for kids.	Problem: children on phones
Middle	Support: phones are used for apps, games, texting. Statement: emergency communication seldom requires a mobile phone. Support: children are supervised.	Problem: Apps, games, distractions, and costs Solution: Don't allow children to use phones
Ending	Summarize: children will use phones irresponsibly and don't need them.	Mobile phones are unnecessary for children and cause problems.
Does It Advance My Purpose?	Yes, well	Yes, somewhat

4. You might choose the statement and support structure because it advances the purpose better. It expresses a position and states the reasons for that position. There is not a strong statement of the problem in the problem-and-solution structure, so it is less effective.

5. The purpose is to show an understanding of states of matter. No audience is specified, but the audience is likely a teacher or evaluator who will evaluate the writer's knowledge.

6. Responses will vary. The following is an example of a completed idea cluster.

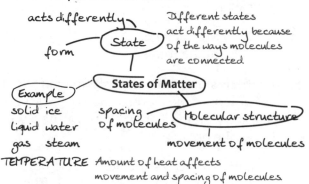

7. **Purpose:** Inform
   Audience: Teacher or evaluator

Structure	Descriptive	Comparison
Beginning	Define states of matter	Define states of matter
Middle	Describe each state of matter: solid, liquid, gas. Describe the state of water and the molecular activity/cause.	Compare examples, behavior, and molecular structure of three states.
Ending	Summarize: what causes states of matter	Summarize: similarities and differences
Does It Advance My Purpose?	Yes, well	Yes, fairly well

8. You might choose the descriptive structure because it fits best with the purpose, which is to inform about the concept of states of matter. While a comparison does help explain the states of matter, it puts more emphasis on similarities and differences and less on explaining the overall concept.

Check Your Skills
pages 45–46

1. A comparison structure is a good organizational structure for this task because the task asks the writer to compare two reviews. This structure allows the writer to draw direct similarities and differences between the reviews. This evaluation can provide evidence for a decision either to eat at the restaurant or not to eat there.

2. You might write:

   Based on the two reviews, I would eat at Annie's restaurant. The first reviewer visited the restaurant with a group of four people, while the second reviewer only talks about one order. Based on the two reviews, four out of the five diners enjoyed their meal. Additionally, the reviewer only criticizes certain elements of the meal: a sauce on the lobster and the dry cake. These might be attributed to the reviewer's particular taste or minor mistakes in the kitchen. While the second reviewer mentions that lobster is the most expensive item on the menu, there is no indication of the price. The first review mentions that the price was less than $10 per person and that the portions were large. This review is more useful and makes the restaurant sound like a good deal. Although the reviewers mention a few minor problems with the food (undercooked potatoes, stale cake, and a sauce that the second reviewer disliked), the restaurant would be worth trying.

3. A statement and support structure is a good choice for this task because it allows you to explain the quotation in statements and use modern-day examples to support those statements. This structure fits well with the prompt.

4. You might write:

> The quotation by Patrick Henry states that in-fighting and divided factions is bad for the country, a truth that is evident in today's ineffective congress. The quotation says that factions will destroy our union. Today, U.S. politics is divided severely along party lines. When the Republicans control the House and the Democrats control the Senate, almost no legislation can pass through Congress. The severely divided factions of the political party destroy the government's ability to operate. Patrick Henry states that division will make us weak and that we need strength to fight enemies. The U.S. certainly continues to go to war, but the problem of terrorism remains unsolved. Perhaps if U.S. politics were not so divided, politicians could use their joint efforts to successfully counter the dangers that face the country. A divided country, fighting about distracting issues, does little to solve any problem.

Focus: Draft — *page 47*

Developing a Thesis Statement — *page 49*

Developing a Thesis Map

Practice It! *pages 52–54*

1. A thesis statement is similar to a map because it shows where your writing is headed and how you might get there.

2. a. The purpose defines what the writer will tell the reader.

3. b. The organization helps determine the content and order of the thesis.

4a. The thesis statement lacks information about the content of the writing, such as the scope of what the writer will discuss or how the discussion will be organized.

An improved thesis statement would be, "I will discuss the history of computers, from the first programmable computer in 1936 through today's experiments in quantum computing."

4b. The thesis statement is missing any ideas about why creativity is important to writing or what the writer will discuss about creativity.

An improved thesis statement would be, "Creativity is important to good writing because it allows writers to explore and expand on their ideas."

5a. The happiest surprise I have ever received was an acceptance letter to college, which changed the course of my life.

5b. Hand-washing is important because it prevents the spread of diseases, such as colds and the flu.

5c. Every four years, when voters elect a new president, they prove the effectiveness of the United State's representative democracy.

5d. Unpaid internships and apprenticeships should be widely available to high school students so that teenagers can learn new career skills and explore career options.

5e. I would like to be remembered for contributing to society through volunteerism and changing my community for the better.

6a. *The Grand Budapest Hotel* is a sad but enjoyable film.

6b. The ensemble cast was excellent. The directing was stylized and beautiful. The story was moving and well-told.

6c. The movie *The Grand Budapest Hotel* is sad but enjoyable, with a moving story that is conveyed through excellent acting and beautiful direction.

7a. Allowing Russia to take over Crimea will cause more difficulty in the future.

7b. The quotation from Machiavelli warns against avoiding war when avoidance will cause trouble to escalate. Russia's invasion of Crimea is such a case.

7c. Machiavelli's warning against avoiding a necessary war applies to the Russian invasion of Crimea, which will cause future troubles if swift action is not taken.

8a. Smoking in public restaurants and bars should not be allowed.

8b. Second-hand smoke is harmful to health. Harmful behavior should be regulated.

8c. Because second-hand smoke harms others, smoking in public restaurants and bars should be banned.

Check Your Skills   pages 55–56

1. The passage makes an argument in favor of tattoos as self-expression, but it ignores the reality of public perception against tattoos.

2. The passage's argument in favor of tattoos as self-expression considers tattoos an example of freedom of speech, a right that is upheld by the First Amendment.

3. There is a limited amount of fossil fuel, particularly oil, on Earth because fossil fuels are created over millions of years from a limited amount of organic material.

Drafting an Introduction   *page 57*

Catch—Hook, Line, and Sinker

Practice It!   *pages 60–62*

1a. Quotation: "If people see the Capitol going on, it is a sign we intend the Union shall go on." —Abraham Lincoln

Fact: President George Washington originally selected the location for Washington, D.C.

Anecdote or Description: Looking down the National Mall, the Washington Monument seems breathtakingly tall, from its mirror in the reflecting pool to its pointed tip.

Surprising Statement: The famous cherry trees of Washington, D.C. are actually a gift from Japan.

Question: Can you imagine seeing Dorothy's ruby slippers and a gown worn by Martha Washington in one excursion?

1b. Important: Touring Washington, D.C. can teach you about history and politics.

Interesting: A trip to Washington, D.C. can reveal hidden treasures of U.S. culture.

2a. The obvious solution of increasing worker compensation is not always the most effective solution to employee retention.

2b. Worker retention is important because it is costly and inefficient to have a high employee turnover.

2c. Because there is evidence that employees who leave are looking for career advancement, a career development program is the best route to improve retention.

2d. You might write:

The obvious solution of increasing worker compensation is not always the most effective solution to employee retention. The proposal to increase worker compensation has no evidence to show its effectiveness. Still, worker retention is crucial to any firm. A high employee turnover is costly and inefficient. The best approach is to identify and act on the factors that cause employees to leave. Because there is evidence that employees who leave are looking for career advancement, a career development program is the best route to improve retention.

3a. Are political parties really an unavoidable evil? James Madison states that they are.

3b. Balance between political interests is important because if one political group becomes too powerful, that group can become tyrannical.

3c. James Madison proposes keeping political parties in check by maintaining a balance of power and wealth; however, today lobbying and money in politics may be creating an oligarchy.

3d. You might write:

Are political parties really an unavoidable evil? James Madison states that they are. He warns that political parties must be combatted. Balance between political interests is important because if one political group becomes too powerful, that group can become tyrannical. James Madison proposes keeping political parties in check by maintaining a balance of power and wealth; however, today lobbying and money in politics may be creating an oligarchy.

Check Your Skills   pages 63–64

1. You might write:

Are the freedoms outlined in the Bill of Rights subject to change with popular opinions? On the contrary, a right is timeless. It can either be respected by the government or infringed. Maintaining our rights is essential to maintaining a free society. The author of the passage supposes that because we do not need a militia of private citizens, we do not need gun rights. The author's position is invalid because gun rights do not depend on our need of a militia and because the author gives no substantial evidence of the harms of gun ownership.

2. You might write:

Albert Einstein wrote, "All of science is nothing more than the refinement of everyday thinking." Science is an extension of the logical thought people use to make good decisions. Over the last few hundred years, the scientific

method—a procedure for systematically studying the world—has given us technological advancements that affect every aspect of life. Although science sometimes seems complex, it is easy to understand the basic steps of the scientific method: to make predictions, to test those predictions, and to analyze the results of those tests.

3. You might write:

Imagine sitting in the audience of a Miss Universe pageant. The audience applauds as the contestants come on stage. The participants look glamorous in fabulous dresses. They answer questions with polished smiles. They perform music or dance. It may be excellent entertainment. However, even when the contestants are singing or answering questions, the focus is on beauty rather than talent or personality. The argument that ultimately, pageants are a negative influence for society is strongest because, when looked at truthfully, pageants are all about beauty.

Drafting Body Paragraphs   *page 65*

Building Body Paragraph Blocks

Practice It!   *pages 68–70*

1. D: Historical fiction tells an imaginary story that takes place in the "real" past.

C: In either case, the reader can expect both truth and surprises.

D: Events and people from that time may affect the characters' lives, but the main characters or plot elements themselves are fictional.

T: Fiction and non-fiction are distinctly different genres of writing; however, historical fiction and creative non-fiction don't fit easily into the definitions of fiction as "not true" or non-fiction as "true."

D: Creative non-fiction retells actual events and depicts actual people, but with fictional elements added to enhance the drama of the story.

2. Fiction and non-fiction are distinctly different genres of writing; however, historical fiction and creative non-fiction don't fit easily into the definitions of fiction as "not true" or non-fiction as "true." Creative non-fiction retells actual events and depicts actual people, but with fictional elements added to enhance the drama of the story. Historical fiction tells an imaginary story that takes place in the "real" past. Events and people from that time may affect the characters' lives, but the main characters or plot elements themselves are fictional. In either case, the reader can expect both truth and surprises.

3. NASA should allow privately chartered launches into orbit for those willing to pay for them. Opportunities to orbit the earth are rare; however, there are some who have the financial means and willingness to pay a million dollars or more for the privilege of orbiting the earth. Using this as a fundraiser, the space program can advance other missions without overburdening the average citizen with increased taxes. While there is a market for spaceflight, NASA should move quickly to tap into it.

4a. Exit surveys are an excellent resource for measuring workplace factors that are valuable for employees.

4b. The employees who take exit surveys are the employees that the company wants to retain. The information that exiting employees report deserves study; the exiting workers are telling the company how to improve. Exit surveys showed that 68% of exiting employees are looking for career advancement.

4c. The data from exit surveys should drive decisions about employee retention.

4d. You might write:

Exit surveys are an excellent resource for measuring workplace factors that employees value. After all, the employees who take exit surveys are the same employees that the company wants to retain. The information that exiting employees report deserves study; the exiting workers are telling the company how to improve. An analysis of exit surveys showed that 68% of exiting employees are looking for

career advancement. This data, along with other information from exit surveys, should drive decisions about employee retention.

5a. James Madison's first recommendation is to establish political equality.

5b. Political equality is difficult to measure and enforce. Every person has one vote. However, does that mean each person is politically equal? The rich and powerful often have resources unavailable to the common man, such as lobbyists and money for political contributions. Those who are less wealthy have other political recourse, including unions, political demonstrations, and grass-roots activism.

5c. American society struggles to limit excess political power of the powerful and increase political power of the average citizen.

5d. You might write:

James Madison's first recommendation is to establish political equality. Political equality is difficult to measure and enforce. Every person has one vote. However, that doesn't mean each person is politically equal. The rich and powerful often have resources unavailable to the common man, such as lobbyists and money for political contributions. Those who are less wealthy have other political recourses, including unions, political demonstrations, and grass-roots activism. Complete equality is not possible, but balancing these political outlets is important. American society should try to limit excess political power of any one group, while maintaining political power for all citizens.

Check Your Skills
pages 71–72

1. You might write:

While the Second Amendment mentions militias, this mention is not the sole justification for gun rights. "The right of the people to keep and bear Arms" exists whether or not a militia is necessary in modern society. Gun ownership allows store owners and home owners to protect their property. Firearms give people security in case of emergency. They are tools for hunting and protection. The right to personal power does not depend on its use, whether for a militia or a hunting trip. The author's emphasis of militias is a distraction, as is the mention of scientific investigation.

The passage places an importance on scientific knowledge without providing any. The author attributes suicides, accidents, and violence to gun ownership without citing specific evidence. What studies show that gun ownership increases violence or death? If the author wants to rely on science, then the argument should cite scientific evidence. Overall, the writer's position against gun rights is weak and unsupported.

2. You might write:

The first stage of the scientific method involves making a prediction. Predictions come from observing the world. To make a prediction, ask questions, make observations, and then form a hypothesis. A hypothesis is a tentative explanation for a physical process or observed event. A good way to form a hypothesis is with an "if-then-because" prediction. You might hypothesize that **if** you give a plant more water **then** it will grow faster **because** plants use water to grow. Your prediction leads directly to constructing a test.

A scientific experiment or study seeks to confirm or disprove a hypothesis. Based on the prediction in the hypothesis, design an experiment to test whether the hypothesis is true. The experiment should have one variable (based on the "if" statement). For example, you might have a group of plants that receives a lot of water, a group that receives little water, and a group that receives no water. The water is the variable in the experiment. All other factors (such as soil and sunlight) should be kept the same between the groups, so that you can attribute the differences in the results to one cause.

Analyzing the results of the experiment or study is the third important stage of the scientific method. Gather data from the experiment and determine whether it supports the hypothesis. Did you get the expected results? What unexpected things happened? Based on the results, you will ask more questions and refine or revise your hypothesis. Over time, you may accumulate

enough evidence to form a theory: a well-supported explanation for an observed natural phenomena. Without the scientific method, scientists could not gather reliable support to form sound theories.

3. You might write:

The author of the second passage focuses on the positive aspects of pageants. Pageants do include personality and talent portions. They do provide scholarships and support charitable organizations. However, these aspects are added on to the pageants to try to mitigate the fundamental focus on physical beauty. The terms "beauty pageant" or "beauty contest" aren't used by the second author, even though these phrases are the first ones that come to mind to describe Miss America or Miss Universe. The author specifically leaves out the word "beauty" to de-emphasize that aspect of pageants. Honest self-examination reveals that beauty truly is the focus of pageants, as the first author states, and therefore pageants primarily value women for their looks.

Drafting a Conclusion   *page 73*

Writing a Memorable Conclusion

Practice It!   *pages 76–78*

1a. The main take-away is that Washington, D.C. has both cultural and political sites worth visiting.

One thing the reader should remember is to visit a broad range of spots in the capital.

A new way to state the central idea might be, "Washington, D.C. is a fascinating city, with much more to offer than just political destinations."

1b. A bigger picture might be travel in general. You might write, "Always look for hidden gems when you travel."

How many other worthwhile attractions does Washington, D.C. hold? Traveling isn't only about visiting time-honored destinations such as the Lincoln Memorial or the Washington Monument.

The reader should try to expand his or her ideas about places to visit while traveling.

1c. An ending tone might be contemplative, excited, or sincere.

2a. An employee retention program needs to address the problems that cause employees to leave.

2b. Employers should always listen to their employees about workplace conditions; employees are the ones working in the workplace environment.

2c. A career development program will benefit the company through both increased employee retention and better recruitment for upper management.

2d. You might write:

Employers should always listen to their employees about workplace conditions; after all, employees are the ones working in the workplace environment. An employee retention program needs to address the problems that cause employees to leave, and exiting employees have cited a need for advancement opportunities in their exit interviews. A career development program will benefit the company through both increased employee retention and better recruitment for upper management.

3a. James Madison warns against allowing unbalancing power to any particular political party, and the methods he cites for balancing power involve regulating wealth and advantages.

3b. Madison's ideas sound controversial because they advocate balancing political power by reducing extreme wealth and limiting opportunities to the advantaged. However, an imbalance of power can only be avoided by withholding power.

3c. Regulating the power of political parties is a difficult prospect, but without regulation, political parties are subject to corruption by special interests.

3d. You might write:

James Madison warns against allowing unbalancing power to any particular political party, and the methods he cites for balancing power

involve regulating wealth and advantages. Madison's ideas sound controversial because they advocate balancing political power by reducing extreme wealth and limiting opportunities to the advantaged. However, an imbalance of power can only be avoided by withholding power from some and providing opportunity for others. Regulating the power of political parties is a difficult prospect, but without regulation, political parties (and all areas of government) are subject to corruption by special interests.

Check Your Skills
pages 79–80

1. You might write:

A right cannot be given or taken away by the government. The right to bear arms is a human right to protection and sustenance. All our rights work this way. The right to free speech cannot be taken away, nor can the right to freedom of religion. Whether or not our country needs a militia, our right to bear arms persists.

2. You might write:

As Phillip K. Dick said, "Reality is that which, when you stop believing in it, doesn't go away." The scientific method is important because it provides an objective way to study the world and discern reality from mere belief. The scientific method relies on observation and prediction. By observing the world, you form hypotheses. By predicting behavior, you test those hypotheses. By observing the results, you evaluate those hypotheses. Through observation and prediction, the scientific method allows scientists to generate an objective view of the world.

3. You might write:

Anything that spurs competition is something that society values. Society values physical ability, so we have sports competitions. Society values intellectual ability, so we have Nobel prizes. Society also values physical beauty, so we have beauty pageants. However, when we think of sports trophies and Nobel prizes, we often think of men. When we think of beauty pageants, we think of women. Relegating female competition to beauty can harm the confidence and self-image of women.

Focus: Evaluate   *page 81*

Revising and Editing   *page 83*

Revising with POSE

Practice It!   *pages 86–87*

1. Although it discusses the topic of the quotation, the response does not specifically mention the quotation. It doesn't fulfill the writing task. You might revise the paragraph by referencing the quotation in the beginning and explaining how the example applies to the quotation.

2. Overall, the paragraph has fair structure, with a beginning, middle, and ending. However, the first sentence of the paragraph doesn't provide a strong beginning. It doesn't establish a specific central idea that relates to the prompt. The middle of the paragraph gives a detailed example, and the ending provides a successful conclusion. You might revise the first sentence to provide a stronger central idea that addresses the prompt.

3. The details in the example are appropriate, but they need to be linked to the quotation. The response needs an explanation of how the example reflects the idea in the quotation.

4. The example in the response is effective, and the tone is appropriate. The content of the opening sentence is overly general and fails to add to the response. The beginning of the response should be revised, and it should be related clearly to the quotation.

5. You might write:

In the quotation, Kennedy states that people need to be educated and informed to be free. In this quotation, he is making an important point about freedom; your degree of freedom depends on your ability to make good choices based on knowledge. Consider this example: a person has a curable ailment. Two treatments are available. One is nothing more than a placebo in a fancy bottle. The other is a proven cure. If the person lacks information and education to make a choice, that person can be manipulated by the company selling the

---

placebo. Therefore, that person is not truly free, based on Kennedy's definition. The person can make a choice, but it is not an informed choice. Freedom is what you have when you have the education and information to understand your choice.

6. The response fulfills the writing task. It takes a position and gives reason to support that position. However, starting the response with "yes" is not informative. The beginning should more clearly state the position of the response by reminding the reader of the prompt.

7. The response is reasonably well organized. It has a beginning that states a position, and a middle that gives reasons for that position. The ending restates the central idea. However, the beginning and middle can be revised to more clearly communicate the author's ideas.

8. The details are appropriate and fairly specific. The response could benefit from justifying the generalizations that companies "always want to pay as little as possible." This statement needs to be better supported or restated more thoughtfully.

9. The response is fairly successful in content, but it is not successful in tone. The tone is informal and flippant. The author overuses casual wording such as "right?" and "yes." The response should be rewritten with a more formal tone. Removing the second person "you" is a good suggestion.

10. You might write:

Salaried employees should qualify for overtime pay, the same as hourly employees. All people deserve compensation for work and time. A job is a contract. The company buys your time in return for compensation. A contract where one party can extract extra services without compensation is unfair. Workers should get paid for their extra time. After all, time is valuable. Employers get benefits from workers' time and energy. The only way to get fair compensation is to enact laws that enforce overtime pay for salaried employees.

Answers and Explanations

Editing with FREE

Practice It! *pages 90–92*

1. In the novel *War and Peace*, Leo Tolstoy write, "I cannot conceive of a man not being free unless he is dead."

2-4. The subject "Leo Tolstoy" does not match the verb "write." You might change it to "Leo Tolstoy writes."

5. Responses will vary. The sentence sounds more natural with the correct verb form.

6. He describes is a particular kind of freedom: a personal, inner freedom.

7-9. The sentence has two verbs, "describes is." You might edit the sentence to read, "He describes a particular..." or "What he describes is a particular..."

10. Every person has freedom of though and freedom within the confines of there situation.

11-13. The sentence has two errors. The word "though" is accidentally used instead of the word "thought." The word "there" is also used instead of the possessive pronoun "their."

14. A person in jail can chose to read, study, and improve themselves; a person who is in a wheelchair can choose to train themselves thoroughly and become an athlete.

15-17. The sentence uses the word "chose" instead of the word "choose." The pronoun "themselves" is plural, but it refers to the singular word "person." It might be easiest to rephrase the sentence with the plural "people." "People in jail can choose to read, study, and improve themselves; people who are in wheelchairs can choose to train themselves thoroughly and become athletes." You could also improve the sentence by removing the extra words "who are" and "thoroughly."

18. Responses will vary. The paragraph will be clearer and easier to read without errors.

Check Your Skills *pages 93–94*

1. The paragraph has a weak beginning which doesn't add to the response. It also has several errors that interfere with reading and some informal language. A stronger, more certain analysis of the quotation would improve the response. However, it does address the writing task and has a beginning, middle, and ending.

2. You might write:

John Quincy Adams defines the power of a nation as the individual freedom of the people combined. He reasons that the more freedom the people have, the more powerful the nation is as a group. Adams applies his argument to the political freedom allowed by the government. Critics might argue that the people do not always act together and combine their individual power. People often struggle against each other. However, the quote from Adams implies that this struggle is not a weakness but a strength. Individual liberty causes conflict, but this may ultimately result in better decisions and laws. Therefore, the nation becomes more powerful through individual liberty.

3. One strength of the paragraph is that it cites a study supporting its claim, but the author seems to rely too much on a lengthy direct quotation. Elsewhere, the paragraph includes very general language with little support, such as "really harmful" and "serious problem." The paragraph has a central idea, but the organization would be stronger if the writer's central idea was clearly stated at the beginning.

4. You might write:

Gambling is illegal in our state, but that doesn't mean gambling is not a problem. People spend countless hours and dollars gambling online, and the state needs to address this problem. The 1999 National Gambling Impact Study found that "the high-speed instant gratification of Internet games" can worsen gambling problems. The study also noted that online gambling offers privacy, so gamblers feel free to indulge in bad behavior. This leads to gambling addiction and money flowing out of our state, likely overseas. Our state needs to make it a priority to limit the availability of online gambling and to increase education and outreach for gambling addiction.

Reading Critically   *page 95*

Reading Your Writing Critically

Practice It!   *pages 98–100*

1. From skimming, it might seem that the central idea is that video games have both benefits and drawbacks. However, a closer examination of the text shows that the author believes video games have more benefits than drawbacks.

2. You might note:
   - Benefits and drawbacks—Which is greater?
   - Inexpensive enjoyment—less important
   - Improve skills, educational
   - Study: increase brain regions
   - Violent video games, unclear evidence—What evidence?

3. One of the weaknesses of the passage is organization. It begins with a statement that doesn't clearly show the author's position. Then, it gives less important details before more important details. It also lacks a clear ending or conclusion. One of the strengths is that it cites a study as evidence for the author's position and gives several supporting reasons. However, the statement that evidence on the opposing side is unclear is not specific. It would improve the response to review some of the unclear evidence.

4. You might write:

   Video games are often criticized as encouraging violent behavior or simply wasting time. However, the benefits of video games are often overlooked, and these benefits outweigh the drawbacks. Critics state that video games contribute to violent behavior. However, evidence from studies is unclear. While some studies find a correlation, it is unclear whether violence is caused by video games or violent teens are attracted to video games. Other studies find no link. The benefits of video games are clearer. Some video games are educational, and even video games designed for enjoyment can improve skills. A study by the Max Planck Institute for Human Development and Charité University Medicine St. Hedwig-Krankenhaus shows that video gaming causes increases in the brain regions responsible for spatial orientation, memory formation, strategic planning, and fine motor skills. Are video games a waste of time or an inexpensive source of enjoyment? Although the link between violence and video games is unclear, it is clear that video games can improve important skills. Therefore, video games have an overall benefit for individuals and society.

5. Responses will vary.

6. The central idea is to encourage employees to apply for promotion opportunities.

7. You might note:
   - Promote from within
   - Opportunities for growth
   - Employee account—skills and experience, apply for jobs
   - What kinds of jobs are available?
   - Who can apply to jobs? How?
   - Contact with questions

8. The strengths of the paragraph are that it stays on topic and gives important information in a businesslike tone. The weaknesses are its organization and redundant wording. It might benefit from a clearer statement of the author's purpose at the beginning and a more logical order of ideas. The ending is redundant, so it should be revised.

9. You might write:

   Because our company's policy is to promote from within whenever possible, we encourage you to consider advancement opportunities in the company. To find open positions, log in to your employee account. On the website, you can easily browse job listings. All employees are eligible for any available position. To apply, please update your skills and experience on the website and select the positions of interest to you. If you have any questions about the website, job listings, or how to advance in the company, please send me an email at human_resources@trc.com. We value your talents and hard work, and we hope you find opportunities for growth that suit your interests and goals.

10. Responses will vary.

11. The central idea is that Douglass's quote states that agitation is necessary for freedom. The central idea is somewhat unclear from skimming the text.

12. You might note:
    - Growing crops—metaphor
    - Freedom = crops, agitation = plowing field
    - Protest creates debate, shows freedom. Does debate/protest/disagreement cause freedom or show that people are free?
    - "Can't make an omelette"—is this needed/helpful? Too cliché?
    - Is agitation necessary for freedom or a result of freedom or both?

13. The response could benefit from a stronger opening, since the first sentence focuses on the fact that the quotation uses a metaphor. This is not the most important idea in the passage. The idea that agitation is necessary for freedom and that voices must protest and create debate is a good one and could be expanded. The response's focus on the prompt and the quotation is also one of its strengths.

14. You might write:

The quotation by Frederick Douglass uses a metaphor to show that agitation is necessary for freedom. In this metaphor, freedom is a crop being grown. Agitation, such as protests, is the field being plowed. The ground must be torn up in order to grow the crops; similarly, voices must protest, be heard, and create debate in order to have freedom. Although Douglass's metaphor describes agitation as a source or generator of freedom, agitation is also a result of freedom. When people are free, they will disagree, debate, and protest. When people protest and agitate, they create freedom. Agitation may be unsettling, but it is a necessary condition for, and result of, freedom.

15. Responses will vary.

Check Your Skills pages 101–102

1. You might write:

My skills and experience fit well with the requirements of the project manager position. I have the necessary skills to work well with clients. In a busy retail environment, I handle customer complaints, complete projects for coworkers, and provide excellent customer service. I also can prioritize and organize work. Every day, I must prioritize to organize the store and perform my duties in a bustling, changing environment. Additionally, I can handle deadlines well. While working a demanding job, I earned an associate's degree in business. In addition to the skills taught in my classes, I learned to manage time well to balance both school and work. I will bring to this position both real-world skills learned on the job and knowledge of computers and business learned in class. I have the requisite skills and abilities to be an excellent project manager.

2. Responses will vary depending on experience. You might write:

A project manager needs to be able to balance multiple tasks in a changing environment while providing excellent customer service. My skills in prioritizing, delegating, and communicating make me an excellent candidate for this position. As an executive assistant, I track and prioritize essential tasks, create schedules, meet deadlines, and delegate responsibilities to staff. My communication skills help me successfully help clients, cooperate with associates, and complete tasks for my supervisor. I do a variety of different tasks every day, and I am sure I can do just as well as a project manager.

3. You might revise the example draft as follows:

A successful project manager needs to balance multiple tasks in a changing environment while providing excellent customer service. My experience as an executive assistant has given me the necessary skills in prioritizing, delegating, and communicating. I track and prioritize essential tasks, create schedules, meet deadlines, and delegate responsibilities to staff. My communication skills help me successfully assist clients, cooperate with associates, and complete tasks for my supervisor. Every day is different, with new challenges. I enjoy meeting those challenges through hard work and skill. I know that I can use my experiences to become a valuable member of your team.

4. You might write:

Voter ID laws hinder democracy by restricting voters without reason. A voter ID law requires voters to show identification at their polling place. Proponents state that these laws prevent voter fraud by identifying people who show up to the polls. However, there is no evidence for widespread voter fraud. The true effect of voter ID laws is to suppress voting among minorities and the poor. A report by the U.S. Election Assistance Commission found that there was a statistically significant correlation between voter ID laws and reduced turnout. The scope of this effect is unclear, but any effect on turnout outweighs the effect on nonexistent fraud. Instead of passing voter ID laws that hinder democracy, governments should develop policies to encourage voting.

5. You might write:

Voter ID laws are a good idea and can be done in a way that helps democracy. Critics state that voter ID laws prevent people from coming to the polls. However, showing an ID is not a significant hindrance. As long as the government provides identification and educates the public about voting requirements, voter ID laws can be effective. No amount of voter fraud is acceptable.

6. You might revise the example draft as follows:

Voter ID laws help democracy, as long as they are well-designed. Critics state that voter ID laws prevent disadvantaged or impoverished citizens from coming to the polls. However, showing an ID is not a significant hindrance. As long as the government provides identification cards for voters and educates the public about voting requirements, voter ID laws can be effective policy. No amount of voter fraud is acceptable, and voter ID laws can be a simple and effective way to preserve democracy.

Language and Word Choice   *page 103*

Using SCVIDs

Practice It!   *pages 106–108*

1. **quiet:** low-key, silent, hushed, peaceful, calm, noiseless, subdued

   nice: pleasant, enjoyable, sweet, polite, agreeable, delightful, friendly, lovely, charming

   say: state, mention, question, wonder, shout, utter, speak, pronounce, ask, exclaim, repeat, murmur

   fast: rapid, quick, swift, speedy, hasty, hurriedly, turbo-powered, supersonic, express, breakneck, fleet

   person: woman, man, businessperson, individual, character, doctor, lawyer, server, friend, partner, helper, protagonist, antagonist

2. You might choose words relevant to the topic to help you brainstorm SCVIDs.

   light: rays, electromagnetic spectrum, sunlight, wavelength, waves, energy

   plant: leaves, cells, species

   chlorophyll: molecule, green, pigment, photosensitive

   photosynthesis: process, chemical, carbohydrates, synthesize, generate, oxygen, carbon dioxide, absorb

3. You might write:

Chlorophyll molecules are green pigments in plants that absorb light energy from the sun. Most plants look green because chlorophyll molecules reflect green light but absorb blue and red light. The light energy is used for photosynthesis, a process that changes sunlight into carbohydrates. Through photosynthesis, plants are able to store the energy in sunlight as usable food.

4. Chlorophyll molecules are green pigments in plants that absorb light energy from the sun. Most plants look green because chlorophyll molecules reflect green light but absorb blue and red light. The light energy is used for photosynthesis, a process that changes sunlight into carbohydrates. Through photosynthesis, plants are able to store the energy in sunlight as usable food.

You might write:

Chlorophyll molecules are green pigments in plant cells that absorb specific wavelengths of sunlight. Most leaves look green because chlorophyll reflects green light but absorbs blue and red light. The absorbed light is used for photosynthesis, a process that changes sunlight into carbohydrates. Through photosynthesis, plants are able to store the energy in sunlight as usable food.

5. Chlorophyll molecules <u>are</u> green pigments in plant cells that <u>absorb</u> specific wavelengths of sunlight. Most leaves <u>look</u> green because chlorophyll <u>reflects</u> green light but <u>absorbs</u> blue and red light. The absorbed light <u>is used</u> for photosynthesis, a process that <u>changes</u> sunlight into carbohydrates. Through photosynthesis, plants <u>are able to store</u> the energy in sunlight as usable food.

You might write:

Chlorophyll molecules are green pigments in plant cells that absorb specific wavelengths of sunlight. Most leaves appear green because chlorophyll reflects green light but absorbs blue and red light. The absorbed light is used for photosynthesis, a process that converts sunlight into carbohydrates. Through photosynthesis, plants can store the energy in sunlight as usable food.

6. Responses will vary. SCVIDs can make your meaning clearer and your writing more interesting.

7. You might choose words relevant to the topic to help you brainstorm SCVIDs.

technology: advancements, advanced, computers, science, modern

DRM: software, rights, protection, safeguard, barrier

business: companies, economy, free market, competition, commerce, corporation

choice: freedom, options, alternatives, selection, preference, preferred, best, most desirable

8. You might write:

The writer says that DRM software is bad for the free market and kills competition but does not tell about any statistics or facts about the harm the technology causes. The person writing doesn't take into account the company's right to make proprietary technology and the consumer's right to make free choices. The author talks about regulating companies while ignoring the power of individuals to dictate what is acceptable or not. A person like the author who dislikes DRM technology will not buy it. If there are enough dissatisfied people, the companies using DRM will lose business and be forced to change their business model. There is no need for regulation.

9. The writer says that DRM software is bad for the free market and kills competition but does not tell about any statistics or facts about the harm the technology causes. The person writing doesn't take into account the company's right to make proprietary technology and the consumer's right to make free choices. The author talks about regulating companies while ignoring the power of individuals to dictate what is acceptable or not. A person like the author who dislikes DRM technology will not buy it. If there are enough dissatisfied people, the companies using DRM will lose business and be forced to change their business model. There is no need for regulation.

You might write:

The author says that DRM software is damaging for the free market and kills competition but does not tell about any statistics or facts about the harm the technology causes. The critic doesn't take into account the company's right to make proprietary technology and the consumer's right to make free choices. The author talks about regulation of industry while ignoring the power of individuals to dictate what is acceptable or not. A consumer like the author who dislikes DRM technology will not buy it. If there are enough dissatisfied consumers, the companies using DRM will lose business and be forced to change their business model. There is no need for regulation.

10. The author <u>says</u> that DRM software <u>is</u> damaging for the free market and <u>kills</u> competition but <u>does not tell</u> about any statistics or facts about the harm the technology <u>causes</u>. The critic <u>doesn't take into account</u> the company's right to <u>make</u> proprietary technology and the consumer's right to <u>make</u> free choices. The author <u>talks about</u> regulation of industry while <u>ignoring</u> the power of individuals to <u>dictate</u> what <u>is</u> acceptable or not. A consumer like the author who <u>dislikes</u> DRM technology <u>will not buy</u> it. If there <u>are</u> enough dissatisfied consumers, the companies using DRM <u>will lose</u> business and <u>be forced</u> to change their business model. There <u>is</u> no need for regulation.

You might write:

The author claims that DRM software is damaging for the free market and destroys competition but does not provide any statistics or facts about the harm the technology causes. The critic ignores the company's right to create and sell proprietary technology and the consumer's right to make free choices. The author demands regulation of industry while ignoring the power of individuals to dictate what is acceptable or not. A consumer like the author who dislikes DRM technology will not buy it. If there are enough dissatisfied consumers, the companies using DRM will lose business and be forced to change their business model. There is no need for regulation.

1a. Possible answers: curved, wound

1b. Possible answers: huddling, clumping, converging

1c. Possible answers: evaporated, vanished

1d. Possible answers: checkerboard, quilt-like, vast

1e. Possible answers: singing, roaring, thundering, booming

1f. Possible answers: cheered, celebrated

2. You might write:

The atmosphere always contains some water. When air is near the Earth, the water present is typically in the form of water vapor, an invisible gas. Warm air, including water vapor, rises. When this air moves away from the warm Earth, it cools and cannot hold as much vapor. The excess vapor condenses onto minute particles. A tiny droplet forms around each atmospheric particle. The droplets combine to become clouds. A similar process creates fog on cold days.

---

3. The following is an **effective** response. It uses SCVIDs to describe the moon landing in 1969.

In July 1969, astronauts Buzz Aldrin and Neil Armstrong arrived on the moon, marking a historic moment in space science. Armstrong took the first steps on the lunar surface, uttering his famous words, "That's one small step for man, one giant leap for mankind." The landing in the Sea of Tranquility was the culmination of the Space Race, a war of technological advancement that began when the Soviet Union launched Sputnik, the first human-made Earth satellite. The moon landing was broadcast live world-wide, and Americans were glued to their television sets to see their flag planted an alien landscape. The technological accomplishment of visiting the moon fulfilled the goal President John F. Kennedy outlined for the nation in 1961.

The following is an **ineffective** response. It uses general words and often repeats terms.

In July 1969, two men got to the moon, which was a historic moment in history. Armstrong was the first one to step on the moon, saying,

"That's one small step for man, one giant leap for mankind." The moon landing was the end of the Space Race, a race for space technology that started when the Soviet Union sent up Sputnik, the first human-made Earth satellite. The moon landing was broadcast live on TV around the world, and Americans watched on TV to see the moon landing. The moon landing fulfilled the goal President John F. Kennedy gave in 1961.

4. The following is an **effective** response. It uses SCVIDs to describe a procedure for requesting time off from work.

When you are planning a trip, do not wait until the last minute to request vacation time. Submit your request four to six weeks before the event. The procedure is simple. First, check the office calendar. If two coworkers in your department have already been granted leave during your preferred time period, select different dates. Vacation time cannot be approved if it will cause a staff shortage. Next, complete the online Annual Leave Request Form on the company website. When you submit the form, it will be automatically emailed to human resources and your direct supervisor. In two to three days, you will receive either an approval or a follow-up email to address any problems.

The following is an **ineffective** response. It uses general or inexact words and often repeats terms.

When you are planning a vacation, do not wait too long to ask for vacation time. Put in your vacation time request four to six weeks before the vacation. The way you get vacation time is simple. First, check the office calendar. If two people in your department have already gotten vacation time during your vacation period, select a different time. Vacation cannot be okay if it will cause too many people to be gone. Next, do the online Annual Leave Request Form on the company website. When you put in the request form, it will go to human resources and your direct supervisor. In two to three days, you will get either an okay or a follow-up email for any problems.

Voice and Tone page 111

Developing a Voice

Practice It! *pages 114–115*

1. The author is a student and the audience is a professor or teacher. The audience is an authority who is judging the author. The tone should be formal and show the author's knowledge.

2. You might describe the author as excited, informal, unsure, or inconsistent.

3. Phrases that could be changed to make the writing more confident include "I recall" and "it is said."

4. You might write:

As counterintuitive as it seems, every chemical element on Earth was formed in a star. In the core of each star, nuclear fusion reactions create all the elements that surround us, including carbon and iron. Hydrogen and helium formed quickly after the Big Bang, and then stars formed as gravity drew particles together. As clouds of gas and dust became denser, they became hotter, eventually becoming stars. At the core of stars, hydrogen and helium fused to become heavier elements. Since the carbon formed in the heart of stars is the basis of life on Earth, we are formed of stardust.

5. Responses will vary.

6. The author is an expert and a teacher. The audience members are young learners. The author's tone should keep the learners interested and be informative. It should also be easy for seventh graders to understand.

7. You might describe the author as formal and informative.

8. The phrase "seems to have" could be changed to make the writing more confident.

9. You might write:

What did President Franklin Roosevelt mean when he called December 7, 1941 "a date which will live in infamy"? He was condemning the actions of the Japanese, who had launched a surprise attack on the U.S. base at Pearl

Harbor in Hawaii. In the attack, Japanese planes dropped bombs on unsuspecting American ships. Imagine the horror of bombs dropping from the sky and soldiers rushing to try to fight back. Before the attack, the U.S. wasn't a participant in World War II, but the Japanese were worried that the U.S. military could interfere with the war in Asia. This concern lead the Japanese to attack Pearl Harbor and try to destroy U.S. forces in the Pacific Ocean. The attack backfired, though. Instead of keeping the U.S. out of the war, it led to the U.S. joining World War II and ultimately defeating the Germans and Japanese.

10. Responses will vary.

Developing Tone

Practice It!   *pages 118–120*

1. An appropriate tone would be friendly and informative. Because the email is to a friend, a tone of friendly disagreement and discussion is more appropriate, and probably more convincing, than an angry, attacking, or condescending tone.

2. You might describe the tone as condescending, patronizing, or arrogant.

3. Words and phrases that show the author's tone include "patently ridiculous," "obviously," "anyone would realize," "clearly," and "next you'll say."

4. You might write:

I can't agree with the argument that unions are "anti-capitalism." Unions are a part of the free market because the free market is based on free actions by individuals, whether they are business owners, consumers, or employees. Workers joining together in a union is a natural market reaction to unfair wages and working conditions. Regulations that limit employee actions are similar to regulations that limit business owners' actions. They both regulate the free market by limiting the actors in the market. I respect your opinion about free markets, but if the goal is free-market capitalism, all people—workers, owners, and consumers—must be free.

5. Responses will vary.

6. An appropriate tone would be businesslike and persuasive. The passage is for a town meeting, so it should be formal. However, it should sound natural and confident when spoken in order to persuade the audience.

7. You might describe the tone as uncertain or questioning.

8. Words and phrases that show the author's tone include "I think," "not really a lot," and "doesn't it?"

9. You might write:

E-cigarettes are a new technology, and we know little about their long-term effects. Smoking cigarettes is certainly harmful, but is smoking an e-cigarette really safe? An e-cigarette gives off water vapor, not smoke, and advocates proclaim that it is safe. But it still delivers nicotine, a harmful, addictive substance. What are the long-term effects? There are no long-term studies to provide evidence about the harm e-cigarettes are doing to young smokers. Shouldn't we be cautious? Shouldn't our town discourage young people from smoking e-cigarettes until we know what harm is being done?

10. Responses will vary.

11. An appropriate tone for this passage would be businesslike and informational. The passage is part of a company handbook, so it should be formal and provide clear information in a direct way.

12. You might describe the tone as condescending or lecturing.

13. Words and phrases in the passage that show the author's tone include "clearly," "don't think," and "you're thinking too narrowly."

14. You might write:

The concept of a stakeholder is an essential one. A stakeholder is any person or entity who is affected by a policy or action. A stakeholder is not necessarily a customer or employee. Stakeholders also include investors, bosses, coworkers, suppliers, or members of the community. Anyone our company affects might be a stakeholder in a decision. Every proposal, report, or memo that is written should include consideration of stakeholders. The more thoughtful the company is about stakeholders, the better the company's policies will be.

15. Responses will vary.

Check Your Skills
pages 121–122

1a. Possible answers: exciting, thrilling, incredible, improbable, fantastical

1b. Possible answers: immense, honest-to-goodness

1c. Possible answers: ancient, rare, samples of

1d. Possible answers: high-tech, cutting-edge, novel, intriguing

1e. Possible answers: extinct, long-gone, vanished

2. The following is an **effective** response. It has an appropriate formal tone and confident voice.

Free trade agreements sound as if they would be effective, but the inequalities between countries requires more thoughtful regulation than free trade agreements allow. The arguments opposing free trade agreements are more compelling because the differences in wages, wealth, and industrial development between countries is extreme. Those in favor of free trade agreements want to create one single economy, but this requires equal partners. With unequal economic partners, wealth and industry will not be distributed equally. Given the current state of the world, arguments in opposition to free trade are stronger.

The following is an **ineffective** response. Its tone is inappropriate for the writing task, and the author's voice lacks confidence.

It seems like free trade agreements might work okay, but different countries are different, poor or rich, and it just seems that we need more than just free trade. I mean, the people who don't like free trade agreements are saying that jobs will go to low-paying countries and small industries will have trouble getting off the ground. That really makes sense, right? I

mean, there is a big difference between rich countries and poor ones. The people who want free trade are trying to make one big economy, I think. That seems like what they're saying. That just can't be done with really rich countries and really poor ones both competing together, can it? It just seems to me that the arguments against free trade are stronger.

3. Responses will vary. When you evaluate your voice and tone, think about adjectives that describe you as an author and adjectives that describe the attitude of your writing.

Unity and Cohesion
page 123

Evaluate Unity with TOS

Practice It!
pages 126–128

1.

Target Your Purpose (Central Idea)	
The purchase of Alaska was criticized but beneficial.	
Ordered Elements	**Specific Relationships**
Seward was criticized for buying unexplored land.	Examples of criticism
Alaska increased the size of the U.S. by 20%.	Maybe a benefit? Why is it a benefit?
Seward barely got the votes to purchase Alaska.	Example of criticism
Gold was discovered.	Economic benefit
Petroleum pipeline is a profitable resource.	Economic benefit
Alaska became the 49th state in 1959.	No relationship

2. The order can be improved by grouping the examples of criticism and then grouping the benefits. The sentence about Alaska increasing the size of the U.S. should either be removed or explained as a benefit. The sentence about Alaska becoming the 49th state needs to be replaced or revised. The paragraph would benefit from a concluding statement relating to the central idea.

3. You might write:

The $7.2 million purchase of Alaska from Russia on March 30, 1867 was widely criticized, but ultimately beneficial. Secretary of State William H. Seward was criticized for buying the large, mostly unexplored land, and critics called the deal "Seward's folly." The reluctance to buy Alaska is illustrated by the Senate vote about the purchase. Seward barely convinced the Senate to approve the purchase, a decision that passed by only one vote. However, Alaska increased the size of the U.S. by about 20 percent, providing the country with a vast pool of unexplored resources. Gold was discovered in Alaska in the 1880s and 1890s, bringing an influx of people. Today, Alaska's petroleum pipeline provides a profitable mineral resource. By January 3, 1959, when Alaska became the 49th state under President Eisenhower, the once-denounced purchase was a precious national asset.

4.

Target Your Purpose (Central Idea)	
Solar power can benefit rural areas of developing nations.	
Ordered Elements	**Specific Relationships**
In developed nations, solar power is popular.	No relationship
Without infrastructure, it gives power for cooking, water purification, and irrigation.	Examples of benefits for rural areas
Increased use in sub-Saharan Africa	Unclear? Perhaps show benefits of this?
Increases food security and allows development	Examples of benefits for rural areas
Environmentally friendly	General benefit—relate to developing nations?
Help eliminate poverty in rural areas	Conclusion

5. The examples of benefits for rural areas should be put together. The benefit of environmentally friendly technology for rural areas of developing nations should be clarified. The increasing use in sub-Saharan Africa should be tied to the central idea or removed. The mention of popularity in developed nations should be removed.

6. You might write:

Solar power can change a rural village in a developing nation, providing essential technology with little investment. In an area without access to infrastructure, solar power provides energy for cooking, water purification, and drip irrigation. The availability of solar energy increases food security and allows economic development. Because of these clear benefits, use of solar power in sub-Saharan Africa has successfully increased in recent years, providing economic improvements. Expansion of solar power in developing areas will provide long-term benefits without environmental costs of traditional power supplies. Ultimately, solar power can help eliminate poverty in rural areas with little access to technology.

7.

Target Your Purpose (Central Idea)	
A third political party is necessary to prevent gridlock.	
Ordered Elements	**Specific Relationships**
Partisanship prevents progress.	Reason a third party is needed
A political party is bound by similar interests.	Definition of a party—no relationship
Two parties cause an impasse.	Reason a third party is needed
The U.S. historically has two parties.	No relationship—background information
The parties have no reason to compromise.	Reason a third party is needed—include better support?
A vote between two people with opposing ideas leads nowhere.	Example illustrating why two parties causes gridlock
Republicans and Democrats are the two political parties.	No relationship—background information

A third party is needed to "break the tie." Three parties allows compromise.	Statement of central idea
Two parties can join together to compromise and create a majority.	How a third party works to prevent gridlock, encourage progress
The existence of political parties is inevitable.	No relationship—background information

8. The statement of the central idea would work better at the beginning of the paragraph to form an introduction. The reasons why a third party is needed should be moved together. The information with no relationship to the central idea can be removed. The background information isn't needed unless it can be tied to the central idea. The example of how a third party works to prevent gridlock can follow the reasons why two parties cause gridlock. The ending of the paragraph needs a conclusion.

9. You might write:

In a two-party system, partisanship does nothing but prevent progress; a third political party is a necessity. When there are only two parties in a political system, an impasse is inevitable. Democrats and Republicans, the two major parties in the U.S., have no reason to compromise. The party with more votes can carry through legislation and doesn't need to compromise with the minority party. If one party controls the Senate and the other controls the House, a stalemate is the result. Imagine taking a vote between two people on opposite sides of an issue. No progress is made. A third party is needed to "break the tie." In a system with three political parties, compromise works. Two parties can join together to compromise and create a majority. Political parties are inevitable; they can't be eliminated. Therefore, the best solution to gridlock is to establish a third major political party.

Check Your Skills *pages 129–130*

1a. The following is an example of an **effective** response. It is cohesive, including relevant support, and organized around a central idea.

Dear Ms. Holmes:

I am writing to apply for the position of community event organizer at the Adams Morgan Community Center. I have the experience, knowledge, and skills to be a valuable team member in this position.

I recently completed my bachelor's degree in social work, and during my studies, I completed a thesis paper about the value of community-building events. I understand not only the necessary planning and budgeting involved in creating a community event, but also the effects of a successful gathering on a community. Local picnics, dances, or shows can open doors between community members, building solidarity and creating a network for tackling community projects.

Over the last summer, I organized a showing of three classic films in Orrison, Maryland. This project involved working with the parks department, local schools, and community leaders. I also managed the budget, staff, rights acquisitions, and equipment for the event. As a result of the film series, the high school and parks department came together to organize a film studies camp which will benefit community youth for decades to come.

I hope to work on similar projects with the Adams Morgan Community Center. I look forward to hearing from you soon and learning more about this position.

Sincerely,

Conrad Marquez

The following is an example of an **ineffective** response. It lacks a clear, logical organization of ideas, and it lacks a conclusion.

Dear Ms. Holmes:

I am writing because of the job listing for the position of community event organizer at the Adams Morgan Community Center. I recently completed my bachelor's degree in social work.

I know that community centers often hold community events, and some of those events include shows, films, or dinners. I once completed a thesis paper about the value of community-building events.

There is planning and budgeting involved in creating a community event. Over the last summer, I organized a showing of three classic films in Orrison, Maryland. I realize that a community event can bring a community together and create a network for tackling community projects.

In the film series I organized, I acquired the rights to the films to show in the park. I worked with the parks department, local schools, and community leaders. In addition, there was equipment that needed to be rented and managed. The high school and parks department eventually organized a film studies camp which will benefit community youth for decades to come. I also managed the budget and staff for the event.

Sincerely,

Conrad Marquez

1b. Responses will vary. Your response should explain the logical progression of ideas in your writing and how each idea relates to the central idea.

2. The passage has some unity and cohesion, but it can be improved. The central idea of the passage is that community service is important in K–12 education. This idea could be made more specific by including a recommendation to include community service in every grade school and high school. The passage lists several reasons why community service is an important part of K–12 education, but these reasons could be tied more closely to the central idea. The sentence that mentions students who think community service is a waste of time should be removed or revised. It doesn't fit with the author's central idea. The final sentence should also be revised. A better conclusion would focus on the desirability of including community service in education.

Fluidity   *page 131*

Creating Fluidity: Find and Fill Gaps to Create Flow

Practice It!   *pages 134–136*

1. The beginning seems choppy and unnecessarily wordy. The sentences beginning "children should" and "the nurse will" are repetitive. There are also two sentences that start "teachers should" and "the teacher should," which are repetitive.

2. You might add time transitions to this passage to emphasize the order of events. You could use the transition "first" for the third sentence. The sentence "The nurse will write a health report" could have a transition such as "after examining the child."

3. The first two sentences could be combined. "When an elementary child feels sick during the school day, teachers should follow these procedures." The fourth sentence can be restructured. "In case of faintness, a buddy should accompany the sick child to the nurse." The fifth and sixth sentences can be combined. "After examining the child, the nurse will write a health report and send it to the teacher." The final sentence can be restructured. "That afternoon, the teacher should make sure the health report goes home to the parent or guardian."

4. You might write:

   When an elementary child feels sick during the school day, teachers should follow these procedures. First, the sick child should get a hall pass from the teacher to see the nurse. In case of faintness, a buddy should accompany the sick child to the nurse. After examining the child, the nurse will write a health report and send it to the teacher. That afternoon, the teacher should make sure the health report goes home to the parent or guardian.

5. Most of the sentences in the paragraph seem short and choppy. There are two sentences about the Civil Rights Movements and two sentences about women's rights that could be combined. The sentences that begin with "college students" sound choppy and repetitive.

6. The final sentence could begin with a transitional phrase, such as "with its widespread social change." The fourth sentence could begin with a transition such as "at the same time" or "in addition."

7. The two sentences about civil rights can be combined. "The Civil Rights Movement, led by Dr. Martin Luther King, came to a climax." The next two sentences can also be combined. "At the same time, with Gloria Steinem heading the newly formed National Organization of Women (NOW), women began to agitate for their rights." The two sentences about college students would be better combined. "College students began to agitate against the conservative norms of their parents and launched what is now called the "Sexual Revolution.""

8. You might write:

The 1960s was a time of great change in American culture. The Civil Rights Movement, led by Dr. Martin Luther King, came to a climax. At the same time, with Gloria Steinem heading the newly formed National Organization of Women (NOW), women began to agitate for their rights. College students began to agitate against the conservative norms of their parents and launched what is now called the "Sexual Revolution." With its widespread social change, the 1960s changed the course of the twentieth century.

9a. We tested two groups and found no significant difference in the results.

9b. The election resulted in a close victory for the incumbent.

9c. New breakthroughs in cancer research appear in the media every day but take years to develop into usable therapies.

10a. During the ten-hour council meeting, dozens of people spoke.

10b. Extreme weather events, which can be costly and deadly, may occur more frequently in the future.

10c. School shootings are traumatic for communities. Unfortunately, the causes of school shootings are controversial.

11. Responses will vary. The following example response uses transitions and varying sentence structures to achieve fluid writing.

The percentage of U.S. citizens who are imprisoned is higher than any other country in the world. While the U.S. represents 5% of the world population, it has almost a quarter of the world's prisoners. In 2009, the U.S. had 742 prisoners per 100,000 citizens. These numbers are alarming. Politicians always seem to receive praise for being tough on crime, but a hard-line stance has caused America's prisons to swell. The result of increased sentencing, often for non-violent offenses, is a costly, overcrowded prison system. In contrast, the Netherlands closed 19 prisons in 2013 due to a lack of prisoners. Decreased crime and the use of electronic tagging has allowed the Netherlands to save countless tax dollars and achieve a low incarceration rate of 163 people per 100,000. The United States needs to review its justice system and develop fair, effective laws, because endlessly escalating sentencing only creates costly social problems.

12. You might advise your friend to read her work aloud and listen for the choppy areas. It might help to read the paper together and identify problems with the writing style. You might demonstrate for your friend specific examples of how adding transitions or modifying sentence structure can improve her writing. You might give your friend advice on how to choose transitions or combine sentences.

Check Your Skills
pages 137–138

1a. Possible answers: Early in the day, That day

1b. Possible answers: However

1c. Possible answers: That night, In the evening

1d. Possible answers: During the play, Later

1e. Possible answers: Then, Sadly, After waiting for the perfect time

2. c. Velocity is a measurement of an object's speed and direction of movement.

3. c. The new law is confusing because its language is meant to deceive readers.

4. You might write:

In 1939, Germans made advancements toward developing an atomic bomb. After learning of these advancements, scientists Albert Einstein and Enrico Fermi warned President Roosevelt of the dangers. Roosevelt agreed to start American research into atomic weapons, and eventually this research effort was named the Manhattan Project.

5. The following is an **effective** response. It includes transitions and variations in sentence structure.

The argument that organ donation should be opt-out instead of opt-in is a strong one. The author's solution to organ donation shortages is an opt-out program where people are donors by default. This solution preserves individual choice by providing the option to opt-out of the program while greatly increasing organ donation. As support, the author cites the programs in Germany and Austria which show the effectiveness of an opt-out program in increasing organ donation. However, the author says opt-out programs have "no down side." If citizens are not aware that they are organ donors by default, such a program could be criticized. The argument would be stronger if the author addressed this issue.

The following is an **ineffective** response. It is choppy and lacks transitions.

The author's argument for opt-out organ donation is a strong one. The author's argument suggests an opt-out program where people are donors by default. The author's solution preserves individual choice. The solution provides the option to opt-out of the program. The solution also greatly increases organ donation. The author cites the programs in Germany and Austria. The programs show the effectiveness of an opt-out program in increasing organ donation. The author says opt-out programs have "no down side." Opt-out programs can be criticized. Citizens might not be aware that they are organ donors by default. The argument would be stronger if the author addressed this issue.

6. Responses will vary. Your response should include examples of transitions and varied sentence structures that provide fluidity in your writing.

Clarity   *page 139*

Using POP to Clarify Writing

Practice It!   *pages 142–144*

1. The purpose of the paragraph is to ask for copyright reform to prevent lawsuits for certain uses of copyrighted material. The statement of the purpose at the end of the paragraph is confusing and could be clarified. A clearer statement of the types of changes the author wants would also help.

2. The paragraph starts by stating that copyright law needs reform. The introduction could be improved by explaining how or why the law should be reformed. The middle of the paragraph includes examples of problems with copyright law. The sentence "They will threaten a lawsuit against anyone for any use of the song" disrupts the list of examples and should be moved or revised. The ending calls for reform, but it is stated unclearly.

3. The sentence about online videos has an unclear pronoun, "it's." The phrasing of the sentence that starts "When there is a problem…" is confusing. The meaning and wording need to be clarified. The last sentence starts with a dangling phrase and also needs to be clarified.

4. You might write:

Copyright law needs reform because the current laws allow large companies to prosecute individuals and small businesses for harmless uses of copyrighted materials. The copyrighted song "Happy Birthday" cannot be used at restaurant birthday parties without paying a fee. Music industry organizations threaten to sue bar owners for unauthorized performances by cover bands. Online videos can get taken down because a copyrighted song is playing in the background. The prevalence of threats of lawsuits against individuals and small businesses demonstrates that copyright laws are too stringent. Copyright law should define clearly harmless, allowable uses of copyrighted material, such as a non-professional casual performance of a song or an insignificant use of music in a not-for-profit video. If such laws are put into place, the music industry and other large industries won't be able to take advantage of small businesses and individuals.

5. The purpose of the paragraph is to explain the causes and effects of antibiotic-resistant bacteria. The opening statement doesn't clearly address the purpose. A summary or concluding statement would also help show the purpose of the paragraph.

6. A clearer organization could help the paragraph. The paragraph does present causes of antibiotic-resistant strains of bacteria and then effects of those bacteria. However, the sections of the paragraph aren't clear, and the paragraph lacks a strong introduction and conclusion. The paragraph could begin with an overall statement about the causes and effects of antibiotic-resistant bacteria, followed by causes that resulted in these strains, followed by the effects, and finally a concluding statement.

7. The author uses the words "these" and "they" without clarifying what the pronouns mean. Reducing the use of the pronoun "these" will help.

8. You might write:

Antibiotic-resistant strains of bacteria are a public health problem that is primarily caused by misuse of antibiotics. Antibiotic-resistant bacteria developed because of the widespread misuse of antibiotics. Antibiotics are overprescribed, and patients often fail to take their full course of antibiotics. This causes drug-resistant bacteria to survive and reproduce. The excessive use of antibiotics in farm animals also contributes to the development of antibiotic-resistant strains. In some cases, strains of bacteria become so resistant that modern medicine has no effective treatment. When antibiotic-resistant bacteria spread, they cause dangerous and often deadly infections. Antibiotic-resistant bacteria are a

result of scientific advances to fight disease, and new advances will be needed to combat these hazardous strains.

9. The purpose of the paragraph is to document how to customize invoices. The main goal is communicating a procedure. The purpose would be better served by breaking down the procedure into simple steps. Complex sentences interfere with communication in this paragraph.

10. The paragraph starts abruptly by talking about a specific template file. An introduction explaining the purpose of the paragraph will help clarify the writing. The order of the paragraph should clearly reflect the order of the procedure. It would make more sense for the instructions for opening the file to appear before the instructions for modifying the file. A concluding or summary sentence at the end would also help the paragraph organization.

11. The main issue with phrasing is long sentences with too much information. Shorter, clearer sentences will help readers understand the author's meaning.

12. You might write:

Company invoices can be easily customized with TT Accounting software. To customize your company's invoices, you will modify the template and logo image used to generate invoices. The invoice template is called invoice.tpl. This file can be found in the "templates" folder in the "TT Accounting" folder. However, you can easily open and modify the template from the software interface by clicking on the templates tab and choosing the invoice.tpl file. Once you open the template, you can modify the text, layout, and form fields that will appear on the invoice. Simply save the modified template to update all future invoices. You can also modify the logo on your invoices by replacing or editing the default logo file, logo.jpg, which is located in the "images" folder in the "TT Accounting" folder. Once you customize your invoices, they will enhance your company's professional image.

Check Your Skills *pages 145–146*

1. d. One common email scam is phishing. In a phishing scam, criminals send fake emails, supposedly from banks or other institutions.

2. c. The hospital visiting hours end at 6:00 P.M.

3. c. As I was going to the office in the morning, the weather was cold and rainy.

4. a. Because of their portrayals of families, TV shows often promote stereotypes.

5. The following is an **effective** response. It has a clear purpose, clear organization, and clear phrasing.

The arguments supporting home schooling are more effective than those opposing it because home schooling provides personalized attention that can be more effective than traditional schools. Home schooling is a valid alternative to public or private schools which cannot meet the needs of every student. A well-run home school provides personal instruction that is custom-tailored to both the student and the parent. The opposing arguments are primarily concerned with quality control and poorly implemented home schools. These are not reasons to oppose home schooling. Instead, they are reasons to regulate home schooling appropriately. Through smart, unobtrusive regulation, quality can be maintained in home schools. Overall, the arguments in favor of home schooling are strongest, since the objections to home schooling can be overcome through legitimate regulation.

The following is an **ineffective** response. It lacks a clear purpose, clear organization, and clear phrasing of its ideas.

Supporting home schooling, the arguments show that home schooling is okay. You can teach children at home through home schooling or you can send them to private or public schools. There, students have what they need. They can be well-run. Providing students with custom-tailored education, the student and parent are both happy. Against home schooling, quality control and poorly implemented home schools are the problem. It isn't why there are reasons to oppose home schooling. Regulating home schools, the schools can be effective. Quality is what the needs are for schools. That's the reason for good schooling for students.

6. Responses will vary. When you evaluate the clarity of your response, discuss how well it fulfills the purpose, how well it is organized, and how well its phrasing communicates your meaning.

Focus: Submit page 147

Proofreading page 149

Proofreading: The Language Microscope

Practice It! pages 152–154

1–3. The paragraph has the following errors:
- "Researchers carefully designs" should be "Researchers carefully design."
- The first sentence is a comma splice.
- The word "die" is misspelled. It should be "dye."
- The word "effects" is misspelled. It should be "affects."
- The word "effected" is misspelled. It should be "affected."
- The last sentence is a comma splice.
- The word "affects" in the last sentence is misspelled. It should be "effects."

Reading aloud can help you find comma splices and mismatched subjects and verbs (such as "researchers designs"). This technique is not as effective for commonly confused words such as "effect" and "affect." Using a piece of paper to focus on one line or reading backwards can be effective for finding commonly confused words.

4. The writer seems to have problems with comma splices and commonly confused words, especially the words "effect" and "affect." You might advise the writer to check for these errors.

5–7. The paragraph has the following errors:
- The words "you're are" should be "you are" or "you're."
- The words "a list of task" should be "a list of tasks."
- "Whenever you are bombarded with a list of tasks" is a fragment. It can be combined with the following sentence.
- The word "frist" is misspelled. It should be "first."
- The word "than" is misspelled. It should be "then."
- The word "brake" is misspelled. It should be "break."

- "In between these smaller tasks" is a fragment. It can be combined with the following sentence.
- In the last sentence, the word "you're" is misspelled. It should be "your."

Reading aloud can help you find repeated words (such as "you're are"), typos (such as "a list of task"), and fragments (such as "in between smaller tasks"). Using a piece of paper to focus on each line can help you find typos, fragments, and misspellings, including commonly confused words. Reading backwards can be especially helpful to find misspellings that aren't commonly confused words, such as "frist."

8. The paragraph has several careless misspellings or typos. You might advise the writer to type more carefully and to check each word for typos. The author also has two fragments and should check for fragments when proofreading.

9. Responses will vary. Tracking the specific errors that you make will help you eliminate these errors and improve your writing.

10. Responses will vary. You may find different proofreading methods useful for different types of errors.

11. You might advise your friend to spellcheck and proofread papers before submitting them. You could suggest several proofreading methods, including reading aloud, using a ruler or piece of paper to focus on a single line, and reading backwards to find typos and other errors. Reviewing your friend's paper to see what types of errors he or she made is a good suggestion. You might tell your friend to keep track of common errors to check before submitting a paper.

12. A spelling error on a job application could mean that your application is immediately discarded. Employers are looking for applicants who care about the position and who are good professional communicators. A spelling error on a job application shows either carelessness or an inability to proofread successfully.

Check Your Skills   *pages 155–156*

1. Their are many possible ways to reform immigration laws. Because the availability of illegal jobs encourages immigration. One important reform is to crack down on employers who higher illegal immigrants, especially at lower then minimum wages.

The corrected paragraph would read:

There are many possible ways to reform immigration laws. Because the availability of illegal jobs encourages immigration, one important reform is to crack down on employers who hire illegal immigrants, especially at lower than minimum wages.

2. Though interpretation of the U.S. Constitution, the Supreme Court determines what can or can't be law. Supreme Court decisions have lead too integrating schools, overturning abortion laws, and enforcing Miranda rights. Those who disagree with court rulings often criticize "activist judges," on on the other hand, the majority of lawmakers and voters may not respect the inherent rights of the minority.

The corrected paragraph would read:

Through interpretation of the U.S. Constitution, the Supreme Court determines what can or can't be law. Supreme Court decisions have led to integrating schools, overturning abortion laws, and enforcing Miranda rights. Those who disagree with court rulings often criticize "activist judges." On the other hand, the majority of lawmakers and voters may not respect the inherent rights of the minority.

3. I have supporting my family for two years with out a college degree. This experience have taught me the value of hard work, persistence, and planning. It has also shown me the value of education. I plan too put my hard work, persistence, and planning skills work to help me succeed in college.

The corrected paragraph would read:

I have supported my family for two years without a college degree. This experience has taught me the value of hard work, persistence, and planning. It has also shown me the value

of education. I plan to put my hard work, persistence, and planning skills to work to help me succeed in college.

4. b. Replace **Birds'** with **Birds**

5. c. Replace **consisting** with **consisted**

6. The paragraph contains the following errors:
   - The word "teh" is misspelled. It should be "the."
   - The word "then" is misspelled. It should be "than."
   - The word "a" is repeated.
   - In the last sentence, two main clauses are joined incorrectly. A comma is needed before the word "and."

The corrected paragraph would read:

Based on our market research report, television advertising is not proving successful for our camping and outdoor gear marketing. Focus groups show that our target audience spends more time on the Internet than watching television. Our advertising department is currently developing a pilot Internet advertising program, and the marketing department will present a plan for viral Internet marketing next week.

7. The paragraph contains the following errors:
   - The word "todays" is possessive. It should have an apostrophe: "today's."
   - The word "socity" is misspelled. It should be "society."
   - The word "chose" is misspelled. It should be "choose." These are commonly confused words. "Chose" is past tense, and "choose" is present tense.
   - The word "there" is misspelled. It should be the possessive pronoun "their." These are commonly confused words.
   - The word "grate" is misspelled. It should be "great."
   - The word "benifit" is misspelled. It should be "benefit."

The corrected paragraph would read:

Stay-at-home fathers are becoming more and more common in today's society. Many fathers choose to stay at home because their partners have better jobs or because they cannot find work. In either case, a stay-at-home dad can be a great benefit to the children.

Publishing   page 157

The Publishing Process

Practice It!   *pages 160–162*

1. The venue is the company's blog, which uses blog publishing software.

2. The publishing requirements are:
   - A title.
   - A permalink (a direct URL), which will be automatically generated but can be changed manually.
   - The text and images of the post.
   - Optional categories and tags to describe the post and make it easy for readers to find.

3. You should write a title: "New Spring Candles!"

   You might choose a category: "Sales & Specials."

   You might also add images to the post.

4. You should preview the blog post using the "Preview" button in the upper right. After making any needed changes, publish the post by using the "Publish" button.

5. The venue is the college class. The professor defines how the paper should be submitted and the requirements of publication.

6. You can determine the publishing requirements by referring to the MLA style guide. Style guides give specific requirements for formatting written works.

7. The works cited need to be formatted and listed alphabetically by the author's last name.

   Fletcher, George P., and Steve Sheppard. *American Law in Global Perspective: The Basics.* Oxford: Oxford University Press, 2004.

Nelson, William E. *Marbury v. Madison: The Origins and Legacy of Judicial Review.* Lawrence, KS: University Press of Kansas, 2000.

Stone, Geoffrey R. *Constitutional Law.* 5th ed. New York: Aspen Publishers, 2005.

8. Before publishing, you would check that the paper is correctly formatted according to the MLA guidelines, including the title, headers and footers, font, margins, citations in the text, and works cited. To publish your paper, you would print it, check that the printout is correct, and turn it in to the professor's mailbox.

9. Responses will vary. Examples of publishing your writing could include mailing a letter to a company, submitting an article to a newspaper or magazine, sending in an application, printing a newsletter, or sending an email.

10. Responses will vary depending on the newspaper. For *The New York Times*, letters should:
    - Be exclusive to *The Times*, not open letters or third-party letters.
    - Be 150 to 175 words.
    - Refer to an article that appeared in *The Times* within the last seven days.
    - Include the writer's address and phone numbers.
    - Not include attachments.
    - Be sent to letters@nytimes.com or to inytletters@nytimes.com for *The International New York Times*.

11. Responses will vary. The publishing step can be simple for venues that are open to many people, such as submitting a letter to the editor or sending an email.

Check Your Skills

pages 163–164

1. The email should be brief. Since you are attaching the cover letter, you do not need to go over your qualifications. You might write:

To hr@mitchfieldchemicals.com
Subject Application to Research Group Assistant Position
Dear Ms. Lozano: I am writing to apply to the research group assistant position. My cover letter and résumé are attached, as requested. I look forward to hearing from you soon. Thank you for your time and attention. Sincerely, Jason Kirkland
Send [résumé file] [cover letter file]

2. To finalize and send your job application, check the email address, file attachments, subject line, and email text. Then, click the "Send" button.

3. You might write:

Most writing is ultimately meant for a reader, and publishing is important because it delivers the writing to the reader. The first step in publishing a written work is to identify the venue. A venue is the place or way in which the writing is published. For a letter, the venue could be email or a physical letter. For an article, the venue is the magazine, newspaper, or website where the article will be published. The next step is to understand the requirements of the venue. For a college paper, the professor will require formatting according to specific style guides. For a business email, a subject line and formal style is required. For a job application, the company will provide guidelines for submission. Most publishing venues have their own specific requirements. The final step is to ensure that the publishing guidelines are followed and to submit the work. No matter the writing task, from emailing a client to writing an autobiography, it will need to be published. While publishing is sometimes as simple as hitting a "Send" or "Submit" button, it is important to be aware of publishing requirements. Neglecting publishing requirements can lower a grade on a paper, cause a publisher to reject a manuscript, or make a client miss an important email.

Organization

page 165

Organizing Short Answers

page 167

Organizing a Short Answer Using the Writing Process

Practice It!

pages 172–175

1a. Central Idea: In a study on the effect of regular exercise on clinical depression, a control group suffering from depression would not exercise regularly so that scientists could more accurately measure the effects of exercise.

Details: A control group is not affected by the factor being studied. Comparing the experimental group to a control group allows scientists to effectively test an independent variable. An experiment with a control group can account for complex factors that might affect the experimental group.

1b. You might write:

> **Beginning:**
> A study on the effect of regular exercise on clinical depression should include a control group suffering from depression that does not follow a regular exercise routine so that scientists can more accurately measure the effects of exercise.

> **Middle:**
> A well-designed study uses an experimental group and a control group. The control group is not affected by the factor being studied, the independent variable. In this case, the independent variable is regular exercise. Comparing the experimental group to a control group allows scientists to effectively test the independent variable. In a study on the effect of regular exercise on clinical depression, scientists should compare changes in clinical depression among the control group (which does not get regular exercise) with changes among the experimental group (which does get regular exercise). An experiment with a control group can account for complex factors that might affect the experimental group, such as changes in environment or life events that might affect depression.

Ending:
If scientists designed a study that only tracked depressed individuals who took regular exercise, they might find that 25% of those individuals experienced improvement in their depression. But what does that number mean? If a control group showed 5% improvement, the study's results would be far different than if a control group showed 25% improvement also. The control group gives the study context.

2a. Central Idea: Based on the Doscero Industries company policy, Kara should report her concerns to her manager's supervisor.

Details: "Doscero Industries encourages an open environment where employees can voice their ideas and concerns." "If a concern involves the manager's performance directly, the employee should voice this concern to the manager's superior." "The company will act promptly to respond to improper behavior and will not tolerate any retaliation."

2b. You might write:

Beginning:
Based on the Doscero Industries company policy, Kara should report her concerns to her manager's supervisor.

Middle:
The company professes to want employees to voice their concerns, stating that it "encourages an open environment." Certainly, the company's official position is that Kara should communicate her ethical concern that her boss is favoring another employee. Since the issue directly involves her manager, policy states that Kara should contact her manager's supervisor. By writing an email to the supervisor and including references to the employee manual, she can maintain documentation of her complaint and her compliance with company policy. Kara might be concerned about retaliation from her manager, but the manual clearly states that the company "will not tolerate any retaliation."

Ending:
Any employee who has an ethical concern about a direct superior is in a difficult position, but the Doscero Industries company policy gives Kara a clear course of action to address the situation.

You can use some direct quotes in your response, but don't rely on them. Restate ideas from the passage to show that you understand.

Check Your Skills   *pages 176–178*

1. The following is an example of an **effective** response. The beginning explains the amplified greenhouse effect. The middle identifies the arguments for reduced growth in the future and evaluates those arguments. The ending makes a big-picture observation about the results of climate change.

According to NASA, scientists have identified a phenomenon, known as the amplified greenhouse effect, that is changing the growing season and amount of vegetation in northern latitudes. The reduction of polar ice and snow increases the greenhouse effect, causing increased warming in northern areas and more green growth. The article presents an argument that increased plant growth may not continue. First, side effects of growth such as forest fires and drought may slow growth. Second, availability of water and sunlight may limit growth of plant life. These arguments are logical, since these are well known and clearly observable factors that affect plant growth in other areas. The article does not provide data about forest fires, infestations, drought, and available resources for plant growth, so it seems that there are many unknown factors affecting the potential future landscape of northern areas. Ecosystems are complex. While current warming trends and changes in seasonal growth can be observed, the long-term effects of climate change are not as easy to predict.

The following is an example of an **ineffective** response. It includes some poor word choices (i.e., "the idea of the amplified greenhouse effect" instead of simply "the amplified greenhouse effect," "ground" instead of "Earth") and fails to evaluate the arguments the article gives for why plant growth might not continue to increase. For extra practice, try revising this response.

The idea of the amplified greenhouse effect occurs through the interaction of gases such as carbon dioxide that trap the heat against the ground, causing polar ice and snow to melt. Although trees are already growing where there was once snow, scientists report that the increase in plants might not continue the same. Ironically, the warming effect that is causing the increase in plant life is likely to have negative effects, such as forest fires and droughts, that will stop more plant growth. While the northern latitudes may become warmer and lose their ice pack, they may not be as green as we would expect.

2. The following is an example of an **effective** response. It includes details from the article that explain why arctic and antarctic ice is expected to melt.

The greenhouse effect causes warming of the Earth because of gases and clouds in the atmosphere. An increasing greenhouse effect is projected to cause ice melt in the arctic and antarctic. The diagram of the greenhouse effect shows that radiation from the sun is either absorbed by the Earth or reflected into the atmosphere. Some of the reflected radiation is trapped as heat by clouds and gases in the atmosphere. According to the article, increased water vapor, carbon dioxide, and methane trap heat near the Earth's surface. This causes ice to melt in both northern and southern latitudes, affecting arctic and antarctic ice. Once ice and snow has melted, the article notes that the exposed land and ocean is less reflective. More heat is absorbed by the Earth, and this also causes increased warming and, in turn, more ice melt. The factors limiting plant growth do not limit ice melt, which may continue as long as the Earth continues to warm.

The following is an example of an **ineffective** response. It is repetitive, lacks good organization, and relies on a long quote from the article without explaining it or expanding on it. For extra practice, try revising this response.

The greenhouse effect is a way that the Earth is getting warmer, and because the Earth is getting warmer, ice will melt. Ice melts in warm temperatures. The article says that "increased concentrations of heat-trapping gases, such as water vapor, carbon dioxide, and methane, cause Earth's surface, ocean, and lower atmosphere to warm." The sun shines on the Earth, and it makes the Earth warm. Some of the warmth gets trapped because of "clouds, carbon dioxide, and other gases." This means the arctic and antarctic ice will both melt.

3. The following is an example of an **effective** response. It includes details from the passage as well as evaluations and responses to the arguments in the passage. It makes original arguments in favor of the proposed bill.

Dear Senator:

I am writing in opposition to the proposed bill to cut military spending over the next five years. The Department of Defense is especially crucial in a time of instability in many parts of the world, including the Middle East. I understand that proponents of this bill note that China and Russia spend only $150 billion annually on their militaries, but the amount of military spending by other countries does not necessarily indicate our military need. The United States military has been overextended through conflicts in the Middle East, so clearly our military is not too large. Opponents of the bill note that Medicare, Medicaid, and Social Security make up a larger percentage of the budget than military spending. While this does not necessarily mean that these programs should be cut instead of the Department of Defense budget, it shows that there are other parts of the budget to examine for potential spending reduction. I strongly encourage you to vote against the proposed bill.

Sincerely,

A Concerned Taxpayer

The following is an example of an **ineffective** response. It gives little information and does not critique the argument from the passage in any way. It does not acknowledge the opposing arguments. For extra practice, try revising this response.

Dear Senator:

I am writing in favor of the proposed bill to cut military spending over the next five years. I hope you vote in favor of it. I discovered that our military spending is more than four times China and Russia combined. That is an unbelievable statistic. Why are we spending so much money on defense? Please vote in favor of this reasonable bill to cut unreasonable spending.

Sincerely,

A Concerned Taxpayer

Organizing Extended Responses
page 179

Developing an Organized Extended Response

Practice It! pages 184–187

1a.

Central Idea:	Details or Explanation:
Jefferson said institutions must "keep pace with the times," and the changing times require that the Constitution be amended to limit the powers of corporations.	The Founding Fathers likely never foresaw corporations would be considered as "citizens" with rights.
Supporting Idea: Corporations are not citizens.	**Details and Evidence:** "inhuman, legal entities without inherent rights" vs. "associations of citizens"

	The Supreme Court considers corporations "associations of citizens." Corporations are not citizens in other ways, i.e. going to jail, voting.
Supporting idea: A constitutional amendment is needed because the Supreme Court made the ruling that corporations deserve free speech.	**Details and Evidence:** The Supreme Court rules on constitutionality, so only a constitutional amendment can counter the ruling. Jefferson: "new discoveries are made, new truths disclosed" Citizens United is a new way of looking at corporations.
Conclusion: Changing the Constitution is not a light decision.	**Details or Explanation:** Citizens United immediately/ significantly affected elections, so a constitutional amendment is worth pursuing.

1b. You might write:

Jefferson professed that institutions must "keep pace with the times," and the changing times require that the Constitution be amended to limit the powers of corporations. Mr. Kittridge makes a strong argument that it is wrong to assign corporations rights. The Founding Fathers likely never foresaw that corporations might be considered citizens, and so a constitutional amendment is appropriate to adapt to unforeseen changes in society.

Mr. Kittridge makes the argument that corporations are not citizens and should not have rights. His position is in opposition to the Supreme Court decision that classifies corporations as "associations of citizens." While groups of private citizens certainly have the same rights as individuals to freedom of speech and assembly, a corporation is clearly not merely a group of citizens. As Kittridge points out, a corporation is a legal entity that protects owners from business liabilities. The purpose of a corporation is to conduct business and make money, and so a corporation has self-interest to promote. However, that same corporation has no empathy, civic duty, or personal liability. Defining a corporation as an "association of citizens" with human rights is misguided at best.

A constitutional amendment is needed because the Supreme Court made the ruling that corporations deserve free speech. The Supreme Court rules on constitutionality, so clarifying the Constitution with an amendment seems the best way to counter the Citizens United decision. Jefferson said that changes in government are needed when "new discoveries are made, new truths disclosed." Modern corporations are a new truth in society, and the government needs rules that clearly define corporations as different from individuals.

Changing the Constitution is not a light decision, and Jefferson points out that "frequent and untried" changes could be hazards to government. Citizens United immediately and significantly affected elections with an influx of financial contributions, so it requires a strong response. A constitutional amendment defining corporations as entities without rights meets Jefferson's criteria for necessary change.

1c. When you evaluate your work, look for strong organization with supporting ideas clarified by strong details and evidence.

2a.

Central Idea:	Details or Explanation:
The arguments against zero-tolerance policies are stronger.	Zero-tolerance policies try to eliminate problems with biased decision making or student excuses, but the problems they cause are serious.

Supporting Idea:	Details and Evidence:
Zero-tolerance policies attempt to deal with real problems, but they cause serious issues.	Witness reports are unreliable, and teachers can be biased. "Zero-tolerance" creates unfair circumstances, i.e. expulsion for minor offences. Victims may be punished along with bullies.
Supporting idea: The best way of dealing with violence is not necessarily expulsion or suspension.	**Details and Evidence:** Violence doesn't go away when students are kicked out of school. Violence signifies emotional, psychological problems.
Conclusion: The idea of the punishment fitting the crime is an important one.	**Details or Explanation:** Treating all situations with one broad-stroke solution rarely works. Each circumstance needs an appropriate response.

2b. You might write:

It is easy to understand how a zero-tolerance policy might be appealing. Any of us might, in a moment of frustration, cry, "Why would they allow violent students in our schools?" Zero-tolerance policies attempt to increase safety and security while eliminating problems with biased decision-making. However, the arguments against such policies are stronger, since zero-tolerance policies cause unjustified results and serious problems. It is questionable whether they provide effective solutions.

Zero-tolerance policies address real issues of teacher or administrator bias, unreliable witness reports, and student lies. Addressing each conflict on its own merits is a difficult task. If punishments could be reliably automated to eliminate human error, it might be a good thing. A zero-tolerance policy, however, does not dole out punishments well. Bullied students may be punished for defending themselves or even simply for being attacked. Instances of unfair expulsion or suspension are worse than potential bias in punishment. They rob students of their education.

The best way of dealing with violence is not necessarily expulsion or suspension. As opponents of zero-tolerance policies note, violence is merely pushed out of the school instead of being properly addressed. Violence signifies emotional, psychological, social, or even physical problems. Students involved in violent instances need help more than expulsion. An important piece of evidence is missing from the proponents' arguments for zero-tolerance policies: evidence that the policies are effective in reducing violence and improving education. On the other hand, there is evidence that students can be hurt unfairly by these policies.

The idea of the punishment fitting the crime is an important one, and treating all situations with one broad-stroke solution rarely works. Each circumstance is different and needs an appropriate response to help both the instigators and victims of violence.

2c. When you evaluate your work, look for strong organization, with supporting ideas clarified by strong details and evidence.

Check Your Skills   *pages 188–190*

1. The following is an example of an **effective** response. It addresses and evaluates the arguments in the passage, and it has a clear position.

> Based on the positions stated in the passage, the evidence in favor of banning or regulating energy drinks is strongest because energy drinks can cause serious health problems. Those in favor of regulation have strong evidence of harmful health effects, and arguments against regulation ignore those hazards.
>
> Serious health effects such as convulsion, anaphylactic shock, and even death have been documented by the Food and Drug Administration, a reliable source. The example of the high school student who suffered a seizure and nearly died as the result of consuming an energy

drink brings this threat home. Any teen could suffer the same reaction. Can these drinks be considered safe? The additional reports of energy drinks harming pregnant women are also significant. The proponents of energy drinks categorize them as healthy, noting ingredients such as antioxidants and herbal remedies. This makes the drinks even more dangerous. Children, teens, and pregnant women are likely unaware of the risks.

The arguments against regulation in this passage fail to take into account the health risks of energy drinks. Opponents compare regulating energy drinks to anti-tobacco campaigns. Both products are harmful, and both need regulation. Both are represented by companies with a financial interest, and those companies will fight regulation on every level. Energy drink proponents state that the risk of death from an energy drink is less than risk of death from cigarettes. The argument is that energy drinks are not risky enough to ban, but the risks the FDA has compiled include death and miscarriage. Should the "free market" be free to advertise products as healthy when they could cause death?

The controversy should not be over whether to regulate products with proven health risks. The controversy should be over how to regulate those products. At a minimum, consumers need to be aware of the risks associated with energy drinks.

The following is an example of an **ineffective** response. It does not have enough specific details and a clear progression of ideas. It does use the passage to construct an argument, but it needs better organization and clearer support. Try revising this response for extra practice.

> Energy drinks aren't good for you, and so banning them is probably a good idea. The idea of something giving you a seizure is really bad and harmful. Companies will always want to advertise their products, and they aren't the ones who are going to tell you that something is bad for you. Like the passage says, banning energy drinks is like banning tobacco. Maybe tobacco is worse, but both are being banned for the same reasons. Both have health hazards. Energy drinks can cause seizures, miscarriages, and death. Tobacco can cause lung cancer,

emphysema, and death. Those under 18 years old shouldn't be able to buy either one. We can trust the FDA to say what's good for us, and it's pretty obvious that energy drinks aren't.

2. The following is an example of an **effective** response. It has a clear and well-supported position.

A regulation banning energy drinks with more than 100 milligrams of caffeine per serving is beneficial because the problem with energy drinks is an excess of caffeine. A ban on excess caffeine goes to the heart of the problem, making it a better choice than a regulation preventing anyone under 18 from buying energy drinks. This type of regulation is difficult to enforce and does not address the core issue. The problems with energy drinks are better addressed by attacking the source of the problem: excessive caffeine in the drinks.

The health dangers from energy drinks are due to high levels of caffeine. The dangers aren't limited to teenagers and children. Pregnant women are at particular risk, since fetal distress syndrome and miscarriage are possible hazards. A ban on high-caffeine energy drinks would help address these significant dangers.

A regulation banning higher-caffeine energy drinks is also easier to enforce. Alcohol and cigarettes, though illegal for teens, are still accessible. Limiting caffeine levels of drinks is enforceable at the level of the manufacturer, distributor, and retailer. Businesses already must deal with regulations for safety. Adding this additional regulation is not an undue burden and benefits the health of the community.

The manufacturer is the one most responsible for the hazards of high-caffeine drinks. It makes sense to require manufacturers to reduce caffeine levels or stop selling their drinks. No consumer needs a drink with more than 100 milligrams of caffeine per serving. A ban on high-caffeine drinks is a sensible solution which addresses the cause of negative health effects from energy drinks.

The following is an example of an **ineffective** response. It does not choose a clear position, although it does address some arguments for each regulation. It needs more development and a strong central idea. This response also includes casual and indecisive language, such as "I guess." Try revising this response for extra practice.

A regulation banning high-caffeine drinks might be a good idea, or stopping teenagers from buying high-caffeine drinks might be a good idea too. If you don't have high-caffeine drinks available to buy, you won't buy as much caffeine. But I guess you could buy a lot of drinks at once and still get a lot of caffeine. That might be kind of dangerous. If you don't let kids buy energy drinks, they wouldn't drink them. Pregnant women or adults could still have seizures, miscarriages, or other health problems from too much caffeine. That's also a problem but maybe not the one the regulations are trying to solve. If you had both regulations, then you would have less danger of people having "caffeine toxicity" like it says in the passage. I guess I would be in favor of either of the regulations being put in place.

Organizing Workplace Documents *page 191*

Workplace Documents: Type, Purpose, and Audience

Practice It! *pages 195–200*

1. A memo should include:
   - A heading area at the top with "TO:" (the recipients' names and job titles), "FROM:" (the senders' names and job titles), "DATE:" (the date the memo is sent), and "SUBJECT:" or "RE:" (describing briefly the subject of the memo).
   - A body with a beginning, middle, and ending.
   - Attachments, if needed.

2. The purpose of the memo is to give the clients an introduction to the planned campaign and invite them to a presentation of the campaign. The audience is the client, the people in charge of marketing at Klean Floss.

3. You might write:

TO: Myra Sommers, Marketing Manager, Klean Floss

FROM: Nancy Tang, Project Manager, JTM Marketing

DATE: June 22, 2014

SUBJECT: Klean Floss Marketing Campaign

Introduction

Overview of the marketing campaign
- Benefit of a clean feeling
- Mail-in offer for a free sample
- Television, direct mail, and email
- Budget of $285,000

Invitation to the presentation
- Purpose to review the campaign in detail
- July 5 at 2:00 P.M. at JTM Marketing

Conclusion and thanks

4. You might write:

TO: Myra Sommers, Marketing Manager, Klean Floss

FROM: Nancy Tang, Project Manager, JTM Marketing

DATE: June 22, 2014

SUBJECT: Klean Floss Marketing Campaign

The advertising department at JTM has reviewed the Klean Floss product and marketing history, and we have developed a proposed campaign that will be effective in meeting your goals for the product.

The campaign will focus on the benefit of a clean feeling and include a mail-in offer for a free sample. It will target television, direct mail, and email, with an anticipated budget of $285,000.

We would like to invite you to a presentation on July 5 at 2:00 P.M. at the JTM Marketing office to review the campaign in detail. We look forward to meeting with you and thank you for this opportunity.

5. Evaluations will vary. You might decide to highlight the important information about the date and time of the meeting. Since it is at the end of the draft, you could highlight it through formatting. You could also include section titles in the memo.

TO: Myra Sommers, Marketing Manager, Klean Floss

FROM: Nancy Tang, Project Manager, JTM Marketing

DATE: June 22, 2014

SUBJECT: Klean Floss Marketing Campaign

The advertising department at JTM has reviewed the Klean Floss product and marketing history, and we have developed a proposed campaign that will be effective in meeting your goals for the product.

Campaign Overview

The campaign will focus on the benefit of a clean feeling and include a mail-in offer for a free sample. It will target television, direct mail, and email, with an anticipated budget of $285,000.

Presentation

We would like to invite you to a presentation to review the campaign in detail. The presentation is scheduled for:

Location: JTM Marketing Offices

Date: July 5, 2014

Time: 2:00 P.M.

We look forward to meeting with you and thank you for this opportunity.

6. Documentation about how to use software can be formatted in a series of steps. You might divide the documentation into common tasks that users need to perform. You could include the following sections:
- Introduction
- Sending Email
- Organizing Emails
- Common Questions

7. The purpose of the document is to give information that will help the reader use the email software. The audience is composed of coworkers. The organization should be easy to follow and should allow the reader to find information to answer specific questions or do specific tasks.

8. You might write the following outline:

Introduction
- Email software type
- Where to find email software

Sending Email
- How to compose email
- How to forward or reply
- How to manage email addresses

Organizing Emails
- How to use labels
- When to delete emails

Common Questions
- How large an attachment can I send?
- What if email isn't working?

9. You might write:

Introduction

The company uses a company Gmail account for all email communications. To access your Gmail, go to https://mail.google.com. You must log in with your company Gmail account. Be sure that you are not logged in to your personal Gmail account.

Sending Email

To compose a new email, click on the red "Compose" button on the left. You can also compose an email by selecting "reply," "reply all," or "forward" from the drop-down menu in the upper right-hand corner of an email. When you choose "reply all," be aware of how many recipients will receive your email.

When you compose an email, the first step is to choose recipients. Start typing an email address or name. If the address is in the company address book, the correct address will appear below your cursor. If you are sending an email to a new contact, you can add this contact by clicking on the email address after you have typed it in the recipient list.

Be sure to include a subject line and check your attachments before sending your email.

Organizing Emails

It is important to keep your emails organized. To accomplish this, create labels to sort emails that you have addressed but do not want to delete. Click on "Create new label" in the lower left to create custom labels. You can create labels to indicate the client, task, or urgency of the email. By applying labels to emails, you can easily sort your email and find the email you need.

Keep all client and internal emails, as well as vendor emails directly related to a job. You may delete advertisements, newsletters, unneeded vendor emails, or any other non-work-related emails.

Common Questions

How large an attachment can I send?
You can email attachments up to 25 MB in size, but because some clients have lower size limits for the email attachments they can receive, we recommend limiting attachments to 10 MB in size.

What if email is not working?
If email is not working, contact the IT department for support.

10. Evaluations will vary. Subheads can help to organize an instructional document. If a procedure has clearly defined steps, you can consider using a bulleted or numbered list to show the steps.

11. A business letter in block format has a double space between each paragraph. Paragraphs are not indented. The letter has the following parts:
- The sender's name and address
- The date
- The recipient's name and address
- The salutation followed by a colon
- The body, with a beginning, middle, and ending
- The closing, followed by a comma
- Space for a signature
- The sender's name and title
- Notations of enclosures, if needed

12. The purpose of the cover letter is to give an overview of the information in the attached quarterly report and to make recommendations based on the report. This is a persuasive task because you want the CFO to accept your recommendations. The audience is the CFO, Margo Foster, who shares your interest in the business's success. The letter should be formal, since it is a business letter to an executive in the company. The organization will reflect the persuasive purpose.

13. You might write:

James Redfin, Manager
Topping Sporting Goods
1599 Spring St.
Atlanta, GA 30301

August 3, 2014

Margo Foster, CFO
Topping Sporting Goods Corporate Office
679 Langer Ave.
New York, NY 10007

Dear Ms. Foster:

Introduction: Overview of the success of the store and need for expansion.

Propose expanding marketing budget. Explain expanded profit based on expanded marketing budget.

Propose hiring a cashier. Explain need for a new cashier to maintain customer service.

Conclusion: Attached quarterly report.

Sincerely,

James Redfin, Manager

Enclosure: Quarterly Report, Second Quarter 2014

14. You might write:

James Redfin, Manager
Topping Sporting Goods
1599 Spring St.
Atlanta, GA 30301

August 3, 2014

Margo Foster, CFO
Topping Sporting Goods Corporate Office
679 Langer Ave.
New York, NY 10007

Dear Ms. Foster:

I am pleased to send you the Quarterly Report for the Atlanta store for the second quarter. As you will see, our store has performed above expectations again, and I propose that we continue to expand our marketing budget and staff to sustain our growth.

Last quarter, marketing expenses rose by 3%, fueling a 16% growth in profit over the same time period. Based on the excellent response to our marketing, I recommend raising the marketing budget by an additional 2% this quarter.

Because of the increased business, I also recommend hiring one additional cashier to maintain strong customer service. A good experience without a long wait time will keep customers coming back to the store. The costs for an additional cashier are included in the projections at the end of the quarterly report.

Details of my proposals are included in the attached report. I look forward to meeting with you to discuss future growth.

Sincerely,

James Redfin, Manager

Enclosure: Quarterly Report, Second Quarter 2014

15. Evaluations will vary. The recommendations are important information and should be clear. It should also be clear that the detailed quarterly report is attached.

Check Your Skills   *pages 201–202*

1. The following is an example of an **effective** response. It briefly delivers the important information in a well-organized way. It includes necessary elements for an email, including a subject line.

To: XYZ Corporation Employees

Subject: City Fitness Gym Memberships

To all full-time employees:

XYZ Corporation is concerned with the health and fitness of its employees. To encourage good health, the company will subsidize 75% of the cost of a membership at City Fitness gym. Please take advantage of this offer and spend at least a few minutes at the gym each week. Regular exercise can reduce stress as well as improve heath.

To take advantage of this offer, please bring proof of membership to the human resources office. Expenses will be reimbursed on your next paycheck. Thank you in advance for participating.

Sincerely,

Ned Parada
Human Resources Assistant

The following is an example of an **ineffective** response. It does not include formatting for an email. It also does not mention the offer at the beginning of the email, which makes the email unclear.

XYZ Corporation is offering a benefit to employees. The corporation is concerned with the health and fitness of its employees. Let me know if you have any questions about this offer.

To take advantage of this offer, please bring proof of a gym membership to the human resources office. The company plans to subsidize 75% of the cost of a membership at City Fitness gym. Expenses will be reimbursed on the next paycheck. Thank you in advance for participating.

Please take advantage of this offer and spend at least a few minutes at the gym each week. Regular exercise can reduce stress as well as improve heath.

2. The following is an example of an **effective** response. It is formatted as a memo and clearly states the most important information at the beginning of the memo. The subject line also alerts the reader to important information. It has a formal stye that is appropriate to the audience.

TO: Sierra Dental Health Employees

FROM: Tom Quevedo, Office Manager

DATE: August 3, 2014

SUBJECT: New Cancellation Policy

As of today, Sierra Dental Health is implementing a new cancellation policy due to a large number of last-minute cancellations. Under the new policy, any client who cancels less than 24 hours before the scheduled appointment will be charged a $25 cancellation fee.

Handling Existing Appointments

The cancellation policy applies to new appointments. Existing appointments will not be subject to the policy, since the clients were not told of the cancellation policy at the time the appointments were scheduled. If there is any uncertainty about a cancelled appointment, please contact me.

Informing Clients of the Policy

Whenever a client schedules a new appointment, inform the client of the cancellation policy. When we appropriately set client expectations, we can deliver excellent customer service.

Please contact me with any questions or concerns about the new policy.

The following is an example of an **ineffective** response. It does not have complete formatting or a clear subject. The organization is poor, since the information about the cancellation policy doesn't appear until the end of the memo. The information is difficult to find.

TO: All Employees

SUBJECT: An Important Change

It is important to appropriately set client expectations, so that we can deliver excellent customer service. Because of this, whenever a client schedules a new appointment, inform the client of the new cancellation policy.

Sierra Dental Health has had a large number of last-minute cancellations that cause problems for all the staff, from dentists to receptionists. To deal with these problems, the office is implementing a new cancellation policy.

The cancellation policy applies to new appointments. Existing appointments will not be subject to the policy, since the clients were not told of the cancellation policy at the time the appointments were scheduled. If there is any uncertainty about a cancelled appointment, please contact me.

Under the new policy, any client who cancels less than 24 hours before the scheduled appointment will be charged a $25 cancellation fee.

Developing Ideas, Arguments, and Evidence
page 203

Developing Ideas
page 205

Expand Your Ideas

Practice It!
pages 208–210

1. **Central Idea:** The argument to fund NASA is stronger because of the benefits of space exploration.

   Supporting Ideas: Space exploration helps with social problems because of technology development. Space exploration is not excessively expensive.

   Details: 0.6% of budget; "intangible benefits"; solar panels; heart monitors; water-purification systems

2. You might write:

   Because of the benefits of space exploration, the argument of NASA supporters is stronger than the argument to defund the space agency. The argument's strength lies in its refutation of the idea that space exploration does not contribute to solving real-world problems. Space exploration does help with social problems because it promotes technological development. Far from having only "intangible benefits," space exploration has given us solar panels that may provide cheap, accessible energy and heart monitors that can reduce long-term health care costs. Water-purification systems can provide fresh water to third-world countries and rural areas. It is short-sighted to ignore these benefits, especially when space exploration is not excessively expensive. A budget of $18 billion may sound enormous until you realize that it is only 0.6% of the national budget. The wide-ranging benefits of solar panels, cancer therapy, and light-weight materials are worth the investment.

3. Evaluations will vary. Evaluate the development of your ideas. Does your writing include related ideas? Does your writing make connections between your ideas and details?

4. **Central Idea:** The parasite D. medineses depends on hosts throughout its life cycle.

   Supporting Ideas: Larvae are eaten by copepods, which transfer them to human hosts. Larvae infest humans and grow to maturity in human hosts.

   Details: Larvae infect humans through water containing infested copepods. Larvae grow in stomach and intestine walls. Roundworms mature and mate in humans, and males die there. Female roundworms create and emerge through a blister, usually in the foot. Copepods eat larvae, which develop in them until they can infect humans.

5. You might write:

   The parasite D. medineses, known as roundworm, depends on two hosts throughout its life cycle: copepods and humans. Larvae are eaten by copepods, which transfer the larvae to human hosts. The immature roundworms are dependent on copepods for an environment where the larvae can develop until they can infect humans. Then the larvae are transported into humans through water containing infested copepods. Roundworms are dependent on human hosts through the rest of their life cycles. The larvae grow in human stomach walls and intestine walls. Roundworms mature and mate in humans, and males die there. Female roundworms use human hosts to transport their larvae to copepods by creating and emerging through a blister, usually in the foot. At every point in its lifecycle, a roundworm is dependent on a host, except for the brief period when released larvae wait to be ingested by copepods.

Check Your Skills
pages 211–212

1. The following is an example of an **effective** response. It contains supporting ideas and specific details from the passage that develop the central idea.

   The arguments supporting a minimum wage increase are strong because they include strong evidence of increased spending due to minimum wage increases. The opposing arguments seem logical. However, they include no hard evidence to support their logic. To argue an economic issue, specific evidence and economic studies are essential.

The opposing arguments in the passage rely entirely on logical reasoning about what might happen. Opponents say that businesses would hire fewer workers, but they do not present evidence of this behavior in the past. The claim that a minimum wage increase would cause increased prices is logical, but it would be a much stronger claim with specific evidence linking wages and price increases.

The passage also presents logical arguments supporting a minimum wage increase. The argument that minimum wage earners will spend their additional income, fueling the economy, is logical. The difference is that this argument is backed by evidence from an economic study by the Federal Reserve Bank of Chicago. Supporters also compare the current minimum wage to the current federal poverty level, which puts the wage level in objective perspective.

The presented arguments against the minimum wage increase could be compelling, but because the passage lacks concrete evidence for these arguments, the arguments in favor of the minimum wage are stronger. Speculating about economic issues is problematic, since economics is a complex field. Hard evidence based on scientific study is needed.

The following is an example of an **ineffective** response. It has a strong central idea and some supporting ideas, but it does not develop its ideas. It lacks details. Practice your writing skills by rewriting and editing this response to improve it.

The arguments in the passage that oppose minimum wage increases are stronger. The opponents to minimum wage increases present more arguments, and the arguments are based in strong logic. It is obvious that minimum wage increases will cause problems for businesses and consumers. The supporting arguments have some evidence in their favor, but it is unlikely that a minimum wage increase will actually spur the economy. The arguments opposing minimum wage will cancel out any benefits mentioned in the arguments supporting a minimum wage increase. Overall, it is clear that an increase in the minimum wage would be bad for economic growth. A minimum wage increase is a bad idea.

2. The following is an example of an **effective** response. It demonstrates how both arguments presented in the passage reflect King's quotation. The ideas are developed with details.

By using terms such as "spiritual death," "revolution of values," and "social vision," King puts his emphasis on moral values. Though the passage tackles the economics of minimum wage increase, both positions include moral arguments.

The argument in favor of a minimum wage increase echoes King's position, which calls for an "adequate wage" for every American. Comparing the minimum wage to the poverty level highlights the value-based foundation of the argument. The call for a "living wage" is a call for social equity.

The opposing argument also presents a value-based argument. The claim that the poor would be hurt most by a minimum wage increase is based in social values. Lost jobs and increased prices are long-term concerns. If those harms outweigh the benefits of a minimum wage, then the socially responsible position is to oppose minimum wage increases.

King's focus on social values is reflected in both arguments. The question is not whether our nation should pursue policies that help lift families out of poverty but how to define those policies.

The following is an example of an **ineffective** response. It lacks specific details that develop the ideas. Try revising and editing this response to improve it.

In the quotation, Martin Luther King, Jr. focuses on social values, while the passage about minimum wage increases weighs both economic and value-based arguments. Both arguments touch on social values. The argument in favor of a minimum wage increase asks for the same thing as King does, a living wage. However, the argument against a minimum wage increase argues that minimum wages hurt the poor in the long run. It takes the position that long-term effects are just as important as immediate benefits. The social benefits and costs of any policy need to be examined carefully.

Developing Strong Support   *page 213*

STAR Support

Practice It!   *pages 217–218*

1. c. The movie theater used to show a double feature every Saturday night.

   This answer does not describe a benefit of renovating the movie theater or a desire to renovate the theater.

2. a. How renovating drive-in theaters has spurred economic growth in similar towns

   Facts about economic growth in a similar situation would support the developer's case that renovating the theater would spur economic growth.

3a. The only fact that the argument includes is that the theater caused traffic in the 1980s. This fact is not very specific. It doesn't have specific information about how bad the traffic was and what caused it. Other statements are very general. The idea that the theater would encourage underage drinking seems to be speculation. The lack of specific facts makes the argument less convincing.

3b. The only fact that the argument includes is about traffic in the 1980s. Many things could have changed in recent years, such as expanded roads or nearby construction. The lack of timely evidence makes the argument less convincing.

3c. The accuracy of the facts is difficult to judge. There is no source given for the increased traffic in the 1980s. The idea that teens will drink in their cars is unsupported. The idea that it is unfair for taxpayers to pay for business development is opinion. The lack of clearly accurate facts makes the argument less convincing.

3d. The facts that the argument provides are relevant, but there are too few well-supported facts to make a convincing argument. Traffic, potential drinking, and costs to taxpayers are all relevant issues. The arguments are weakened by the lack of specific, timely, and accurate evidence.

4a. The best example of specific evidence in the passage is the example of two people who were severely injured walking along the shoulder of the road. This example shows that the danger of walking on a road without sidewalks is real. However, statistics comparing injuries on streets with and without sidewalks would be stronger evidence, since statistical evidence is more reliable than the anecdotal evidence of individual stories. A combination of statistical and anecdotal evidence is often the most convincing.

4b. One sentence that is irrelevant is, "We require bicyclists to wear helmets; we should have roads with sidewalks." Requiring helmets for bicyclists is not clearly analogous to installing sidewalks.

4c. One statement with questionable accuracy is, "Our citizens should not be afraid to walk to the park or the grocery store." There is no evidence in the passage that citizens are afraid to walk. Another statement of questionable accuracy is that the benefits of sidewalks outweigh the costs. The author does not provide information about the costs of sidewalks, and there is no way to compare costs and benefits.

5. You might write:

   The argument in the passage is somewhat supported. It provides specific evidence of some injuries to pedestrians walking on streets without sidewalks. The anecdotal example in the passage is recent and relevant. Its accuracy could be checked. The argument also includes some questionable statements, such as that citizens are afraid to walk the streets. The author's argument would be better supported by statistics about the number of accidents on roads with and without sidewalks as well as by facts about the costs of installing sidewalks.

Check Your Skills *pages 219–220*

1. The following is an example of an **effective** response. It uses STAR Support to evaluate the arguments in each passage.

The passage that supports privatization of national parks provides the most relevant and specific evidence, citing both the current mismanagement of parks and the success of private companies in other venues. However, both passages lack specific examples or data to support their argument. The passage supporting privatization has stronger evidence because it cites more comprehensive and valid evidence than the opposing passage.

The passage supporting government-run national parks has little evidence and relies mainly on general statements of opinion. It does state that privatization in the past has resulted in less public access at greater cost. Since this evidence specifically relates to national parks, it could be strong evidence. However, the author does not mention where and when this happened. Its timeliness and accuracy is unknown.

The opposing passage states that private business is more efficient in running telephone services and utilities, but it also fails to give specific examples comparing government-run utilities to privately-run ones. The passage also cites mismanagement of parks by government. It gives some specifics, such as understaffing and roads in disrepair. However, this evidence could be much more specific. How many parks are currently understaffed? Where and when were visitors endangered? The author only states that his examples are from the 20th century. A 100-year timeframe can't be considered timely. Finally, the passage states that industry outperforms government in creating vacation destinations. This statement also lacks specific evidence, although destinations such as Disneyland or Las Vegas come to mind. How do these private destinations compare to the Grand Canyon or Yellowstone?

Although both passages lack specific evidence, the second passage provides more relevant specifics than the first. To ultimately determine which position is better policy, it would

be necessary to examine specific evidence of privately-run versus publicly-run parks, utilities, and vacation destinations.

The following is an example of an **ineffective** response. It doesn't clearly address the arguments in the passages. Try revising and editing this response for extra practice.

Definitely, parks should be supported by the government. If the parks are understaffed, it's because the government isn't funding them with enough money. On the other hand, what are companies going to do with parks? They just want to make money, and they'll definitely charge more money, build on land that should be preserved, and cause us ultimately lose control of public lands. Who knows? Maybe they'll start logging in Yellowstone and build casinos in the Grand Canyon. That's not a good road to follow.

Evaluating Arguments *page 221*

Describe the Claim, Evidence, and Speaker

Learn It! *page 224*

4. You might write:

While the author makes a clear claim that two years of college education should be free to U.S. students, the support is weak and insufficient. The claim is somewhat reasonable. The government provides many services and could expand public education by two years. However, this would incur significant costs and changes in the educational system. One piece of evidence that is specific, timely, accurate, and relevant is that over 60% of jobs will require degrees by 2018. Other statements in the passage are vague, such as the idea that students would quickly decide on majors. This idea isn't supported by specifics and seems mainly to be speculation. It has no source. The statement that college graduates often cannot find jobs undermines the idea that two years of free college is a solution. The author acknowledges that opposition exists but does not address any counterarguments. Overall, the evidence seems insufficient, especially since it does not address the costs of the proposal.

Answers and Explanations

1. The claim that holiday parades are a waste of resources is clear. It is stated in the first sentence. It is a reasonable claim, depending mainly on a value judgment, since the benefits of parades (such as a sense of community) are difficult to quantify.

2. The evidence in the first paragraph, which states that there are possible alternatives to parades, is somewhat irrelevant. Why are other events less wasteful? The evidence in the passage includes some examples of negative results of parades: traffic, trash, and expenses for police. The evidence would be more specific if the author provided total costs for various parades compared to other events. The timeliness and source of the evidence is unknown, since the evidence is not very specific.

3. The speaker is unknown, and the lack of specific evidence indicates that the speaker is not an expert. However, the speaker does acknowledge an opposing viewpoint, mentioning that parades are festive and happy.

4. You might write:

   The argument in the passage has some strengths, but it lacks specific and compelling evidence. The claim is clear and reasonable: that holiday parades are wasteful. The speaker acknowledges that parades are festive and happy and suggests alternatives. However, simply suggesting that there are alternatives to parades does not make a clear argument for the claim. Other events substituted for parades may be as costly as parades. The evidence that parades block traffic, create trash, and require overtime from city workers is logical. However, it is not specific. How much do parades cost? How much waste do they produce? How detrimental are the effects on traffic? Without more specific and relevant support, the overall argument is weak.

5. The claim in the passage is clear: that the U.S. should allow driverless cars in every state. It is a reasonable claim, since some states already have such laws.

6. The evidence in the passage generally provides specific, timely, accurate, and relevant details. The author mentions states that have laws allowing driverless cars. This would be more relevant if the author explicitly explained the results of these laws. However, the author does give examples of the safety and successful testing of driverless cars. Driverless cars have navigated Lombard Street and traveled 300,000 miles with only one accident, caused by another car. These details would be more compelling if the author included a source. The author does mention a 2012 video posted by Google, showing a blind man using a driverless car. This evidence is specific and timely. Google, as a company, is interested in promoting self-driving cars, but there does not seem to be a strong reason to doubt the story in the video and the benefits of driverless cars to the disabled.

7. The speaker in the passage is unknown. The speaker does provide some specific details that show knowledge of the subject. However, the speaker does not acknowledge any potential counterarguments.

8. You might write:

   The passage provides a strong argument in favor of legalizing self-driving cars by showing the high benefits and low risks of these cars. The speaker clearly states the claim and provides detailed evidence. Several states already have laws allowing driverless cars, and although the author does not explain the results of these laws, he or she does give details about tests of self-driving cars. After 300,000 miles of testing with only one accident, caused by another car, driverless cars seem safe. The author also gives an example of a blind man using a driverless car. This example shows the benefits of self-driving cars. The argument could be improved by addressing possible counterarguments, but overall, it makes a strong case for a clear claim.

Check Your Skills
pages 227–228

1. The following is an example of an **effective** response. It evaluates each passage, noting positive and negative aspects, and makes a clear judgment about which gives the stronger argument.

The passage opposing royalty makes a strong case against this outdated custom, which is contrary to fundamental ideas of democracy. The passage supporting royalty includes specific evidence. However, when its evidence is weighed against the serious issues that a royal class poses for a society, the evidence seems less relevant and compelling.

The author who argues in favor of royalty makes a clear claim: that royalty should be preserved. The example of Great Britain is a good one. The constitutional monarchy provides a parliamentary democracy while maintaining a royal family. The author's evidence primarily revolves around the popularity of British royalty. Millions watched the marriage of Prince Charles and Lady Diana, and while this example is not very current, the recent birth of Prince George shows the ongoing popularity of the royal family. However, the popularity of royal events is rather frivolous. The author does not address counterarguments, and this is very detrimental to the pro-royalty position. After all, what was the cost of Charles and Diana's royal wedding?

The passage opposing royalty makes a stronger case. It has a clear claim: that royalty is anti-democratic. A monarchy is clearly a delineation of an upper-class by birth, and this goes against fundamental principles of democracy. The author quotes Graham Smith's writings on CNN. This quote points out that the royal family is not subject to Freedom of Information laws. It also puts a dollar amount, over two hundred million pounds a year, on the monarchy. These are weighty points that need to be addressed. The author's argument that a lack of royalty drives innovation and individuality is not well supported, but the problems with royalty are clearly stated.

When a royal family is no longer in complete political control, what is its value or detriment to society? The arguments in favor of royalty are about valuing culture and sharing popular cultural experiences. The arguments against royalty are concerned with secretive political influence, high expenses, and a lack of democratic equality. These arguments are stronger because they are significant and potentially damaging to society. Culture can still be preserved without preserving a royal class.

The following is an example of an **ineffective** response. It lacks good organization and a clear evaluation of each argument. Try revising this response for extra practice.

A royal family is okay to have if they do not make the laws. The first argument is that 750 million people watched Prince Charles and Lady Diana's wedding. That shows that lots of people like British royalty, and they don't care so much about the expenses. If people want something, why not give it to them. There is a good argument that culture is the benefit of royalty. When people in the U.S. want to read about royalty on the news all the time, that is showing that royalty fill a role that people want. If people want something, then you shouldn't try to take it away from them.

The main thing is, does royalty actually cause problems? We pay for lots of things just because people enjoy them. Cities build football stadiums because people like football. What's the harm in having a royal family so that people can have something they enjoy? The dresses at big events are nice and something every girl dreams of when she is little. Why can't there be a little bit of culture that people will like?

After looking at the evidence, it's good to see that it's okay to have a royal family. People in Britain still vote and have a legislature just like the U.S. Everyone can enjoy their royal families and watch them on TV. It's not hurting anyone, so it's okay.

Citing Evidence and Connecting with Claims

page 229

Building a Chain of Evidence

Learn It! *page 231*

5. You might write:

> I recommend interviewing Angela Goren for the sales position because of her familiarity with the company and her success in sales. In her last position, Angela received a promotion after six months, which demonstrates her success in sales. She also may need less training, since she is already familiar with the company's products. In addition, Angela has a BA in communications. Because of this, she may have good communications skills that will help her show clients the benefits of our products. Angela is the most promising candidate.

Practice It! *pages 232–234*

1a. The argument that wet conditions were created by impact events is more logical because it includes supporting evidence.

1b. There were obvious impactors in the past. In CO_2 atmospheres, greenhouse potential is limited by clouds, and no carbonate has been detected. Methane requires a source. SO_2 may not build up to high enough levels.

1c. Because there are clear indications of large impactors in the past, there is evidence for impact events that may have caused a wet climate.

There is no evidence for CO_2 as the cause, since no carbonate has been detected, and clouds in CO_2 atmospheres make this explanation less likely.

With no known source of methane, the idea that methane is the cause lacks evidence.

The cause is unlikely to be SO_2 since there is no evidence the levels would have been high enough.

1d. Since three pieces of evidence have to do with the composition of Mars's atmosphere and the lack of evidence for hypotheses that focus on atmospheric composition, it is logical to group them together. You might start with your claim, and then discuss the evidence in favor of impact events. Then, you could discuss all three atmospheric gases together.

2. You might write:

> The passage gives two potential reasons that early conditions on Mars were warm and wet: the atmospheric composition and large impact events. Of these two potential reasons, impact events seem more likely, because the passage includes evidence in support of this hypothesis. There is evidence supporting the existence of large impacts in the past. In fact, the passage calls these impacts "obvious." This is the only positive evidence in the passage.
>
> There is no evidence in the passage that methane, CO_2, or SO_2 might have caused a warm and wet climate in Mars's past. All three gases pose problems. No carbonate has been detected that would support the existence of large amounts of carbon dioxide. Additionally, CO_2 would form clouds, which would limit its warming effects. Since there is no known source of methane on Mars, the idea that methane is the cause lacks evidence. The cause is also unlikely to be SO_2 since there is no evidence that the levels would have been high enough. Impact events are the only proposed reason for Mars's early climate that have any supporting evidence in the passage.

3. Evaluations will vary. Evaluate your claim and evidence. Is the evidence clearly connected to the claim?

4a. Claim: The argument against removing drink machines from schools is stronger because there is no evidence that banning sugary drinks reduces obesity.

Evidence: When all sugary drinks were banned, students still consumed the same amount.

The objective of removing soda machines is to combat childhood obesity.

4b. Because banning sugary drinks did not result in lower consumption, the policy is not effective.

There is evidence that sugary drinks contribute to obesity, but there is no evidence in the passage that banning them from schools reduces obesity.

4c. You might start with the claim, and then discuss the evidence that banning sugary drinks does not lower obesity. Then you would end by pointing out that reducing obesity is the goal, and that the evidence doesn't show a resulting lower obesity.

5. You might write:

Since sugared drinks provide empty calories, it might seem logical that schools shouldn't serve them to students. However, the argument presented against banning sugary drinks demonstrates that the policy is ineffective. The study cited in the passage found that when all sugary drinks were banned from schools, students still drank the same amount of sugar. Because banning sugary drinks did not result in lower consumption, the policy is not effective. There is evidence that sugary drinks contribute to obesity, but there is no evidence in the passage that banning them from schools reduces obesity. Opponents of banning sugary drinks suggest health education as an alternative. If health education is more effective, then it is the policy that should be pursued.

Check Your Skills

pages 235–236

1. The following is an example of an **effective** response. It has a clear claim and makes connections between the evidence and the claim.

When businesses are in conflict, which businesses should government favor? Should ISPs be given freedom to control the information traveling over their service? Should websites be free from potential regulation or pressure from ISPs? The conflict over net neutrality highlights this issue, and the passage presents arguments both opposing and supporting net neutrality. Overall, the arguments in favor of net neutrality are stronger because they identify serious potential dangers.

The arguments supporting net neutrality are strong, but they are based on potential dangers of a lack of regulation. They would be stronger arguments if they were supported by evidence of these dangers, but the court ruling eliminating net neutrality rules is recent. It is prudent to consider the potential harms of eliminating regulation before deregulation creates damage.

Net neutrality prevents ISPs from controlling specific information that travels through the Internet. The arguments in the passage mention several ways ISPs could control information: by charging websites and web services, by banning or charging competitors, by blocking content for political reasons, or by banning negative commentary about their business. These are all examples of controlling and limiting information, infringing on individuals and businesses. Allowing ISPs to control information in these ways gives too much power to ISPs.

The arguments opposing net neutrality, on the other hand, favor deregulation for ISPs. The weakness of this argument is that it has a limited perspective. Deregulation can lead to innovation, but innovation and free-market growth do not make up for potentially dangerous abuses. If opponents do not address these abuses, the arguments against net neutrality are not convincing.

The Internet is a new and society-changing technology. It is difficult to make good choices regulating it. However, the potential costs of unregulated ISPs, as outlined in this passage, outweigh the potential benefits of deregulation.

The following is an example of an **ineffective** response. It lacks clear connections between the evidence and the claim. To practice your writing, try revising and editing this response to improve it.

Net neutrality is a good idea, and the arguments in favor of net neutrality are stronger. Those in favor of net neutrality put forth several reasons that net neutrality is a good policy. ISPs could charge websites so that people can access those websites if there is no net neutrality. Supporters of net neutrality also say that ISPs could block services or posts, while those against net neutrality mostly are in favor of freedom for ISPs.

They want ISPs to have the ability to choose their business practices. Proponents of net neutrality counter that unregulated ISPs could interfere with the business practices of web services. Overall, net neutrality is a beneficial type of regulation.

2. The following is an example of an **effective** response. It makes a clear connection between the quotation and the passage, and it cites supporting evidence.

In the quotation, Thomas Jefferson outlines the limits and responsibilities of good government. He defines the purpose of government as stopping "men from injuring one another." Beyond that, government should give citizens freedom. The difficulty is in defining the line between protecting citizens from injury and abstaining from controlling and regulating. The passage on net neutrality illustrates the difficulty of defining this line.

The arguments in favor of net neutrality focus on protecting citizens from injury. Charging websites for bandwidth could result in limited access to services and limited competition. Blocking political content or criticisms of ISPs interferes with freedom of speech. Jefferson identifies protection from injury as the purview of government, but these are potential injuries. How significant are they? Could they be curtailed with other regulations that would leave ISPs "free to regulate their own pursuits"?

On the other hand, opponents to net neutrality reflect Jefferson's concerns about government regulation. Opponents point out that free ISPs can make better decisions and manage Internet bandwidth. Jefferson says that the government should leave men free and able to enjoy the fruits of their labors. This is what ISPs will be able to do without the regulation of net neutrality. The better ISPs will benefit from their policies.

Both positions on net neutrality reflect different aspects of Jefferson's quotation. The conflict between them is a conflict between freedom from regulation and protection from injury, the two ideas in the quote from Jefferson.

The following is an example of an **ineffective** response. It makes a link between the quotation and the passage, but it lacks evidence from the passage. To practice your writing, try revising and editing this response to improve it.

The quotation from Jefferson argues in favor of a limited government that does not interfere with industry, and the arguments opposing net neutrality reflect this argument. Small government is a good idea because when individuals and business have more freedom, the result is a better marketplace. Competition creates better products and services. Jefferson advocates for a government that only focuses on preventing harm and lets each person work as he or she pleases and reap the rewards. The sentiment is pro-capitalist and anti-regulation. It supports many of the arguments opposing net neutrality.

Drawing Conclusions   *page 237*

Getting a KICK from the Evidence

Practice It!   *pages 240–242*

1. Based on the passage, you know how computer programs score essays. They find computer-readable features such as length, grammar, and spelling that correspond with human scores. You also know arguments in favor of and opposed to computer-scored essays. Computer scoring is quick, inexpensive, and accurate, and it is used in conjunction with human scoring. On the other hand, opponents are concerned that computer scoring could cause students to focus on elements of writing such as length and spelling while ignoring content and strong communication skills.

2. Based on the evidence and the arguments, you can infer that administrators might be in favor of computer scoring, since administrators are likely concerned with budgets and efficiency. You might infer that computer programs don't score the quality of the content and that changes in student tactics could affect the program's accuracy.

3. You might compare the goals or values of opponents and proponents. While opponents are concerned with the quality of student writing, proponents are concerned with efficient testing. You might also compare computer grading to human grading. Computer grading measures performance indirectly by measuring computer-readable aspects of writing that correlate to good writing. On the other hand, human grading measures performance directly by evaluating the content and form of the writing as a reader.

4. Key ideas are:
   • Computer scoring analyzes essays and their scores to find computer-readable elements that can be used to predict scores.
   • The benefits of computer scoring are that it is quick, inexpensive, and accurate.
   • The objection to computer scoring is that it measures student performance indirectly, relying on correlations between good scores and computer-readable factors.

5. You might conclude that while computer scoring is accurate, it could fail if student writing behavior changes. Computer grading, therefore, needs to be used in conjunction with human grading to make sure the accuracy is maintained.

6. Based on the passage, you know that texting is common. You know that advocates of texting believe that the increased use of written language will increase literacy. A study concluded that texting involves a rich linguistic environment. You know that opponents of texting are concerned that texting creates poor language habits. In support, the passage cites a newspaper article that reported students using texting language in school exams.

7. Based on the evidence and arguments, you can infer that a rich linguistic environment helps language develop. You can infer that advocates of texting are not concerned by the use of acronyms and other shortcuts in texting. You can infer that opponents believe the use of acronyms and other shortcuts contributes to poor literacy.

8. You can compare advocates' and opponents' attitudes to the language of texting. While advocates find the language of texting rich enough to develop literacy, opponents regard it as illiterate, encouraging bad language habits. You might also compare the support for the two positions. The study that supports proponents concluded that texting includes rich language. The support for opponents is a newspaper article, not a study, so it is not as rigorous. It gives examples of students using texting language on exams, but this isn't strong evidence that texting language reduces student literacy.

9. Key ideas are:
   • Texting is common.
   • Supporters believe that more practice using language increases literacy.
   • Detractors believe that shortcuts in texting language decrease literacy.

10. Based on the evidence, you might conclude that the argument in favor of texting is stronger. The study cited to support proponents is stronger evidence than the article cited to support opponents.

11. Based on the passage, you know that a study showed that a compound can reduce muscle aging and related illnesses in mice. This treatment could eventually help heal human ailments, such as diabetes and arthritis. In turn, this would reduce medical costs and improve quality of life. Possible negative consequences of longer life could include overpopulation, stagnation, and unemployment, as older people remain in their jobs longer.

12. You can infer that the potential treatment would not be ready for years, if ever. You can also infer that the treatment would not cure all ailments, only muscle-related ones. You might infer that many factors affect lifespan and population and that there is little reliable information about potential social problems.

13. Based on the evidence and arguments, you could compare those who are in favor of this treatment to those who speculate about possible problems. Those in favor are thinking

narrowly about one treatment and its imme-diate benefits. Those who are opposed are thinking widely and speculatively, imagining a worst-case scenario about the future. Those in favor are thinking about benefits to individuals, and those opposed are thinking about societal problems.

14. Key ideas are:
    - A study shows a potential treatment for muscle aging and related illnesses.
    - Combatting aging-related illnesses reduces death, increases quality of life, reduces health care costs, and increases lifespan.
    - Combatting aging-related illnesses could cause problems such as overpopulation and unemployment, as the older generation remains in place.

15. Based on the evidence, you might conclude that the potential negative consequences of coun-teracting aging could be countered with social policies, so they don't outweigh the benefits for individuals.

Check Your Skills   *pages 243–244*

1. The following is an example of an **effective** response. It draws a conclusion based on the evidence in the passage. It compares the opposing and supporting arguments to reach a conclusion.

The argument opposing the *Journal News* releasing the names and addresses of registered pistol owners is strongest because the potential dangers of this action outweigh the benefits. The *Journal News* created a danger to individu-als that outweighs any potential benefits. While government transparency is important, it does not justify putting individuals in danger.

Opponents claimed that the newspaper put individuals in danger by releasing the names and addresses of gun owners. By advertising gun ownership, the newspaper made it easier for potential criminals to target homes with registered weapons. Compared to this concern, the argument that readers "were interested" to know about gun owners seems unimportant.

Stating that freedom of information is univer-sally good is naive. Information can cause harm as well as benefits.

The arguments in favor of the actions of the *Journal News* are weak and general. The argu-ments that oppose those actions are specific and outline a real potential harm.

The following is an example of an **ineffective** response. It fails to connect its conclusion with the evidence in the passage.

The argument opposing the *Journal News* releas-ing the names and addresses of registered pistol owners is strongest. It is not good to release the names and addresses of individuals. That does harm to individuals instead of helping them.

A newspaper gives information to readers, but sometimes there is too much information. Information that could harm people shouldn't be released. No one wants their names and addresses released. The newspaper did a poor job by putting individual names and addresses on their website.

Support for the newspaper's actions is mis-guided. When a newspaper takes action to harm readers, it should be held accountable for its actions. The newspaper should not release indi-viduals' names and addresses.

2. The following is an example of an **effective** response. It draws a conclusion about the relationship between the quotation and the passage: that the passage gives an example illustrating the idea in the quotation.

The quotation from Sydney Smith states that knowledge is neither good nor bad; its value depends on how it is used. The example of the *Journal News* releasing the names and addresses of gun owners illustrates Smith's point. The knowledge of names and addresses is not good or bad in itself. However, it can be used for good or bad purposes. Critics of the *Journal News* raised concerns that criminals could use the names and addresses that the newspaper published. Burgling a house because a gun is kept there is an example of misusing knowledge for wrong purposes, rendering "depravity more depraved." On the other hand, if the police use the names and addresses of gun owners to find a criminal, this increases "the strength of virtue" of the knowledge. Whether the actions of the *Journal News* were good or bad depends on the consequences of releasing the information. The knowledge released is power, as Smith states. That knowledge can be used for good or for evil.

The following is an example of an **ineffective** response. It fails to draw a conclusion about the relationship between the passage and the quotation.

The quotation from Sydney Smith states that knowledge is neither good nor bad; its value depends on how it is used. The passage about the *Journal News* talks about whether it is good or bad to release the names and addresses of gun owners. Critics of the *Journal News* raised concerns that criminals could use the names and addresses that the newspaper published. However, the newspaper argued that readers were interested in the information, which was freely available under the Freedom of Information Act. Critics also raised concerns that the information on the website could be inaccurate and that it implied that gun ownership was negative. On the other hand, supporters argued that free distribution of information is always a good thing. Smith argues in the quotation that information can either "render depravity more depraved" or "increase the strength of virtue." In other words, Smith states that information can be either good or bad.

Issues in Revising and Editing   *page 245*

Obstructions to Communication   *page 247*

FREE to Fix Obstructions to Communication

Practice It!   *pages 250–252*

1. The following sentence is problematic:

   Having asthma, any individual should look for which triggers are the ones which trigger that one's asthma attacks or worsen them, also.

2–3. The sentence has several errors that you might find through reading aloud and checking for common errors. The phrase "having asthma" is awkwardly placed. Although it does refer to "any individual," the word order is unnatural. The phrase "which triggers are the ones which trigger that one's" is awkward because it repeats the words "trigger," "which," and "one" and uses the pronoun "one" in an unclear way. The verb "worsen" should be "worsens," and the word "also" seems awkwardly placed at the end.

4. The corrected sentence might read:

   Individuals with asthma should identify triggers that cause or worsen their asthma attacks.

5. The following sentence is problematic:

   These results of the poll show that there is enough interest in a car share program in our community and among our community members to make one a financially viable choice for our community.

6–7. The main problem with this sentence is wordiness. "These results of the poll" could be stated more simply: "the poll results." The phrase "in our community and among our community members" is redundant. The writer uses the phrase "our community" three times.

8. The corrected sentence might read:

   The poll results show that there is enough interest in a community car share program to make it financially viable.

9. The following sentence is problematic:

Remaining controversial, how to fix the current complex tax system and make it simpler continues to be elusive.

10-11. The phrase "remaining controversial" is awkward. It applies to a lengthy noun phrase, "how to fix the current complex tax system and make it simpler." This lengthy phrase with an awkward modifier is confusing. Focusing the sentence's content and creating a simpler structure will help clarify the meaning. The phrase "remaining controversial" is also redundant with "continues to be elusive." Although "elusive" and "controversial" have different meanings, the author is trying to convey a similar idea with both.

12. The corrected sentence might read:

The best method to simplify the current complex tax system remains controversial.

Check Your Skills   *pages 253–254*

1. b. to get an oil change for my 2005 Toyota Corolla.

   This response has the most logical word order.

2. c. while I was there.

   This response clearly communicates who was there.

3. a. Because of his help, I avoided the inconvenience and expense of a blown tire.

   The other responses contain illogical word order and dangling modifiers.

4. c. excellent customer service that I received.

   This response has logical word order. The phrase "that I received" is clear and modifies "customer service."

5. d. by causing the body's natural defenses to develop immunity.

   The vaccines cause the body's defences to develop immunity to the diseases. This choice states the idea the most correctly and succinctly.

6. a. These imitation infections

   The sentence needs a subject, and the other options are modifying phrases or clauses.

7. c. After a patient receives a vaccine,

   This phrase clearly tells who receives the vaccines. The other phrases are dangling modifiers.

8. a. and should not cause concern.

   This is the simplest way to complete the sentence. The other choices are unnecessarily wordy, awkward, or illogical.

Word Usage   *page 255*

Using FREE to Fix Word Usage

Practice It!   *pages 258–260*

1. Start with the first sentence.

   Gravitational attraction from the sun and the moon are responsible for tides.

2-3. The subject "gravitational attraction" and the verb "are" do not match. The prepositional phrase "from the sun and the moon" between the subject and verb makes this hard to catch. You can catch this error more easily by removing the prepositional phrase. "Gravitational attraction are responsible for tides" sounds wrong.

4. You can revise the sentence by correcting the verb.

   Gravitational attraction from the sun and the moon is responsible for tides.

   You might decide to revise the sentence to more clearly connect the subject and verb.

   Tides are caused by gravitational attraction from the sun and the moon.

5. Continue with the second sentence.

   The moon's gravity has their strongest effect on the side of the Earth that is closest, but water nearest the moon is pulled toward the moon.

6-7. The pronoun "their" is incorrect. It should be "its," since it refers to "the moon's gravity." Also, the connecting word "but" has the wrong meaning for the sentence. The two ideas are not in contrast to each other. The connecting word "and" is appropriate.

8. The corrected sentence might read:

The moon's gravity has its strongest effect on the side of the Earth that is closest, and water nearest the moon is pulled toward the moon.

You might decide to make the sentence less wordy.

The moon's gravity has its strongest effect on the closest side of the Earth, pulling the nearest oceans toward the moon.

9. Continue with the third sentence.

The moon's gravitational force was ginormous enough to form a bulge of water near the moon.

10-11. The word "ginormous" is inappropriate because it is informal. The verb "was" is incorrect because it is in the past tense. It sounds like the moon's gravitational force has stopped forming a bulge of water.

12. The corrected sentence might read:

The moon's gravitational force is substantial enough to form a bulge of water near the moon.

13. Continue with the fourth sentence.

On the other hand, the sun causes a second bulge of water near the sun.

14-15. The transition "on the other hand" has the wrong meaning for the sentence. Its meaning is similar to "however," since it shows contrast. In this case, a transition such as "similarly" is a better choice, since the sun has a similar gravitational effect to the moon.

16. The corrected sentence might read:

Similarly, the sun causes a second bulge of water near the sun.

17. Finish with the fifth sentence.

As the Earth, sun, and moon rotate, the tides don't never cease to rise and fall.

18-19. The sentence contains a double negative, "don't never cease."

20. You can correct the sentence by eliminating the double negative.

As the Earth, sun, and moon rotate, the tides continuously rise and fall.

21. Responses will vary. The better you understand the errors that you are likely to make, the easier it will be to correct those errors.

22. Responses will vary. Subject-verb agreement errors can be difficult to find when a phrase comes between the subject and verb. Pronoun errors can be difficult to find for some nouns such as titles that appear plural but are singular.

Check Your Skills
pages 261–262

1. d. On that date,

The meanings of the other transitions are inappropriate to the sentence.

2. c. The tree

The pronoun "it" is unclear, since the previous sentence mentions a fence, a tree, and a car. The pronoun "they" and the phrase "the fence and the tree" cannot be correct since they don't match the singular verb.

3. a. will cost

The other verbs are the wrong tense or do not match the subject of the sentence.

4. d. which

The pronoun "it" would make this sentence a comma splice. The pronouns "they" and "who" do not match the noun "estimate."

5. a. use

The other verbs are the wrong tense or do not match the subject of the sentence.

6. d. not a good idea.

The other choices contain double negatives.

7. b. hidden problem with a lottery

The other answer choices have informal language that is inappropriate to the passage.

8. d. since

The other connecting words do not have the correct meaning for the sentence.

Spelling, Capitalization, and Punctuation   *page 263*

Using FREE to Fix Language Mechanics

Practice It!   *pages 266–268*

1. Start with the first sentence.

   Their are four basic laws of Supply and Demand, each describing the affects of a different relationship of supply and demand.

2–3. The word "their" should be "there." The term "Supply and Demand" should not be capitalized. Also, the word "affects" is incorrect. It should be "effects."

4. The corrected sentence might read:

   There are four basic laws of supply and demand, each describing the effects of a different relationship of supply and demand.

   You might decide to simplify and clarify the sentence.

   The four basic laws of supply and demand describe the effects of different relationships between supply and demand.

5. Continue with the second sentence.

   First, if demand increases and supply, does not change, a shortage occurs, leading too higher prices.

6–7. This sentence uses an unnecessary and confusing comma. The word "too" is also misused. It should be "to."

8. The corrected sentence might read:

   First, if demand increases and supply does not change, a shortage occurs, which leads to higher prices.

9. Continue with the third sentence.

   Second, if demand decreases and supply does not change; a surplus occurs and this leads to lower prices.

10–11. This sentence incorrectly uses a semicolon. It also joins two main clauses incorrectly by using the word "and" without a comma.

12. The corrected sentence might read:

   Second, if demand decreases and supply does not change, a surplus occurs, and this leads to lower prices.

   You might structure the sentences describing the laws of supply and demand the same way.

   Second, if demand decreases and supply does not change, a surplus occurs, which leads to lower prices.

13. Continue with the fourth sentence.

   Third, if demand does not change and supply increase's, a surplus occurs, which causes lower prices.

14–15. This sentence has an incorrect apostrophe. The word "increase's" should be "increases."

16. The corrected sentence might read:

   Third, if demand does not change and supply increases, a surplus occurs, which causes lower prices.

   You might structure the sentences describing the laws of supply and demand the same way.

   Third, if demand does not change and supply increases, a surplus occurs, which leads to lower prices.

17. Finish with the last sentence.

   Finally, if demand does not change and supply decreases, a shortage occurs, than this situation causes higher prices.

18–19. The word "than" is used incorrectly. It should be the word "then." This is also a comma splice. Two sentences cannot be joined using only a comma and the word "then."

20. The corrected sentence might read:

   Finally, if demand does not change and supply decreases, a shortage occurs. This situation causes higher prices.

   You might structure the sentences describing the laws of supply and demand the same way.

   Finally, if demand does not change and supply decreases, a shortage occurs, which leads to higher prices.

21. Responses will vary. You can correct spelling errors and commonly confused words by looking up words that you know are problems. Try to identify memory techniques to help you remember correct spellings or commonly confused words.

22. Responses will vary. Commonly confused words often sound alike but are spelled differently. Errors with these words can be difficult to find.

Check Your Skills   pages 269–270

1. b. their children

   The word "their" is a possessive pronoun, meaning belonging to them. The word "they're" means "they are." The word "there" means "in that place." It is also used as the subject of sentences that begin "there is" or "there are."

2. a. might mean for a child's development.

   The word "child's" is a possessive noun meaning belonging to a child. When a noun is singular, such as child, make it possessive by adding an apostrophe and the letter s.

3. d. answer, but opponents

   The other options incorrectly join two main clauses. Two main clauses can be joined by a comma and a conjunction such as the word "but."

4. d. spatial awareness and learning skills.

   The terms "spatial awareness" and "learning skills" are not proper nouns and do not need to be capitalized.

5. b. philosopher Aristotle

   The word "philosopher" is not a title and should not be capitalized. The name "Aristotle" is a proper noun and should be capitalized.

6. a. objects that produce

   No comma is necessary in this sentence.

7. d. made from iron

   The correct spellings are "made" and "iron."

8. b. are fascinating examples of

   The correct word choices are "are" and "of."

Sentence Structure   page 271

Using FREE to Fix Sentence Structure

Practice It!   pages 274–276

1. Start with the first sentence.

   In 2014, the United Nations' International Court of Justice ruled that Japan's Arctic whaling was a commercial program, it was not a scientific endeavor.

2–3. This sentence is a comma splice.

4. The corrected sentence might read:

   In 2014, the United Nations' International Court of Justice ruled that Japan's Arctic whaling was a commercial program, not a scientific endeavor.

5. Continue with the second sentence.

   After the United Nations ruled that the whaling program was not scientific; Japan cancelled its 2014 Antarctic whaling hunt.

6–7. The subordinate clause and the main clause are incorrectly joined with a semicolon instead of a comma.

8. The corrected sentence might read:

   After the United Nations ruled that the whaling program was not scientific, Japan cancelled its 2014 Antarctic whaling hunt.

9. Continue with the third sentence.

   Since many types of whales are endangered species.

10–11. This is a fragment. It can be combined with the following sentence, or the word "since" could be removed to make this a complete sentence.

12. The corrected sentence might read:

   Many types of whales are endangered species.

   If you combine the two sentences, the corrected sentence might read:

   Since many types of whales are endangered species, Japanese whaling, a historic, part of culture, and commercial tradition, has been a controversial issue.

This sentence still needs improvement, but it can be addressed in the next section.

13. Continue with the fourth sentence. If this was combined with the fragment preceding it, the revised sentence will read:

Since many types of whales are endangered species, Japanese whaling, a historic, part of culture, and commercial tradition, has been a controversial issue.

If you did not combine the fragment with this sentence, you might have added a transition.

Because of this, Japanese whaling, a historic, part of culture, and commercial tradition, has been a controversial issue.

14-15. The words "historic," "part of culture," and "commercial" are not parallel and sound awkward. You can replace "part of culture" with "cultural."

16. The corrected sentence might read:

Since many types of whales are endangered species, Japanese whaling, a historic, cultural, and commercial tradition, has been a controversial issue.

You might decide to simplify the structure of the sentence.

Since many types of whales are endangered species, the historic, cultural, and commercial tradition of Japanese whaling has been a controversial issue.

17. Finish with the last sentence.

While whaling are still controversial, international bans on whaling are proceeding.

18-19. The subject "whaling" does not match the verb "are."

20. The corrected sentence might read:

While whaling is still controversial, international bans on whaling are proceeding.

You might decide to clarify the sentence by using a different connecting word for the subordinate clause.

Although whaling is still controversial, international bans on whaling are proceeding.

21. Responses will vary. If you have difficulties with correct sentence structure, try using shorter, simpler sentences.

22. Responses will vary. To find sentence structure errors, identify pairs of subjects and verbs. Then, identify which subject-verb pairs are main clauses and which are subordinate clauses.

Check Your Skills   *pages 277–278*

1. d. are unusually high.

   The other choices contain incorrect verbs for this sentence.

2. a. occurs, it

   The other choices incorrectly join the subordinate clause to the main clause.

3. a. droughts in the West Pacific.

   This choice creates parallel structure with "floods in the U.S." and "tropical cyclones in the East Pacific."

4. d. invaluable because they allow

   The other choices create a sentence fragment or incorrectly join a main clause and a subordinate clause.

5. a. illegal, and

   The other choices incorrectly join two main clauses.

6. b. argue

   The other verb choices do not match the subject of the sentence or are the incorrect tense.

7. d. sanctions because

   The other choices create a sentence fragment or incorrectly join a main clause and a subordinate clause.

8. b. opportunity. Despite

   The other choices create run-on sentences.

Writing Practice *page 279*

Practice in Everyday Writing *page 281*

The Writing Process for Everyday Writing

Practice It! *pages 286–289*

1.

Purpose:	Audience:
To persuade the college to accept you as a student by showing your ability to succeed	The college entrance exam reader or admissions officer

Beginning:	
Introduce self and desired major: biology	

Middle:	
Interest in major: growing up in desert, visiting mountains	
Experience: part-time work at a nursery, volunteer work at arboretum	
Goals: environmentally sound urban landscaping and building green communities	

Ending:	
What I learned from experience and how the degree will help me contribute to society	

2. You might write:

Through a lifetime of working with plants and gardens, I have developed a strong interest in biology, the field I hope to pursue. Growing up in a desert community with nearby mountains, I was fascinated by the lush pine forests every year when we went camping. I began working in my home garden at a young age, where I learned how to care for plants with limited water resources. As I became older, I began working part time in a local nursery where I learned more about local plant life, invasive weed species, and city regulations regarding plants. In the last two years, I have volunteered at the city arboretum and gained experience with local plant conservation and community education. In college, I hope to deepen my understanding of plant biology so that I can study environmentally sound urban landscaping and building green communities. My experiences have shown me how important plant life

is to the human experience in an urban environment. Plants enrich us, relax us, and feed us. I hope to enhance the relationships between humans and plants in urban areas, and a biology degree is the first step toward that goal.

3. Evaluations will vary. The prompt asks for a wide range of information about your experiences and your desired major. Be sure that your response addresses all these requirements:
   - What your intended major is
   - How you became interested in the major
   - Your relevant experience, including activities, employment, volunteer work, or internships
   - What you have learned from your experience

4.

Purpose:	Audience:
To persuade the company that you are a good candidate for the job	The hiring manager of Parken-Todd Media Group, Inc.

Beginning:	
Introduce self and desired position, communication manager	

Middle:	
Creative and enthusiastic: example of previous work experience as a copy writer	
Write, edit, and proofread web content: example of experience with blog writing	
Team member working with web team, project manager, and social media team: strong team skills	
Manage web communications plan and documentation: organized and detail-oriented	

Ending:	
Thank the company, hope to have an interview soon	

5. You might write:

To Whom It May Concern:

My name is Edwina Baker, and I am applying for the position of communication manager at Parken-Todd Media Group, Inc. I was excited to see this position listed on the Parken-Todd website.

I currently work as a copy writer at CMD Communications, and I particularly enjoy the creative aspect of my work. I am enclosing samples along with my résumé. I write a wide variety of copy and maintain strong enthusiasm and creativity for every task.

I also have significant experience with web content. I produce my own copy writing blog, The Writing Word, at www.writingword.com.

I have strong team skills and am ready to work effectively with the web team, project manager, and social media team at Parken-Todd. I am organized and detail-oriented and will be an effective manager of the web communications plan and documentation.

Thank you for your time and attention. My résumé and samples are attached, and I look forward to the opportunity to interview for this position.

Sincerely,

Edwina Baker

6. Evaluations will vary. A cover letter is most persuasive when it shows how you can fulfill each of the job's requirements that are mentioned in the job description.

7.

Purpose:	Audience:
To persuade readers to disagree with the article	Readers of the newspaper

Beginning:

The article is flawed, since publicly funded elections will not work and since big money doesn't necessarily translate into votes.

Middle:

Human beings still vote in elections, not corporations.

As money increases in politics (on both sides) the goal is still to create an effective message. People still decide which message is worthwhile.

Publicly funded elections put a burden on the taxpayer and limit the ability to communicate.

Successful candidates can raise money without the bureaucracy of public funding.

Ending:

Money doesn't control elections. Money only makes it possible to communicate ideas.

8. You might write:

The article "Take Money out of Politics" blames all the problems with politics on one thing: money. It pretends that there is a simple solution to the complex political issues that our country faces. However, the basic premise of the article is flawed. Publicly funded elections will not work, and big money doesn't necessarily translate into votes.

As easy as it is to blame wealthy individuals and corporations for political failures, money does not buy votes. Human beings still vote in elections, and one individual equals one vote. Money does play a role, but as money increases in politics (on both sides) the goal is to distribute an effective message. People still decide which message is worthwhile. If the result is a broken political system, then we need better ideas more clearly communicated to the voting public.

The author suggests that publicly funded elections are a solution, but this opinion is misguided. Public funding of elections puts a burden on the taxpayer and limits candidates' ability to communicate effectively with voters. Candidates who will be successful lawmakers will also be successful at raising money without the bureaucracy of public funding.

Money doesn't control elections. Money only makes it possible to communicate ideas. Politics needs money so that the public can be informed and make good decisions. Money, used correctly, will enhance politics and not destroy it.

9. Evaluations will vary. You can write a letter to the editor either agreeing or disagreeing with the article. In either case, you should communicate a clear position and effective supporting evidence from the article and your own experience or knowledge.

Check Your Skills

pages 290–292

1. The following is an example of an **effective** response. It is appropriate for its audience and accomplishes its purpose.

Dear Valued Customer:

As AAA Landscaping approaches its 25th anniversary, I wanted to write a personal letter to thank you for your business and loyalty. In a quarter of a century, our family-owned business has helped the city improve its green open spaces, advocated for organic and sustainable growing, created gardens throughout the community, and helped countless individuals make good landscaping choices. The only way that AAA has accomplished these goals is through the patronage of loyal customers like you.

In honor of our 25th anniversary, AAA Landscaping is giving you 25% off all your purchases the week of August 11 through 17. Just mention this letter when you make your purchase. We look forward to seeing you soon and to another 25 years of growth.

Sincerely,

Jonas Andrews
AAA Landscaping

The following is an example of an **ineffective** response. It starts overly formally, which is inappropriate to the purpose and audience. It ends abruptly, without a good conclusion.

Dear Sir or Ma'am:

I am writing to notify you of AAA Landscaping's 25th anniversary. Thank you for your business and loyalty over that time. I wanted to notify you of a few things our business has done. We have helped the city improve its green open spaces, advocated for organic and sustainable growing, created gardens throughout the community, and helped countless individuals make good landscaping choices. Thank you again for being a customer.

In honor of our 25th anniversary, AAA Landscaping is giving you 25% off all your purchases the week of August 11 through 17.

Sincerely,

Jonas Andrews
AAA Landscaping

2. The following is an example of an **effective** response. It has an appropriate formal tone and provides all of the needed information.

Dear Mr. Linman,

I recently received a notice that my property at 9180 Northside Drive needs weeding to comply with city zoning codes. The notice number is A34991. According to the notice, a second inspection will occur on April 24.

Unfortunately, I will be out of town on vacation from April 12 through April 21. My scheduled trip gives me little time to complete the necessary weeding on my property. I am writing to request an extension until May 1. I will be able to correct the code violations by that date.

Thank you for your time and attention.

Sincerely,

Keela Waterson

The following is an example of an **ineffective** response. It is repetitive, giving unnecessary information, but it lacks important information including the notice number. It neglects to communicate the idea that the writer wants an extension.

Dear Mr. Linman,

I recently received a code violation notice in the mail. This letter said that I need to remove weeds in excess of four inches and excessive weeds adjacent to the sidewalk. I have two sidewalks adjacent to my house, since my property is a corner lot. One of the sidewalks does have some weeds, but the other sidewalk is currently clear.

I understand that I need to comply with the city zoning codes. According to the notice, a second inspection will occur on April 24.

April 24 is not a good date for me. Unfortunately, I will be out of town on vacation from April 12 through April 21. That is not enough time to complete the necessary weeding. There are several spots on my property with weeds in excess of four inches. I will need to put in a good number of hours or hire a gardening firm, which will take a long time. Most of the gardening firms in the area are booked up, since spring is a busy time for gardeners. I cannot finish the job by April 24.

Thank you for your time and attention.

Sincerely,

Keela Waterson

3. Responses will vary widely depending on the article chosen. The following is an example of an **effective** response. It summarizes the article, explains why it is important to the blog readers, gives the writer's opinion, and provides a link to the article.

Recently, a California State Senate committee passed a bill that would require labeling of genetically modified foods (known as GMOs). The bill will now go to the California legislature. While food safety is important, GMO labeling bills encourage misinformation about GMOs.

Proponents of the bill say that it encourages informed consumers. However, when GMOs are labeled, it implies that they are inferior food or somehow harmful. In actuality, GMOs are completely safe for human consumption. Without GMOs, growing enough food to sustain the world's population would be nearly impossible.

Learn about this proposed bill and contact your state representatives. California does not need more extraneous labeling. You can read about this bill on the Capital Public Radio website: http://www.capradio.org/articles/2014/04/22/california-genetically-modified-food-labeling-bill-passes-senate-committee/

The following is an example of an **ineffective** response. It only summarizes the article without giving any reason for the blog post. The blog post is redundant. It doesn't show why the author is writing. Why is this an article that the blog followers should read?

The article "California Genetically Modified Food Labeling Bill Passes Senate Committee" appears on the California Public Radio website. It explains that a California State Senate committee passed a bill that would require labeling of genetically modified foods (known as GMOs).

According to the article, people in favor of the bill say that its isn't about banning GMOs but about providing information to consumers to make informed decisions. The article also says that opponents complain about the expense for food producers. Two other states and the European Union have similar laws.

You can read about this bill on the Capital Public Radio website: http://www.capradio.org/articles/2014/04/22/california-genetically-modified-food-labeling-bill-passes-senate-committee/

Practice for Reasoning through Language Arts *page 293*

Comparing Arguments

Practice It! *pages 298–301*

1. Remember that you can write a response on either side of the issue. For extra practice, try writing two responses arguing for opposing points of view.

Central Idea: The arguments opposed to drilling in the Gulf of Mexico are stronger.	**Explanation:** The arguments against drilling include specifics and respond to arguments in favor of drilling.
Restate a Detail: Oil spills harm fishing and tourism.	**Explanation:** A main argument for drilling is that it will create jobs, but the oil industry can also harm other industries.
Restate a Detail: The Deepwater Horizon spill in 2010 spilled millions of barrels.	**Explanation:** The argument against drilling gives a specific, recent example of harm.
Restate a Detail: Oil drilling is safer with modern technology.	**Explanation:** The argument in favor of drilling doesn't give any support for this statement.

Restate a Detail: There are two and a half years of oil reserves off shore.	**Explanation:** The quantity of oil is specific information, and the number of years of oil supply puts it in perspective.
Conclusion: The argument against drilling has more specific, convincing evidence.	**Explanation:** The argument in favor of drilling needs to address opposing arguments more thoroughly and include specific evidence.

2. You might write:

The passage opposing drilling in the Gulf of Mexico strongly shows the dangers of oil drilling. Opponents of drilling cite specific evidence and respond to the arguments in favor of drilling. The arguments in favor of drilling have less specific support.

Opponents of drilling counter the claims of proponents. One of the main arguments in favor of drilling is that it will create jobs. However, opponents of drilling note that oil spills harm fishing and tourism. Harm to other industries should be considered in addition to the benefits of drilling.

The arguments against drilling also include specific details, including the Deepwater Horizon spill in 2010 that spilled millions of barrels of oil. This is a specific, recent example of an harmful spill. It counters the argument that "with modern technology, oil can be drilled safely." The argument in favor of drilling doesn't give any support for this statement. Another specific detail is that there are only about two and a half years of oil reserves off shore. The quantity of oil is specific information, and the number of years of oil supply puts it in perspective.

The argument against drilling has more specific, convincing evidence than the opposing argument. The argument in favor of drilling needs to address opposing arguments more thoroughly and include specific evidence in order to be convincing.

3. When you evaluate your work, check that the ideas and details are presented in a logical order. Make sure transitions are in place that connect your ideas. Your introduction and conclusion should make your central idea clear. Check for errors and edit for clarity.

4. Remember that you can write a response on either side of the issue. For extra practice, try writing two responses arguing for opposing points of view.

Central Idea: The arguments in favor of pet breeders are stronger.	**Explanation:** Those supporting pet breeders acknowledge problems, but also show the benefits of responsible breeding.
Restate a Detail: 40% of dogs are returned or abandoned.	**Explanation:** This is specific evidence about the results of poor matches between dogs and owners.
Restate a Detail: A lack of compatibility is the reason pets are abandoned.	**Explanation:** Breeders give owners predictable pets, and a good breeder can help match pets with owners.
Restate a Detail: Shelter animals have problems.	**Explanation:** While animals from breeders can have problems, so can animals from shelters.
Restate a Detail: Health problems occur in purebred dogs.	**Explanation:** Responsible breeders could limit health problems through good breeding practices.
Conclusion: The arguments show that breeders can benefit the broader community of pets and owners.	**Explanation:** The large numbers of animals in shelters show the need for breeders, since pets and owners need to be well matched.

5. You might write:

The passage presents strong arguments that show the benefits of getting a suitable pet from a breeder. Supporters of pet breeders acknowledge problems, but they also show the benefits of responsible breeding. On the other hand, the opponents of pet breeders ignore the benefits of responsible breeding.

Proponents of breeders cite specific evidence. The fact that 40% of dogs are returned or abandoned within the first year shows the unfortunate results of poor matches between dogs and owners. A lack of compatibility is the reason many pets are abandoned, and this demonstrates that choosing compatible pets is important. Breeders give owners predictable pets with specific characteristics, and a good breeder can help match pets with owners.

Animals from both breeders and shelters can have problems. Shelter animals can have physical or emotional problems. They may have abandonment issues, or they may have been abused in the past. While health problems in purebred dogs are an issue, responsible breeders can limit health problems through good breeding practices.

The arguments in favor of breeders show that breeders can benefit the broader community of pets and owners. The large numbers of animals in shelters isn't a reason to remove breeders. These figures show the need for breeders, since pets and owners need to be well matched to avoid abandonment.

6. When you evaluate your work, check that the ideas and details are presented in a logical order. Make sure transitions are in place that connect your ideas. Your introduction and conclusion should make your central idea clear. Check for errors and edit for clarity.

Check Your Skills
pages 302–304

1. The following is an example of an **effective** response. It has a clear central idea, a strong introduction, a body with supporting ideas, and a clear conclusion.

Nuclear power is a much-debated source of energy. Both supporters and opponents of nuclear energy are concerned about the environment. Is nuclear power truly the key to a clean energy policy, or do the dangers outweigh the costs? The passage opposing nuclear energy makes a strong argument that nuclear energy is too expensive and dangerous.

Perhaps the most controversial aspect of nuclear energy is the possibility of accidents. Supporters of nuclear energy dismiss disasters, stating that they are preventable. However, the fact that accidents are preventable doesn't mean they will be prevented. Humans are error-prone creatures. The recent disaster at the Fukushima nuclear plant shows that accidents can still happen. The costs are significant.

Both arguments also mention the cost of nuclear energy. The passage in support of nuclear power states that it is cheaper than wind, solar, or oil. It does not include details to support that statement, and the argument opposing nuclear power refutes it. The costs of storing waste and building power plants must be considered when weighing the affordability of nuclear energy.

With promising new technology arising for other types of energy, should nuclear power be pursued? Based on the arguments in the passages, less controversial sources of energy such as solar or geothermal power might be more promising investments.

The following is an example of an **ineffective** response. It has a clear central idea, but it is redundant. It summarizes the passage in favor of nuclear energy instead of analyzing the arguments. It doesn't address the arguments opposed to nuclear energy. To practice your writing, try revising and editing this response to improve it.

Nuclear energy is a good source of power that should be pursued. If nuclear energy can give us good power without downsides, there is no reason not to use it. Nuclear energy could be a big benefit. It is true that nuclear energy is clean energy that doesn't release carbon dioxide into the atmosphere. That means there is less pollution and harm to health. Nuclear energy helps us limit global warming. It also can be done without accidents or harm to the environment. Because nuclear power is cheap, it is a good source of energy. It should definitely be a kind of power that we use all the time.

2. The following is an example of an **effective** response. It has a clear central idea supported by evidence from the passage.

Texting while driving is clearly a dangerous activity. However, policies that make intuitive sense aren't always the best ones. The passage makes a strong argument opposing bans of texting behind the wheel, demonstrating that this type of ban will cause, not prevent, accidents.

The comparison between lowered speed limits and texting bans is apt. A law or regulation by itself won't stop a wide-spread behavior. Texting might be dangerous, but simply banning it won't solve the problem. The study that is cited in the passage shows that the policy is ineffective.

While long-term studies are worthwhile, their absence does not support a ban on texting. Neither do statistics showing the prevalence of texting while driving. The argument in favor of a ban on texting and driving rests almost entirely on statistics that show it is dangerous to text behind the wheel of a car. This is only an argument in favor of curbing dangerous texting. It is not an argument in favor of a specific policy or ban.

Bans on texting and driving deserve further study. Perhaps long-term studies will show that these bans eventually have effectiveness. However, based on the current knowledge, the effectiveness of bans on texting behind the wheel is not proven. The opposite is true—texting bans are harmful.

The following is an example of an **ineffective** response. It needs more development. To practice your writing, try revising and editing this response to improve it.

Texting while driving is a very dangerous activity, and if an activity is dangerous, then we should respond to it with laws. Since 40% of teens have been in cars where the driver did dangerous texting, the problem is widespread. The only evidence shown against bans on texting while driving is one study. A single study does not give a large body of evidence. However, the dangers of texting are extreme, accounting for about one tenth of crashes involving young drivers. Laws against texting while driving protect potentially irresponsible drivers, passing drivers obeying the law, and passengers in both cars. They are important and desirable laws.

3. The following is an example of an **effective** response. It has a strong central idea. It also includes specific information from the passage that is clearly organized. The response has a clear beginning, middle, and ending.

The passage that opposes banning large sugared soda has strong arguments, citing evidence that indicates why bans will be ineffective. Restaurant bans will not control the behavior of heavy soda-drinkers or reduce obesity.

Proponents of soda bans focus on the harms of sugar. While the argument includes specific evidence such as the high incidence of obesity among adults and the cost of obesity, that evidence doesn't show that a ban on large soda would be effective. Even if sugared sodas were the only cause of obesity (and not merely the largest source of calories), would banning large-sized drinks improve health? The argument gives no evidence to show that it would.

The opponents of soda bans acknowledge the lack of evidence on the effectiveness of those bans. One specific piece of evidence that opponents cite is that 80% of sugared sodas are sold in stores. The people who drink large amounts of soda will likely continue to buy large quantities of soda.

When regulating business is ineffective, it is bad policy. Opponents to soda bans state that a ban does not attack the root of obesity, and this statement is true. It may be more difficult to teach healthy eating habits than to institute regulations and bans. However, the easy route is not always the most effective. The arguments opposing soda are stronger because they acknowledge this and argue in favor of effective action.

The following is an example of an **ineffective** response. It does not focus on a clear central idea. The language choices could be improved to give this response a more formal tone and more variety in sentence structure and language. To practice your writing, try revising and editing this response to improve it.

The passage has information about stopping restaurants from serving large sugared soda. The people who support banning sodas have a lot of information about the costs of obesity. Obesity is a real problem and cost a good deal of money. The people who oppose banning sodas note that nobody knows the effects of a ban. A lot of soda is available from stores instead of restaurants. It is difficult to know if policies will help or not. The policy to ban sodas tries to make people eat better. This is a good goal, at least.

Practice in Social Studies Writing   *page 305*

The Relationship Bridge

Practice It!   *pages 310–313*

1.

Bridge End
Issue: Liberty versus safety
Summary: It is not worth giving up liberty to gain safety.
Context: Revolutionary War era

Connection
In her criticism of NSA data collection, Conroy weighs the two conflicting values, liberty and safety, that Franklin compares in the quotation.

Bridge End
Issue: Liberty versus security
Summary: Collecting large amounts of data about U.S. citizens creates the probability of abusing that information. In this case, individual liberty is more important than security.
Context: NSA mass data collection

2. You might write:

In her criticism of NSA data collection, Conroy weighs the two conflicting values, liberty and safety, that Franklin compares in the quotation. Conroy suggests that liberty and safety are conflicting values that must be balanced, and

echoing Franklin's sentiment, states that liberty should outweigh security in regard to NSA data collection. The goal of an intelligence service such as the NSA is to ensure security. Conroy notes that when there is secrecy, there is often a cost to individual liberty. Some limits on individual liberty are acceptable. For example, a secret court might rule that an intelligence agency can place a wire tap on a phone, for example. Even Franklin qualifies his statement about liberty and safety, comparing giving up "essential" liberty to gain "a little temporary" safety. Conroy recognizes that liberty and security need to be balanced but believes that the massive amounts of data collected by the NSA cross a line. Massive data collection is not an issue that Franklin could have anticipated during revolutionary times, but it evokes the issue of liberty versus safety that Franklin identified.

3.

Bridge End
Issue: Blind patriotism versus responding to the country's problems
Summary: Supporting your country means keeping it on the right path, not blindly supporting anything your country does.
Context: Senate discussion, 1872

Connection
Antonio Marquez reflects Schurz's sentiment through his desire to enhance government oversight.

Bridge End
Issue: Oversight of police officers
Summary: Video surveillance of police creates oversight that can prevent abuse of power as well as false complaints and violence.
Context: Video cameras integrated into police uniforms

4. You might write:

Carl Schurz said, "My country right or wrong; if right to be kept right; and if wrong to be set right." This sentiment opposes blind patriotism, instead advocating for government oversight to keep the country on the right track. Antonio Marquez reflects Schurz's sentiment through his desire to enhance government oversight.

He discusses filming police officers on duty. The main argument in favor of video cameras on police uniforms is to create oversight that can prevent abuse of power. While Marquez also mentions preventing false complaints and violent episodes, he focuses on creating oversight for police in their roles as public servants. If the officers are right, oversight will keep them on the right path. If the officers are wrong, oversight will set them right.

Check Your Skills *pages 314–316*

1. The following is an example of an **effective** response. It focuses on and explains the connection between the quotation and the passage.

> The Fifth Amendment affirms in the U.S. Constitution the right to remain silent, that no one "shall be compelled in any criminal case to be a witness against himself." In its ruling in Salinas v. Texas, the Supreme Court seems to qualify this right by stating that defendants must explicitly evoke the right to silence, instead of simply remaining silent. Morgan appeals to the Fifth Amendment and to the idea of "inalienable rights." Rights are not awarded by the government. Instead, they are inherent rights that the government recognizes. It is counterintuitive that a person must declare he or she is using a constitutional right before it takes effect. An inherent right never goes away. It can be recognized, or it can be infringed. When the suspect did not answer a question about his shotgun, he was remaining silent. However, the Supreme Court ruled that he was not using his right to remain silent. Morgan's main point is that the Fifth Amendment right to silence is an inherent right, not one that is switched on and off by a declaration.

The following is an example of an **ineffective** response. It is difficult to follow and does not make a clear connection between the quotation and the passage. To practice your writing, try revising and editing this response to improve it.

> The Supreme Court says that silence can be used as a kind of evidence in a court case. The possibility of using silence is a way of showing how the suspect reacts or how they talk with the

police. This is something that is observed and then told about in a court during a court case, such as the one that is Salinas v. Texas, the case that the Supreme Court ruled on in June 2013. The person used Miranda rights to remain silent when asked about his shotgun and would it match the shells from the murder. It was a serious crime and the person was then arrested and tried, where it was evidence that he wouldn't answer. This is what the problem is, that not answering was used as part of the court case against him.

2. The following is an example of an **effective** response. It makes a clear connection between the passage and the quotation.

> The idea of "tyranny of the majority" refers to the majority overwhelming the rights of minority groups by voting against them. However, creating strangely shaped districts based on demographics to keep one party in power evokes the second part of Baron Acton's quotation, the tyranny of a party that succeeds "by force or fraud." Banner's letter reflects this concern.
>
> Banner notes that democracy depends on the accurate representation of votes. Banner suggests that non-partisan redistricting commissions can draw fair, unbiased district boundaries to prevent a party from conniving to unfairly maintain power. He provides a specific example of such a commission created in California in 2010 to avoid the tyranny of the elected party over district boundaries. More information about the successes of such commissions would better support Banner's position, but the fact that the commission is composed of Democrats, Republicans, and people associated with neither party reflects Baron Acton's concerns. By implementing this solution nationally, Banner hopes to avoid at least part of Baron Acton's concerns and prevent one way that a party can become a tyrant through democracy.

The following is an example of an **ineffective** response. It lacks focus, is redundant and confusing, and does not make a connections between the quotation and the passage. To practice your writing, try revising and editing this response to improve it.

Districts are a normal part of government that allow people to elect officials that represent their particular areas or states. There is never going to be a district that everyone is happy with because everyone wants a district that might vote for them instead of voting for their competitors. There is no way for it to be fair, and it just depends on who is in power right now. Tomorrow someone else will be in power and make their own district lines. That's why it doesn't make any sense having politicians declaring their own political lines, but it isn't something that can be helped. Everyone is biased and someone always is doing the wrong thing. When you make a political boundary, you are making political friends and enemies. It's always the politicians that you can't trust, and everyone is biased. There is no way you can be unbiased or really independent, because everyone has their own opinion that they support.

3. The following is an example of an **effective** response. It explains the meaning of Hamilton's quotation and applies the concept to the blog post. It makes a clear connection between the quotation and the passage.

The quotation from Alexander Hamilton advocates for moderation in government, warning against extremes. In the blog post, Olsen discusses the electoral college, which is an attempt to create a moderate democracy. The electoral college is a form of representative democracy, similar to Congress. Instead of voting directly, each state sends representatives to the electoral college to vote for president. This gives power to the states. It might be considered an "extreme of democracy" to have individuals vote directly for the president. However, the movement towards a direct presidential vote reflects the changes in the U.S. since Hamilton's time. The federal government is more powerful, and the state governments are less independent. Olsen uses a specific example of how the electoral college changed a presidential election. The reason it seems so strange for the presidential election and the electoral college votes to be different is because we think of

the presidential race as a national election, not a decision made between the states. Without strong, independent states, perhaps the more reasonable, moderate choice today would be to eliminate the electoral college. It is no longer an extreme of democracy to vote directly for president.

The following is an example of an **ineffective** response. Its language is confusing, and it does not make a connection between the quotation and the passage. To practice your writing, try revising and editing this response to improve it.

The electoral college is a way to elect the president. It works because it's done by states. It seems like Al Gore got more votes but George W. Bush got more votes in the electoral college. George Bush was elected president. The idea is states have representatives for the electoral college, and really when you vote it goes to vote for the representatives. They say who they vote for in the electoral college. That is what determines who is the next president. It is an extra step in the process of elections that sometimes can go wrong. Most of the time it works fine, though, and it means that each state gets their representation in government. Congress has state representation, too, and just applies it to the electoral college for presidential elections.

Practice in Science Writing   *page 317*

Responding to a Science Prompt

Practice It!   *pages 322–325*

1.

Central Idea:
The experiment will test the hypothesis that the beetles will not infest apple trees.
Detail:
The independent variable is the type of tree.
Detail:
The dependent variable is the infestation caused by the beetles.

Detail:
The experiment will keep two groups of tree branches in a controlled environment, a control group of forest branches and an experimental group of apple trees.
Detail:
The experiment will measure the infestation from beetles and determine whether the type of tree affects the infestation.
Conclusion:
Based on the experimental results, the orchard owners can decide whether they need to take steps to protect their apple orchard from infestation.

2. You might write:

To test the hypothesis that the beetles infesting a local forest will not infest apple trees, the experiment will expose apple tree branches and forest tree branches to beetle infestations in a controlled environment. The independent variable in this experiment is the type of tree, and the dependent variable is the infestation caused by the beetles. The experiment will keep two groups of tree branches in similar environments, with similar temperature, amount of beetles, and other environmental controls. The experiment will include a control group of forest branches and a test group of apple trees. The beetle infestation will be measured by the amount of damage caused to each branch by the beetles. By analyzing the results, the scientist can determine whether the type of tree affects the infestation. If the apple branches are not damaged but the other forest branches are damaged, then the hypothesis is correct. Based on the experimental results, the orchard owners can decide whether they need to take steps to protect their apple orchard from infestation.

3.

Central Idea:
The amount of rainfall in May through August for the year is low.
Detail:
Average May rainfall is just over six inches, while this year's rainfall is 4.26 inches.

Detail:
The rainfall for every month is below the average.
Detail:
The rainfall for July is 0.18 inches, which is near the lowest recorded rainfall in 50 years.
Detail:
The rainfall for June is 2.12 inches, which is near the lowest recorded rainfall in 50 years.
Conclusion:
The rainfall for these four months is much lower than normal, and the rainfall in June and July may be the lowest in over 50 years.

4. You might write:

The amount of rainfall in May through August for the year is low compared to prior years. The rainfall for every month is below the median. Median May rainfall is just over six inches, while this year's rainfall is 4.26 inches. The rainfall for June is 2.12 inches, and the rainfall for July is 0.18 inches. Both of these numbers are near the lowest recorded rainfall in 50 years. Rainfall for August is 3.14 inches, while the median is over four inches. The rainfall for these four months is much lower than normal, and the rainfall in June and July may be the lowest in over 50 years.

5.

Central Idea:
The experiment will test the hypothesis that appliances run with the generic brand of batteries will not last as long as those run with name brand batteries.
Detail:
The battery type is the independent variable, and the length of time until the battery dies is the dependent variable.
Detail:
The experiment will use the same appliance in similar conditions for repeated tests and test each type of battery multiple times.
Detail:
Results will be measured by the amount of time the appliances will run with each type of battery.

Detail:

The name brand batteries are the control group, and the generic batteries are the test group.

Conclusion:

If the generic batteries consistently die more quickly than the name brand batteries, then the hypothesis is correct.

6. You might write:

To test the hypothesis that the generic brand of batteries will not last as long as name brand batteries, each battery will be tested under similar conditions in the same appliance. The experiment will consist of repeated tests so that each type of battery is tested multiple times. The battery type is the independent variable, and the length of time until the battery dies is the dependent variable. Results will be measured by the amount of time the appliance will run with each battery. The name brand batteries are the control group in the experiment, and the generic batteries are the test group. If the generic batteries consistently die more quickly than the name brand batteries, then the hypothesis is correct.

7.

Central Idea:

The results do not show that Chemical A causes Bacteria B.

Detail:

The amounts of Chemical A in Briar Lake are greater than the amounts in Carson Lake.

Detail:

The amounts of Bacteria B in Briar Lake are also greater than the amounts in Carson Lake.

Detail:

At Briar Lake Site 2, the amount of Chemical A is twice as much as at Site 1, but the amount of Bacteria B is less.

Detail:

At Carson Lake, Site 1 has 12 times the amount of Chemical A, but the amount of Bacteria B are almost the same.

Conclusion:

While Briar Lake has more of both Chemical A and Bacteria B than Carson Lake, the results do not show a correlation between Chemical A and Bacteria B at different sites.

8. You might write:

The results of the study do not show that the presence of Chemical A causes increased levels of Bacteria B. The quantities of Chemical A and Bacteria B in Briar Lake are greater than the quantities of both in Carson Lake. However, at Briar Lake, there is no correlation between the quantities of the chemical and the quantities of the bacteria. At Site 2 in Briar Lake, the amount of Chemical A is twice as much as at Site 1. Yet, the quantity of Bacteria B at Site 2 in Briar Lake is less than at Site 1. At Carson Lake, the results are similar. Site 1 has 12 times the amount of Chemical A as Site 2, but the amounts of Bacteria B are almost the same. While Briar Lake has more of both Chemical A and Bacteria B than Carson Lake, the results do not show a correlation between Chemical A and Bacteria B at different sites.

Check Your Skills   *pages 326–328*

1. The following is an example of an **effective** response. It covers important elements of experimental design, including a control group, an independent variable, and a dependent variable. It answers the full prompt and has a beginning, middle, and ending.

To test the hypothesis that either group work or Socratic questioning will improve student performance, the department can design an experiment with three groups of students. The first test group will receive instruction with 30% group work. The second test group will receive instruction with 30% Socratic questioning. The third group will be a control group and will receive the current type of instruction. The groups should be as similar as possible, balanced for factors such as existing GPA and previous science courses, and the course requirements should be the same. The independent variable is the teaching method, and the dependent variable is the student performance. Results will be measured by tracking student grades in all three groups. Based on the hypotheses, the department will expect student performance to be higher for both the group receiving Socratic instruction and the group receiving group instruction. Results can also be compared to the existing grade distribution. The control group is expected to be representative of the existing grade distribution, while the test groups are expected to show higher scores. If the results are as expected, the hypothesis is correct.

The following is an example of an **ineffective** response. It fails at the task of designing an effective experiment, since it tests both types of instruction on one group and does not include a control group. It also does not include constants, to make sure other variables aren't affecting the results.

The department believes that group work or Socratic questioning will improve student performance. To test the hypothesis the department can design an experiment to test both methods. A group of students will receive both Socratic questioning and group work for 30% of class time. The student scores will be tracked. If the students receiving the new types of instruction score higher than previous groups of students shown in the grade distribution histogram, then the hypothesis is true. If there is no change in scores from previous classes, or if grades go down, then the hypothesis is not correct.

2. The following is an example of an **effective** response. It clearly explains the relationship between surface tension and the movement of small, light insects.

Surface tension helps small, light insects move and stand on water because it creates a layer of tightly bonded molecules that help hold up these insects. Since water molecules on the surface are not bound to molecules on every side, they create stronger bonds with the other molecules on the surface of the water. This creates a layer of molecules that will not be broken apart by light-weight creatures such as water striders. The reason that small insects can walk on water is that they do not exert enough force to break the surface tension.

The following is an example of an **ineffective** response. It attempts to summarize the information in the passage, but it does not clearly communicate the idea of surface tension. The writer does not seem to understand the passage well.

Surface tension happens when there are molecules at the top of water. The surface molecules are not completely surrounded. That makes a film on the top of the water. The film on the top of the water is where insects walk. Surface tension is a strong barrier that is tightly bound.

3. The following is an example of an **effective** response. It gives details about all of the animals in the diagram who would be affected by a disease that wiped out the mouse population.

If a deadly disease wiped out most of the mouse population in the diagrammed ecosystem, then the animals who depend on them would be affected and populations would decrease. The owl, wild cat, kite, and snake population would suffer from a lack of food sources. Wild cats might prey more on rabbits, affecting the rabbit population and the jackals that feed on them. Kites would be affected by declining owl and snake populations as well, and lions might suffer from the decline in wild cats and jackals. More than half of the ecosystem would be affected by a disease that wiped out the mouse population.

The following is an example of an **ineffective** response. It lacks details.

If a deadly disease wiped out most of the mouse population in the diagrammed ecosystem, then the animals who depend on them would be affected and populations would decrease. The diagram shows a food web. The organisms in the food web are affected by the mice, and if the mice die, they will cause populations of other organisms to decrease. Organisms further down on the food chain will affect more organisms in the food web. The animals that prey on organisms are affected by the presence or lack of food.

Resources

Use the following resources to continue practicing and improving your writing. Resources for language and grammar can help you avoid mistakes that can hinder communication. Writing prompts can give you extra practice to develop your writing.

The Writing Process, Grammar, and Mechanics

 The Purdue University Online Writing Lab (OWL) has resources covering academic writing, the writing process, and writing grammar and mechanics. Use this resource to improve your language skills.
https://owl.english.purdue.edu/owl/

 HyperGrammar contains information on parts of speech, phrases, clauses, sentences, punctuation, and paragraphs. Find useful references on all aspects of the English language.
http://www.uottawa.ca/academic/arts/writcent/hypergrammar/

Dictionaries

 The Oxford Dictionary website includes definitions, synonyms, grammar references, word origins, games and quizzes, and foreign language dictionaries.
http://www.oxforddictionaries.com/us

 The Merriam-Webster® online dictionary includes a dictionary and thesaurus, as well as quizzes and games, a word-of-the-day feature, and helpful videos about language issues.
http://www.merriam-webster.com/

Common Errors

 Visit the *Common Errors in English Usage* website to explore errors from "a" versus "an" to "your" versus "you're." In addition to an extensive list of errors, this site has a daily calendar and a blog.
https://public.wsu.edu/~brians/errors/errors.html

 Find common grammar errors and FAQs at GrammarMonster.com. Topics include abbreviations, apostrophes, plurals, comparatives, and many more.
http://www.grammar-monster.com/common_grammar_errors.htm

 "Common Mistakes of English Grammar, Mechanics, and Punctuation" by Dr. Jeffrey Kahn, Illinois State University, provides a brief list of common errors, along with examples of right and wrong usage.
http://my.ilstu.edu/~jhkahn/writing.html

Writing Prompts

 Use these four essay prompts from the most recent SAT® test administration for extra writing practice.
https://professionals.collegeboard.com/testing/sat-reasoning/prep/essay-prompts

 This webpage at the Writing Center at the University of North Carolina at Chapel Hill explains how to interpret academic assignments and writing prompts.
https://writingcenter.unc.edu/handouts/understanding-assignments/

 This list of 100 brief persuasive writing prompts at the Writing Prompts website can help you practice using claims and evidence. When you use these prompts, research your topic to find strong arguments.
http://www.writingprompts.net/persuasive/

Word Processing

 Google® Drive allows you to create online documents. You can use this word processor to practice skills including keyboarding, navigating on a computer, and using features such as cut, copy, and paste.
http://www.google.com/drive/apps.html